Strategies for Academic Writing

Strategies
for Academic
Writing

A GUIDE FOR COLLEGE STUDENTS

Irvin Y. Hashimoto
Barry M. Kroll   John C. Schafer

121680

Ann Arbor

The University of Michigan Press

Copyright © by The University of Michigan 1982
All rights reserved
Published in the United States of America by
The University of Michigan Press and simultaneously
in Rexdale, Canada, by John Wiley & Sons Canada, Limited
Manufactured in the United States of America

Library of Congress Cataloging in Publication Data
Hashimoto, Irvin Y. (Irwin Yuiichi), 1945–Strategies for academic
    writing.
    An outgrowth of work begun by the authors at the University of
Michigan's Reading and Learning Center.
    Includes bibliographical references.
    1. Dissertations, Academic. 2. English language—Writing. I. Kroll,
Barry M., 1946–
II. Schafer, John C. III. Title.
LB2369.H33   808'.02   81-19762
ISBN 0-472-08020-2   AACR2

LB
2369
.H33

Acknowledgments

During the several years of work on this book we've had important help from our colleagues, students, and families, only a small part of which can be acknowledged here. But we'd like to repay a few special debts of gratitude. We first developed a number of the concepts and exercises now incorporated into *Strategies for Academic Writing* when we worked at the University of Michigan's Reading and Learning Skills Center, where we wrote a series of mimeographed pamphlets dealing with various problems students had when doing academic papers. We were lucky to have the strong support of the center's director, Rowena Wilhelm, whose encouragement and enthusiasm were vital to the early stages of our writing and testing the materials. Carol Mitchell, of the University of Michigan Press, examined our early pamphlets and encouraged us to transform them into a unified textbook. We've been fortunate to have such a friendly, sympathetic, and patient editor.

The reviewers of our manuscripts have also been helpful. Several anonymous reviewers challenged us to rework substantial parts of our early drafts. And we were greatly helped by Richard Larson's thoughtful and detailed critiques of two earlier versions of *Strategies*. Our colleagues and students have been generous in permitting us to use example assignments and papers. And finally, we thank our wives—Marianne, Diana, and Quynh—for believing in the worth of this project even when we grew tired and discouraged. Their support has been essential.

Contents

Note to Students

There are many different reasons for writing—to entertain yourself, to convey information, to make an object of beauty or pleasure. These different reasons for writing result in many kinds of writing: diaries, scientific reports, poems, or stories. Even in college there are many kinds of writing. As a student you might be asked to write an autobiographical sketch in English, a research paper in history, a report of an interview for psychology, or a technical report for your engineering class. Instead of trying to cover school writing in all its variations, however, we have chosen to concentrate on those kinds of papers that are most typical of the writing done for college courses—papers involving thoughtful analysis and some research on a particular topic, either as a response to a specific assignment (perhaps a problem-solving exercise or take-home exam question) or as a more extensive independent project. We call these academic papers.

To succeed as a student you need to learn to do academic writing. You need to master this kind of writing, first of all, because it is a valuable tool for learning. Learning the subject matter of a discipline involves more than memorizing terminology or acquiring new concepts. Real learning also entails gaining an understanding of the way people in that discipline think: how they deal with the facts in their field, how they organize information to show relationships among facts, and how they view the key issues or divergent theories of the discipline. In writing the academic paper you are learning to select and organize the significant information of that discipline; by doing this, you make the information your own in a way you never do when you memorize facts or formulas.

You also need to master academic writing because it is a major aspect of your performance in many college courses. Teachers view the ability to write a good academic paper as a measure of a student's ability to think about the subject matter of a particular discipline. In a questionnaire survey of faculty members, a professor of applied economics, when asked for a statement about the value of writing skills for students in his discipline, responded: "I really appreciate the time that sutdents take to learn to write well. When I read a well-written essay, I know that the student has really understood the subject matter. But more than that, I know that the student has learned to think about problems in applied economics. It is this thinking process, and not the specific information of the course (which quickly goes out of date), that is the hallmark of an educated person." Other instructors we've talked with in our survey emphasize the extent to which writing skills can affect a student's performance in a college course.

> Technical knowledge is emphasized but writing skills help the students express what they know. Writing skill could alter the grade of some students. (agronomy)
>
> Writing skills are an important factor in the student's success and for his course grade. Organized, lucid prose is a key factor in expressing historical arguments successfully. (history)
>
> The following statement is on the course syllabus: "On all assignments and tests the clarity and correctness of your written expression will be considered in arriving at a grade." (secondary education)
>
> Our department believes that English proficiency is an ongoing thing, so each . . . instructor watches every bit of writing a student does. For us writing and composition skills are very important and do figure into a student's success. (textiles and clothing)
>
> On the term paper and in the essay examinations, I attempt to evaluate the organization and conciseness of the written material as well as the content in assigning a grade. (economics)

The aim of this book is to provide you with a set of strategies that will help you succeed on a number of important problems you are likely to face in doing academic writing. Chapters 1 through 3 emphasize strategies for conceptualizing and developing the body of a paper: devising a plan of attack, using particular methods of development, and deciding on a final arrangement for your main points. In chapters 4 and 5 we suggest strategies for dealing with three major problems that occur when you move from developing the body of the paper to completion of the final draft: writing introductions, writing conclusions, and making certain that all the main points fit together, or "cohere." Throughout these chapters we have made generous use both of actual assignments given by college instructors and of selections from papers written by college students. We have also placed complete student papers at the end of several of the chapters. We do not claim to be experts in the various fields represented, but we feel that the papers included offer good examples of many of the strategies presented in the text. The final chapter follows a student through the writing of an academic paper, thereby illustrating how all the individual strategies work together in an actual writing situation. Following the last chapter you will find answers to a number of the problems you are asked to do in each chapter.

The ultimate test of any textbook is its practicality. We hope you will find yourself not only using the strategies we suggest in this text but also discovering other useful strategies on your own as you cope with the special writing problems of specific academic disciplines.

Note to Teachers

Strategies for Academic Writing has grown out of our conviction that students are often unprepared to write the kinds of reports, examinations, and papers that they face in college classes, even though these same students may be successful in other types of writing and may be proficient in most of the so-called basic skills. We first became aware of this situation several years ago when the three of us worked in a writers' workshop at the University of Michigan. This workshop was a counseling and tutorial serivce, a place where students could drop in for help with their writing problems. The majority of students we counseled were sophomores and juniors who were struggling with the writing demands of academic courses, particularly in the humanities and social sciences. These students had taken freshman English; many were bright, successful students; they typically had few problems with sentence construction—and yet they didn't understand some rather fundamental principles about writing papers for such courses as anthropology, economics, education, history, nursing, philosophy, or psychology. These students were unprepared for the tasks of academic writing. We have since moved to other universities in different regions of the country, yet the problems we see are much the same.

Why do college students write papers which their instructors find to be poorly conceived and inadequately organized? Why haven't they been taught to do academic writing? It's always tempting to look for simple causes, and even easier to try to place the blame on someone else. Thus some college teachers would say that students don't write enough in high school, and that the writing they are assigned often deals excessively with personal experience or "creative" writing. There is undoubtedly truth in these charges, although we know—since all three of us have taught secondary school—that high school English teachers are expected to teach too many things to too many students. Other college teachers would say that freshman English courses don't adequately prepare students to deal with academic writing. There is clearly truth in this assertion, too, although freshman English courses may serve important goals other than simply the pragmatic one of preparing students to write academic papers in subsequent college courses. Finally, instructors in various academic disciplines are usually quick to sidestep any suggestion that *they* should be responsible for teaching students to write in a particular discipline, claiming, with some justification, that they simply don't have time to teach both writing skills and academic subject matter. It is easy to see the effect of this situation: students are rarely taught the skills of academic writing—not in high school, not in freshman English, not in subject area courses. Students are simply expected to be able to write academic papers.

We've attempted to write a book that will teach students some of the skills involved in writing academic papers. We've designed *Strategies for Academic Writing* so that it can be used in several different ways. Although it is not a self-instructional workbook, the text is designed so that students can work through it independently. We've provided answers to many of the exercises, so that students can check their comprehension of key principles. We've tried to make the book easy and enjoyable to read by including some light-hearted examples and exercises. And we've written to students in a simple, straightforward manner and with a casual tone—as if we were talking to them in a writing workshop setting. Because the book is easy for students to read and work through on their own, it could be used in a writing center, where students receive individualized assistance, or as a supplementary text in an academic course, where the focus is on subject matter rather than on writing skills per se.

Strategies for Academic Writing can also be used effectively in a more traditional composition course. However, this book is obviously more specialized than many familiar composition texts. For example, many textbooks devote considerable attention to several modes of discourse: narration, description, exposition, and persuasion. The kind of academic writing we focus on, however, is predominantly expository, sometimes with an argumentative twist. Many composition texts also deal with such basic sentence-level problems as dangling modifiers, subject-verb agreement, faulty parallelism, or wordiness. Such problems can be important for student writers, but our guiding philosophy in teaching composition is that most students should get their writing motors running first and leave the fine tuning for later, after they understand the strategies involved in conceptualizing and producing an academic paper. We do not discuss sentence-level problems in this book. Therefore, if you use *Strategies* in a traditional writing course, you may want to supplement it with material on narrative and descriptive writing (if you believe your students need practice in these modes), or perhaps with a handbook (if you believe your students need a textbook to help them edit sentences).

Although *Strategies for Academic Writing* is not a traditional composition text, neither is it a typical text on how to write a research paper. Such books often devote considerable attention to such details of research writing as how to use the library, how to take notes, how to construct bibliographies, and how to produce footnotes. These details are important, but our focus is instead on the planning and thinking processes involved in writing a broad range of academic papers—from book reports, to take-home examinations, to problem-solving assignments, to research papers. The last chapter in the book lends itself, however, to work on a fairly extensive and formal research paper. In this chapter we trace a student's progress through the writing of a research paper on the snail darter controversy, focusing on the kind of thinking that a student might use in conceptualizing, developing, and organizing such a paper. We show not only the finished paper, but also the sources (in the appendix) that the student used in writing it. We've included these materials for two reasons. First, we felt that if we left the source materials out and just printed the finished paper, we would make the process of writing a research paper appear too tidy and simple. By looking through the sources when they read the account of how the paper was written, students will better appreciate the difficulties that must be overcome as one struggles to understand a complex subject, decide on a manageable point of view, and select and arrange information.

Second, we've included the sources so that teachers can, if they wish, use them to assign their own "controlled sources" paper, using these sources as a casebook on the snail darter controversy. Assignments based on a casebook don't teach students how to find sources in a library, but they do enable them to practice important writing skills: devising an initial plan, organizing information, and arranging it effectively. Because you have the materials, you can check whether students are reading intelligently and quoting their sources accurately. We've used these source materials in our own composition classes and have found that the subject appeals to a variety of students. For example, those who aspire to be lawyers can explore the legal issues, students of government can discuss what the snail darter case reveals about the working of our political system, and students in the biological sciences can concentrate on environmental issues. You might also encourage students to read more widely on the snail darter issue, exploring related topics not adequately covered by the sources in the text. One of our students wrote an award-winning essay describing how the Tellico Dam affected the culture of the Cherokees. She supplemented the information found in the casebook with material from other sources.

We believe that the strategies taught in this book will help students write better academic papers. But we don't have a simple answer to the problem of when and where to teach academic writing. We'd like to see more college-bound high school students working on problems involved in academic writing. We'd like to see some emphasis given to academic writing in college-level composition courses. And we'd like to see more teachers of subject-area courses take responsibility for training students to use writing as a way of wrestling with the problems of a particular field. We hope this book will be used in each of these contexts. For without some coherent instruction, too many students come to view academic writing negatively: as writing that merely regurgitates facts and figures; as writing that addresses a narrow audience (the teacher) for a limited purpose (to get a good grade); and as writing that has to be stilted and boring to sound scholarly. Instead, we hope students will come to view academic writing as an intellectual adventure: a difficult but rewarding struggle to understand concepts, to see relationships, to discover a point of view—in short, as a way to learn how people think in an academic discipline.

1 | *Devising an Initial Plan*

In most academic writing your aim is to convey a body of information about a particular subject. This body of information usually consists of facts you have gathered either from your own observations or by reading authoritative articles and books on a topic. But gathering relevant information can present problems. There is often a great deal of information on a topic, only a small portion of which will be relevant for the paper you end up writing. We have often imagined how much easier writing would be if there were a crystal ball that gave you a vision of your finished paper before you had begun your search for information. This glance at the end product would provide a good basis for knowing what information would be useful. Your search for information could then be selective.

Although we don't know of a reliable crystal ball, what we are going to discuss involves something like that vision of the finished paper. We recommend that you devise a tentative plan for your paper before you have done very much gathering of information. You may wonder how it is possible to devise a plan before you know what your information will consist of. Obviously, there are situations in which you can't have a clue about how the paper will be developed until you do a good bit of preliminary reading. But in this chapter we want to focus on those situations in which it is feasible to devise an initial plan.

By initial plan we mean a scheme for organizing information. The plan is a picture of how you will go about developing the main section of your paper, a flexible guide that helps you know what kind of information is likely to be relevant for the type of paper you will be writing. Although this organizational plan must often be tentative—in the process of gathering information you may discover a better one—it provides an important guide to help you in finding and assessing information.

Plans Based on Standard Formats

Sometimes initial plans are given to you along with your assignment. Some disciplines, particularly those in the social and physical sciences, have standard formats which students are expected to follow when writing papers. In such courses you will have a clear idea how to organize your paper before you begin gathering information. For example, if you are writing a report on an experiment for a course in psychology, you may be required to follow a conventional guide, such as the one recommended by the American Psychological Association:

Title
Abstract (a one-paragraph summary of the content and purpose of the report)
Introduction (a statement of the point and importance of the study)
Method (a discussion of who participated, what materials were used, what procedures followed)
Results (a report of the findings, usually including scores and statistics)
Discussion (an interpretation of the results which draws conclusions and points out the contribution of the study to the field)
References (the books and articles used in writing the report)

Such a format largely determines the order in which you present your information. Other fields also use specific formats for their reports. Part of being a student is learning what formats are typically used in your discipline.

Sometimes a teacher will give you a specific format to follow when writing a paper for a course. Here is an example from a handout in a history course.

Your paper in this course should have the following parts:
  I. Introductory statement
    A. A listing of the categories to be used to develop the essay
    B. Rephrasing of question
    C. A telling quotation
  II. The body
    A. General statement
    B. Specific information as "proof"
    C. Analysis of data (commentary)
      1. Refer to theme of essay
      2. Explain significance of the data
  III. Concluding remarks
    A. Characterize your interpretation
    B. Or summarize your point of view
    C. Try to include a "ho-hum" breaker (a comment suggesting why this subject is significant)

In a number of courses students are asked to do a "problem-solution" paper. Here is a format for writing this kind of paper, provided as part of the assignment for a course in political science.

Situation (What's wrong?)
Proposed solution (What should be done?)
Discussion (Why is the solution a good one?)
Conclusions or recommendations

Yet another assignment for which teachers often provide a set of guidelines is the book review. Here is one instructor's suggested format for a nonfiction book.

I. Summary
   A. Author—Who is he/she; what are his/her qualifications?
   B. Purpose—Is it to inform, evaluate, persuade, communicate an experience, or a combination of these?
   C. Background of book—Are there any special circumstances surrounding its writing or publication that would help explain its importance or impact?
   D. Theme—What is the central idea behind the book?
   E. Summary—Give a brief report of the organization and important features of the book.
II. Evaluation
   A. What you didn't like about the book
      1. Evidence was unsatisfactory—Were the facts slanted? Were there unjustified or unsupported statements?
      2. Author was limited—Were important aspects of the subject neglected? Did author examine only one side of the issue?
      3. Author's purpose or procedures were unclear.
   B. What you liked about the book
      1. Presentation was interesting—Were there especially meaningful or memorable points?
      2. Argument was convincing—Was the thinking clear, logical and free of bias?
      3. Book has implications—Does it raise thought-provoking insights? Is it original?

When there is a standard format for writing papers in a particular discipline, or when a teacher gives you a format as part of an assignment, you have at least some basis on which to devise an initial plan for organizing the information in your paper. The plan can help guide your search for relevant facts. For example, if you are required to write a book review following the format just given, you know something about the kind of information you need to gather.

You need to know about the author. You need to understand the book well enough to summarize its purpose, theme, and organization. And, to evaluate the book, you need to find examples of ways in which the author is biased or objective, dull or thought provoking.

Although in some courses you may be given a format for writing a paper, more commonly instructors leave the organizing of the paper up to you. In such cases, you can often use a general format, like this one:

I. Introduction
   A. Background
   B. Thesis
II. Body
   A. Facts, explanations, or information to support your thesis
III. Conclusion
   A. Summarize the issue
   B. Show importance or relevance

This format outlines the major sections of an academic paper, but it does not specify how the body of the paper—the longest and most difficult section to write—should be organized. Your initial plan needs to include a tentative scheme for organizing the body of the paper.

Plans Derived from Directed Assignments

The assignment often contains clues which direct you to a particular method of organization for the body of your paper. For example, the following assignment suggests a way to organize the paper:

> Trace the changes in child-rearing practices throughout this century in the United States.

This assignment contains a key word, "trace," which directs you to a special kind of organization for the information in your paper—an organization according to time, or chronological order. The next assignment suggests a different kind of organization.

> Compare the major child-rearing practices in the United States with practices in the Soviet Union.

The directive in this assignment, "compare," again gives you a clue to how the content of the paper should be organized. You will have to gather facts about child rearing in both countries, and you will need to arrange these facts in a way that highlights similarities and differences.

Our point is that, when you look carefully at an assignment, you will often see that the assignment is pushing you toward a particular method of organizing your information—toward an initial plan. There are four common methods of organization that you should keep in mind when attempting to devise an initial plan: *categorizing, sequencing, comparing/contrasting*, and *finding causes and effects*. We will discuss these more thoroughly in the next chapter, but we introduce them here so that you can see how certain assignments may push you toward one of these methods.

Many assignments suggest that *categories* should be used to organize information as it is gathered. Sometimes the assignment will give you the categories. An assignment might ask you to

> discuss the distinguishing characteristics of three theories of grammar: traditional, structural, and transformational.

The categories for this assignment are obviously the three theories of grammar. Another assignment might require you to

> discuss the various forms of syncretism that occurred in the ancient Near East, focusing on such categories as religion, politics, economics, literature, social arrangements, science, etc.

From this assignment you know that you will need to find some information under the categories "religion," "politics," "economics," and so forth. Perhaps more often you will have to decide on your own categories. Assignments with the following directives could lead you to a method of organization based on categories: "describe," "assess," "weigh," "examine," "analyze," and "explain." You might be asked to

> examine the political preferences of students at this university by conducting a limited survey.

For this assignment you would need to use some categories of "political preference," perhaps categories based on party (Republican, Democratic, Libertarian, Independent) or perhaps categories based on political philosophy (conservative, liberal, socialist, etc.). These categories would help you design your survey, and would enable you to organize your data.

Some assignments push you toward another method of organization: *sequencing*. Assignments with such directives as "trace," "outline," and "list" suggest that your information should be organized in a sequence. The following assignment indicates that the information you gather should be organized chronologically, or in a time sequence.

> The authors of the United States Constitution made no mention of political parties in that document because they hoped none would appear in the new nation. Yet almost immediately parties became an integral part of American political life. Trace the rise and fall of political parties from the Federalist Era to the Civil War, paying attention to what constituencies (i.e., social classes, occupational groups, geographic regions) the various parties represented.

Some assignments suggest an initial plan in which you must *compare or contrast* points of information. Sometimes the assignment will specifically state that you are to "compare" or "contrast" two things. These two directives give you a fairly clear idea of what the teacher wants you to do for the assignment. The word *contrast* means to look at differences. The word *compare* means to set things side by side and look at the ways they are alike and different. Although the word *compare* at one time meant to look at similarities only, it now usually means to examine either similarities or differences, whichever are more appropriate—or both. (If in doubt, you might want to check with the instructor on a "compare" assignment to see if both similarities and differences are to be discussed.) But the compare/contrast method of organization can also be suggested by other directive words. You might be asked to "assess" two plans for organizing the staff of a factory, or to "distinguish between" two theories of personality, or to "choose the best of" a set of marketing strategies. In each case, the assignment involves organizing your information so that the plans, theories, or strategies are put side by side and compared.

Another method of organization involves thinking in terms of *causes and effects*. Some assignments, such as the following, can lead you to use this method.

> Assume that the United States suddenly discovered enormous reserves of oil and natural gas within its territorial waters. What consequences would this discovery have on U.S. foreign policy?

The assignment leads you to focus on effects. Possible effects might be effects on relations with Middle Eastern nations, effects on relations with European allies, and effects on relations with communist-bloc countries. Other assignments might lead you to search for causes.

A good deal of publicity has been given to the "writing crisis" in American education. Assuming that students really do write less well than they used to, discuss the reasons for a decline in writing achievement.

The causes might include: decreased support for education, changes in teaching styles, and influence of nonprint media. When the assignment tells you to look for causes or effects, you know something about the kind of information you need to gather.

Our point is that many assignments suggest a particular method of organization as an initial plan for gathering your information. But the directive words in assignments are not always specific enough to push you toward a particular method. General directives such as "discuss," "examine," or "analyze" can take on various meanings, depending on the context in which they are used. For example, the directive "examine" can be used to suggest different methods of development.

Examine the factors involved in designing an assembly line for producing a particular product. (Here the assignment involves organization according to categories.)

Examine the rise of the theory of social Darwinism. (Here the assignment directs you toward a chronological sequence.)

Examine two methods of teaching beginning reading. (Here the assignment pushes you toward comparison.)

Examine the reasons for and the consequences of eliminating the Electoral College System. (Here the assignment suggests an organization based on causes and effects.)

From these examples it should be clear that for many assignments you have to look further than the directive words to discover which method of organization is likely to be most useful. Often you have to consider the context in which the directive is used. You need to base your plan on the meaning of the entire assignment, not simply on the directive word.

Some assignments, like the following, suggest that you should break a larger concept down into its parts or factors, even though you aren't explicitly told to "categorize."

Analyze Japan's post–World War II economic success.

In this case the "success" could be divided into its major factors: political stability, labor-management relations, education, etc. Other assignments suggest you should group factors together.

> Find at least twelve magazine advertisements for cigarettes. Discuss
> the appeals used in these advertisements.

After finding the ads, you first list all the appeals you find: outdoors,
ruggedness, women, affluence, freshness, taste, nature, good looks,
sophistication, relaxation, low tar, etc. You then group these appeals
into limited health risk, upward mobility, masculinity and feminin-
ity, etc. When the assignment suggests that you should break a concept into parts or put factors into a group, it guides you toward using
categories.

Similarly, assignments can contain clues which point you toward the other three methods of organization. If an assignment indicates that the information will consist of steps, stages, or events in
time, then an organizational plan based on sequence will probably
be useful. Although the directive word "describe" is vague, the following assignment suggests that you should use sequential organization.

> Describe the process through which a new educational theory be-
> comes part of accepted doctrine and then begins to influence curric-
> ulum development.

If an assignment asks you to focus on ideas, events, or causes which
are clearly alike or different, or if you are to weigh, evaluate, or
critique two concepts, you should adopt an initial plan based on
comparison/contrast. The following assignment directs you to compare two theories.

> Two theories of presidential power are the stewardship and executive
> prerogative theories. Assess the relative importance of these two the-
> ories in the twentieth century.

Other assignments may direct your attention to influences, origins,
or consequences, and thus lead you to organize your information in
terms of causes or effects.

> Discuss the consequences of family planning programs in India.

Problem 1-1. Here are some assignments which suggest an initial
plan for organizing a paper. Discuss the method of organization that
might be appropriate for each.

1. Analyze the skills needed to be a successful football player.
2. Contrast the life of an urban and a rural slave in the year 1820.

3. Choose a work of art reproduced in the text or on view in the gallery and write a descriptive analysis of the form.
4. Explain the process of dental decay.
5. Discuss the effects of consumerism on the American economy.

Sometimes assignments will be more complex than those we have discussed so far. Many assignments suggest that your initial plans should involve more than one method of organization.

> Spain was at war for most of the century following 1550. What was the impact of this warfare on Spain and the Spanish Empire—politically, socially, and economically? In which of these categories were the pressures greatest and why?

This assignment seems to include categorizing (the categories are given: political, social, economic) and also suggests finding effects (the "impact" or effects of a century of warfare). Moreover you are asked to arrange the effects in a sequence according to which areas experienced the greatest pressures.

The following assignment is also long and complex:

> Consider the process by which a person is converted to a new ideology (political, religious, or whatever). What kind of person is the most likely prospect for such a conversion? Why? Describe the psychological process by which a person is converted. If you wish, use a hypothetical case study.

The directive in the first sentence—"consider"—is one of those vague, general directives that gives you little help in devising an initial plan for the paper. The meaning of "ideology" may also need to be clarified. The next part of this assignment, which consists of two questions, is a bit more helpful. These questions begin to narrow the assignment topic from the general "process by which a person is converted" to the specific kind of person who is susceptible to conversion. The next sentence is directive: "Describe the psychological process by which a person is converted." This sentence seems to be the *real* topic for the assignment. Compare this sentence with the first. They are similar, but the third sentence is more specific: the directive is "describe" and the process is identified as "psychological." Although the directive "describe" is vague, the word "process" provides a strong clue to the kind of initial plan that might be useful for this paper. If you are going to be dealing with a process, then you will probably think in terms of various stages in the process, arranged according to some kind of sequence. This means that you will have to find information to fill in all the steps in the process of being converted. Finally, the last sentence in this assignment suggests one way to do the paper: through a hypothetical case study. This sentence raises a number of questions. Do you know what a "hypothetical case study" is? Have you seen a model? Moreover, you should ask yourself how valuable this instructor's suggestion is. Does the teacher really want you to do a case study? Would your paper be considered weak if you decided not to do the case study? Or would the instructor be impressed if you used a different, perhaps more original method to present your information? These are difficult questions. In answering them, consider what you know about the instructor and how confident you feel about tackling the assignment from a particular direction.

Plans Devised from Undirected Assignments

To this point we have been focusing on directed assignments—assignments that contain at least some clues for helping you devise an initial plan for your paper. But some assignments may be so general and undirected that they provide almost no clues for an initial plan. You might encounter an assignment like the following:

> You will be expected to turn in a ten-to-fifteen page project by November 16. Subject matter is your own choice, so long as it deals with something we have wrestled with during the term. Make your subject clear, direct, and meaningful to your own professional interests.

In such a situation, you are on your own as far as a topic and direction for the paper are concerned. However, you can sometimes rewrite an assignment to make it more directed. To do this you can try mimicking the teacher-directed assignments we have been discussing, using some of the same directive words to arrive at a tentative method of organization. For example, suppose you are faced with the following topic for a course in secondary education:

> Most high school teachers encounter the problem of maintaining discipline. Write a paper in which you discuss the topic of discipline in the schools.

You might rewrite this undirected assignment using one of the directives which indicate a method of organization based on a sequence: "trace," "list," or "outline." You would then begin to think in terms of progress through time: historical accounts, sequences of important events, or major developments in the field. You could rewrite the topic as:

> Trace the history of discipline problems in the secondary schools since World War II.

Or you could choose to rewrite the assignment so that it suggests a comparison. You would then try to find issues or problems related to the subject and compare them. For example, you could rewrite the assignment as:

> Compare the problems of discipline in U.S. public schools with problems of discipline in English state-operated schools.

Or you could use a directive which involved categorization, such as "explain," or "analyze." You would then divide the topic into several categories. You might consider rewriting the assignment as:

> Analyze the major contemporary approaches to maintaining discipline in the classroom.

When your initial plan has to be based on a rewritten version of an undirected assignment, this plan should be considered a tentative guide until you see how well it works for organizing the information on your topic. When a teacher gives you a directed assignment, your initial plan is likely to lead you to a firm organizational scheme, because the teacher usually knows a good bit about the available information on the topic and how this information can be organized. However, when you rewrite an undirected assignment you probably have only a preliminary idea of what the important information will be, and perhaps only a "hunch" about a good way to approach the topic. As you gather ideas, facts, or data on the topic, your organizational plan will become more specific.

When you rewrite assignments so that they are more directed, you should try to make certain that your new assignment is a good one. What makes a "good" assignment? This question is not easy to answer, but there are several critieria that can help you assess the quality of an assignment you might be considering.

Complexity. When creating your own assignment, make it manageable. Try to avoid an assignment that contains more points than you can possibly discuss, as does the following:

Describe New York City, its history, the culture of its different ethnic groups, and its relation to important aspects of America's economic and political life.

Such a topic is not manageable because it contains too many points. A person who chooses such a topic could write for a long, long time.

Simplicity. Topics become simpleminded when they point you toward information which is obvious. An assignment such as the following is dangerous because it could lead to statements of the obvious:

Discuss the differences between living in the big city and living in a small town.

It is too easy to resort to the obvious: towns are quieter and safer than cities, but cities have more facilities, such as shopping, cultural events, etc.

Availability of Information. It is easy to find information on some subjects; others may present problems. Sometimes not much has been written on a subject. Or your library may not have key documents or publications. A preliminary search could keep you from wasting your time. If you have trouble finding information but want to pursue the topic anyway, your instructor might know of additional resources, or might suggest alternative topics that could lead you in more profitable directions.

Freshness. One person's oldness is someone else's newness. But you should be aware that there are topics that teachers find stale, boring, or hackneyed. A teacher may express a dislike for papers on abortion, gun control, or capital punishment because these topics appear over and over again in student writing. When in doubt, discuss your idea with your instructor.

Problem 1-2. Evaluate the following topics according to the four criteria: complexity, simplicity, availability of information, and freshness.

1. Discuss the relation of language to thought, the ways the languages of the world differ from each other, and how to teach foreign languages to elementary school children.
2. Describe six important ways that life can be very difficult.
3. Compare and contrast the effects of environmental lobbies on

wilderness preservation programs in Idaho, Montana, and Alaska. In doing so, describe the basic arguments that relate to local residents, business, politics, and future legislation.

4. Discuss the power of positive thinking.
5. Examine basketball as a sport.
6. Analyze how teaching in high school differs from teaching in elementary school.
7. Explain the nutritional difference between white sugar, brown sugar, honey, molasses, and raw sugar.
8. Analyze both the underlying and the immediate causes of the gradual erosion of England's stability between 1550 and 1630.

In this chapter we have emphasized the importance of having an initial plan to guide your work on an academic paper. This plan is sometimes obtained from a standard format, but often must be devised either from clues given in a directed assignment or from your own reformulation of an undirected assignment. When you know something about the methods that are most useful for organizing academic papers—methods based on categorizing, sequencing, comparing or contrasting, finding causes and effects, or some combination of these—you have a guide to help you in gathering and organizing your information. These methods of developing your ideas are so important that we consider them in greater detail in the next chapter.

Problem 1-3. Some of the following writing assignments are simple and directed, while others are complex and undirected. In each case, assess the extent to which the assignment enables you to devise an initial plan for organizing the information for the paper. Which of the four methods of organization might be most successful for each assignment? Do any of the assignments seem to direct you toward more than one method? Do any of the assignments need to be rewritten so that they are more directive?

1. Collect five songs, riddles, proverbs, jokes, or stories (stay with the same genre) from oral tradition, and analyze their significance for the people who know them.
2. Our cities are all facing problems of transportation. As increasing numbers of cars stream into urban areas, buildings must be torn down to make parking lots but little is done to encourage public transportation. Discuss the alternatives to automobile travel, evaluating the difficulties in implementing effective change.
3. Write a short paper in which you discuss Russian imperialism in the third world.

4. State factors which would have a bearing on a patient's attitudes toward his/her oral health (cultural, racial, economic, past experiences, previous oral health education, etc.).

5. What you are required to do for this paper is to write a scenario or short story in which you demonstrate your knowledge of how our political system works. Some possible suggestions follow, but you should not feel compelled to draw upon them.

   a) A takeoff on Dr. Strangelove. You might want to portray a president caught up in events he cannot control and demonstrate his inability to control the people and institutions around him. This scenario might also be appropriate for a Cuban missile crisis or a Lyndon Johnson–Vietnam war type situation. You would probably want to include in your story aspects of public opinion, bureaucratic inertia, presidential-congressional conflict, etc.

   b) A story of someone caught up in the criminal justice system.

   c) A "Mr. Smith Goes to Washington" scenario. This might be the story of someone who gets upset with the political system to the point that he decides to do something about it, like run for office. Such a story might include the role of the political party, money in elections, interest groups, congressional behavior, congressional-bureaucratic relationships, the frustrations of the legislative process, etc. A variant of this one might be one who goes to Washington, not as part of the establishment, but rather as an individual or member of a group outside the establishment to petition the government for a redress of grievances.

   d) You could do a story of someone caught up in a bureaucratic tangle. Perhaps an IRS computer has determined by mistake that he owes $100,000 in back taxes, and he has problems trying to convince the IRS that they have made a mistake or that they have the wrong John Smith.

   The possibilities are practically endless, but remember—the grading criteria for this paper place a premium on creativity and accurate portrayal of those facets of the political system which are relevant to your story. Obviously, no footnotes or other documentation are required and there is no page limit. This paper constitutes approximately 40% of your grade, so do it well. Good luck.

6. One of the major issues in curriculum development is "disciplinarity." Write a paper exploring this issue from the point of view of your own subject matter specialization.

7. Discuss the issues that arise in the regulation of natural monopolies. What solutions to these problems have been adopted in the real world?

8. Go to the visual aids department in the library and check out a filmstrip in your subject area. How could you use this filmstrip

in a lesson for a class you might teach? What are the strengths and/or weaknesses in the filmstrip? Are there areas you would have to emphasize to your class? Would you provide a class study guide? Why or why not?

9. Contrast the positions of conservative and liberal politicians on environmental protection and pollution control.

10. In the preface to *The Nigger of the Narcissus*, Joseph Conrad discusses the task of the artist. In a short paper of approximately 500 words, discuss Joseph Conrad's definition of the artist's task in relation to a poem chosen from your text (one which has not been discussed in class). In explicating the poem make sure that you discuss carefully the theme, imagery, and diction as support for your interpretation. The final paper should be typed and free of grammatical and mechanical errors.

11. Discuss in detail some of the more remarkable features of Egyptian civilization.

12. Examine the pedagogical implications of three different methods of teaching elementary geometry.

13. Assume you are employed in private practice by one dentist and due to limited facilities the entire dental office staff will be relocating. Given an unlimited budget, the dentist would like you to design as well as select all the equipment and resources needed for the preventive dentistry room. The dentist wants a complete budget and the following information with rationale for each:
    a) Floor plan (including location of equipment and resources)
    b) Interior design
    c) Equipment
    d) Resources
    (Note: equipment and resources are to be prioritized.)

14. Select a religious or political leader who made skillful use of propaganda, or a situation in which propaganda was used very skillfully or very ineptly, and analyze:
    a) how propaganda was used by this person or in this situation,

    and

    b) why this propaganda was effective (or ineffective).

15. Propose a problem in our society in which the understandings of a linguistic anthropologist would prove useful. Write a brief proposal for the application of these understandings to the solution of the problem. Include your estimate of budget, time, personnel, and equipment required and a reasonably objective method for evaluating project success or failure.

16. Pick one type of advertisement (print, film, or whatever). What types of products, under what conditions, and to what types of consumers is this type of advertisement good for? Why?

17. Analyze the top ten songs of the week regarding their connection to the culture of the listeners, singers, and songwriters. Consider

both music and lyrics, and keep social and economic relations in mind as a part of culture.

18. Spend a day in jail or the district court and write up your observations in terms that relate language and culture. Note any generalizations that emerge.

19. Observe, compare, and contrast the language used by two of the three major network evening newscasts and the commercial messages that accompany them. (Compare network to network, rather than news to commercial.)

20. Pick a contemporary social problem that we face in our society and discuss its consequences for education.

21. Trace the assimilation of one of the Caucasian immigrant groups into mainstream American life. Compare this pattern of assimilation with that for a non-Caucasian group.

2 | *Using Four Methods of Development*

In the first chapter we introduced four methods of organization and emphasized that you can use them in constructing an initial plan. We showed how this plan can guide your search for information and help you organize that information after you find it. The same methods you use to devise an initial plan are also methods for developing the main points that will make up the body of the paper. Each method is a way of thinking about ideas, events, or processes—a way of developing and organizing your information so that it seems complete and sensible. In this chapter we will explore further these four basic methods of development—categorizing, sequencing, comparing/contrasting, and finding causes and effects—and give you practice in using each of them to organize and develop ideas.

Categorizing

You can get categories either by dividing or grouping. Which process you use depends on how you start your investigation. If you begin with a single event, concept, or object, you can develop your ideas by dividing your subject into parts. For example, if you are examining the concept of political ideology you might decide to divide it into communism, socialism, totalitarianism, fascism, and anarchism. If, on the other hand, you already have a set of items, you might organize them by grouping them according to some criterion. If you were examining the interviewing techniques of major television personalities, you might begin by listing as many newscasters as you could think of. Then you would group them by style, perhaps using such categories as "aggressive," "congenial," and "diplomatic." Whether you divide or group, you end up with categories which you can use to organize and develop the ideas for your paper.

DIVIDING AND GROUPING

Sometimes you will be faced with a large topic which you can develop by dividing it into its major parts. Usually these parts will consist of conventional or commonplace categories. For instance, in discussing the topic of "the automobile," people usually need to divide this large topic into smaller common categories.

make	Chevrolet, Plymouth, Ford
model	Chevette, Reliant, Escort
body type	sedan, coupe, station wagon
size	full-size, medium-size, compact
engine type	V-8, six cylinder, four cylinder

The advantage of such conventional categories is that almost everyone is likely to recognize them. For example, people usually find it easier to talk about cars when they can refer to such common categories as make or model. Academic disciplines also make use of conventional categories to divide up the major topics or issues in a field. For example, in developmental psychology the two categories of "nature" and "nurture" explanations of development are traditionally used to discuss the larger concept of "human growth." When you know the conventional categories in a discipline it can be useful to employ them in dividing your topic into its major parts.

Problem 2-1. What are some conventional ways to categorize the following subjects?

√ 1. Sports
2. College students
3. Pets
4. Rocks

There are disadvantages as well as advantages to using conventional categories: they can appear overused and can lead to a careless examination of your subject. If you were writing a paper on the student population of a particular high school, you might consider dividing these students by using such familiar categories as "college prep," "business," and "vocational" students. Such categories might serve your purpose in the paper, particularly if you were examining the pros and cons of "tracking" students into a particular program. But by accepting too readily these conventional categories you might not take a deeper look at other ways in which these high school students could be divided: by social groups, by extracurricular interests, or even by philosophies of life. By using the conventional categories you might also accept too readily the divisions implied by the grouping, when in reality these categories may be breaking down. Many vocational students, for example, may be preparing to attend a technical college.

When the conventional categories seem overused, or when you simply don't know of any traditional categories for your topic, then you may be able to create your own. Sometimes you may get an insight into a new way to divide up a topic. But inventing divisions for a large topic is a difficult procedure. You can't know what the meaningful divisions are until you understand a great deal about the subject. Therefore, if you can't break a large topic into conventional parts, you may need to use a different strategy for finding categories: gathering specific details on the subject and then grouping these details by common features.

Suppose you were given a simple list such as the following:

bull snake	pig	eagle	lizard
dove	duck	donkey	porcupine
mule	tarantula	grasshopper	mosquito
anchovy	whale	ant	crab
sparrow	cockroach	turtle	red worm

You could group these creatures into categories using the feature "number of legs."

no legs	*two legs*	*four legs*	*six legs*	*eight legs*
anchovy	dove	mule	ant	crab
red worm	eagle	pig	cockroach	tarantula
bull snake	duck	donkey	mosquito	
whale	sparrow	turtle	grasshopper	
		lizard		
		porcupine		

Or you could group them using a different feature, such as "size."

small	*medium*	*large*	*extra large*
ant	duck	donkey	whale
mosquito	porcupine	mule	
etc.	etc.	etc.	

You could also group the creatures according to "diet," "intelligence," "means of locomotion," or "complexity."

Problem 2–2. What are some features that could be used to group these two lists of words?

1. stroll   step   march   hobble
   tread   hike   glide   clip clop
   amble   waddle   lurch   strut
   plod   trot   limp   clomp
   trudge   jiggy-jog stumble along tramp
   shuffle
2. shame   jealousy distress   delight
   excitement joy   affection   fear
   anger   disgust   filial affection parental affection
   hope   anxiety   envy   disappointment

Problem 2-3. The following exercise simulates a situation in which you have a number of facts about a particular event, but you need to create categories that would be useful for sorting out the facts.

John Jones is accused of stealing chickens from Farmer Smith. Jones pleads "not guilty"; he claims that he bought a couple of chickens from a traveling salesman (who left town). Here is the evidence.

Witness: Suzie Bell White swears she saw Jones running down the street with two chickens under his arms.

Witness: Sheriff Smith arrested Jones at the dinner table. At the time, Jones was gorging himself on chicken, biscuits, and gravy.

Exhibit: A bucket with chicken feathers in it, found outside Jones's house.

Witness: Lucky Louie, salesman of encyclopedias, denies knowing or meeting Jones. Picked up nineteen miles down the road, he swears he was never in town.

Witness: Betty Wilson claims to have bought a set of encyclopedias from Lucky Louie.

Exhibit: Sales receipt for 25 volume set of encyclopedias. (Made out to Betty Wilson.)

Exhibit: Chicken bones on a plate, collected by Sheriff Smith from Jones's house.

Witness: Farmer Smith, who swears that two chickens are missing from his coop.

Exhibit: Jones's police record showing four previous arrests for chicken stealing.

Exhibit: Laboratory report: chicken grease found on Jones's hands and face when arrested.

Witness: Psychiatrist Dr. Mindbender testifies that Jones came to him with terrible obsession about chickens.

Exhibit: Footprint, size 9D, outside Farmer Smith's chicken coop.

Witness: Sheriff Smith testifies Jones had mud on his floor. The mud had chicken droppings in it.

Exhibit: Tennis shoe, size 9D, found in bushes behind Jones's house. (Matches footprint found outside Farmer Smith's chicken coop.)

Exhibit: Jones's foot size: 6A.

If you had to decide on whether Jones is innocent or guilty, what categories could you use to sort out the evidence?

Both dividing and grouping are useful methods of devising categories. Sometimes you will be able to divide a large topic into conventional categories; sometimes you will have to obtain your categories by grouping specific details. Often, however, you will find yourself using a combination of dividing and grouping as you constantly reevaluate the usefulness of your categories.

Suppose you were assigned to write a paper on the "outcast" in America. Assume this assignment provides little hint of an initial plan for how to organize the paper. Since you are beginning with a single concept, you decide to begin developing your ideas by dividing the concept into specific categories of people who might be considered outcasts in some respect:

black students in a predominantly
   white high school
physically handicapped people
old people
foreigners
the mentally retarded
religious fanatics

people who dress oddly
people with pronounced
   dialects
fat people
ugly people
alcoholics

This is a fairly good list. But you now have too many categories to use in your paper. Your next task is to group these categories, seeing how they might go together to form a few categories of outcasts. By looking for common features you may create two categories:

1. Outcasts due to differences in physical appearance
2. Outcasts due to differences in behavior

You should make sure that all your outcasts can be grouped within these two categories:

1. Outcasts due to differences in physical appearance: blacks, fat people, ugly people, physically handicapped, people who dress oddly, old people.

2. Outcasts due to differences in behavior: alcoholics, people with dialects, religious fanatics, mentally retarded, foreigners.

During this process, several things may happen. First, you may begin to think of additional examples of outcasts. If blacks are in some cases outcasts, then so are Asian-Americans. If fat people are left out of mainstream American life (who ever saw a fat model on TV?), then so are very short people. If mentally retarded people are outcasts, then so are people with illnesses, such as people who are slowly dying of cancer. If religious fanatics qualify as outcasts, then so do people with unpopular political views. Second, you may have difficulty deciding which larger category certain outcasts fit into. Foreigners may be very different in physical appearance (skin color and dress) as well as behavior. Old people are often different in their actions and ideas as well as appearance. These difficulties in grouping may lead you to question the usefulness of your categories. When you examine the outcasts that get lumped together, you may wish to create new categories based on other features. The point is that by putting your ideas into categories you are not only developing your paper, you are also learning to think more clearly about your ideas—adding examples, seeing similarities and differences, and testing the soundness of your categories.

Let's suppose that as a result of your initial efforts you decide the two categories are too broad. Thus you try out another set of categories.

race	blacks, Asians, etc.
appearance	fat, short, ugly, deformed, old, those who dress oddly
handicap	physical, mental
illness	alcoholism, cancer
background	regional dialect, foreigners
belief	religious fanatics, political radicals

You may feel that categories based on these features more accurately serve your purposes in writing the paper.

LABELING YOUR CATEGORIES

Labeling is an important aspect of categorizing. For example, in the student paper "School Violence" (reprinted at the end of this chapter), the author discusses six factors which might motivate school crime. She helps us understand and remember these factors (or categories) by giving them labels: drugs and rebellion, hostility, malicious play, adolescent emotional problems, poor grades, and school gangs. Her labels undoubtedly helped her think about her subject; they also make her main points clear and memorable.

Sometimes it is easy to find labels for your categories because there are already labels traditionally associated with them. The following problem is designed to provide examples of some of these conventional labels.

Problem 2-4. Provide conventional labels for the following descriptions of categories. (If you don't know the conventional labels, you might try to make up some of your own.)

1. Description of Category
   a) Magazines that are published once every seven days
   b) Magazines that are published twice a month
   c) Magazines that are published once a month
   d) Magazines that are published four times a year
2. Description of Category
   a) A plant that lives only one year and does not grow again the following spring
   b) A plant that produces flowers year after year and need not be replanted
   c) A plant that lasts two years, usually producing flowers only the second year
3. Description of Category
   a) People with large bones and an abundance of muscle
   b) People who are lean and slightly muscled
   c) People who have large stomachs and much fatty tissue on different parts of their body

When there aren't any conventional labels for your categories you will have to try to devise some of your own. What makes a "good" label? Essentially, a label is good if it is *clear* and *memorable*. You can judge the clarity of a label by asking yourself whether a reader could predict what you mean by the label. If you look at the labels used by the author of "School Violence," you will see that they are clear because they enable you to predict what she will include under each category: drugs and rebellion, malicious play, poor grades, etc.

Problem 2-5. See if you can predict the meaning of the sets of labels in the following exercises.

1. In August of 1978, a *Time Magazine* reporter went on the Annual Great Bike Ride Across Iowa and classified the participants in this

event into five categories. He gave each category a label. Can you guess from the label the style of biker it refers to?

a) Bike Nuts
b) Amiable Amateurs
c) Togetherness Families
d) Senior Cyclers
e) Handlebar Hedonists

2. D. R. Olson, in an article entitled "Notes on a Theory of Instruction" in *Cognition and Instruction*, edited by K. Klahr (Hillsdale, N.J.: Lawrence Erlbaum, 1976) used these labels in categorizing the theories he discusses:

a) meddling
b) modeling
c) muddling

Can you predict what Olson means by these three labels?

3. Researchers describing stages in the creative process use the following labels. State what you think they mean by each label.

a) preparation
b) incubation
c) illumination
d) verification

In addition to being clear, it is helpful if labels are memorable. One of the reasons for using labels is to enable your reader to remember your main points. You hope that the labels will stick in the reader's mind. The labels used in Problem 2-5 are probably going to be interesting and memorable for most readers. The labels from the article on the bike ride are striking because of their originality. Olson's labels for theories of instruction are memorable both because they all begin with the same sound (a technique called alliteration) and because they are based on a subtle kind of humor (for example, it is funny to call discovery learning "muddling"). The labels for stages in the creative process all rhyme and some have a metaphorical quality—the process of "incubation" brings to mind an image of an egg getting ready to hatch, an image which accurately reflects the meaning of the stage.

Although some of the best labels are original and memorable, you need to be careful that your labels are not overly humorous or possibly offensive to some groups. For example, the conventional labels for the third set of categories in Problem 2-4 are "mesomorph," "ectomorph," and "endomorph." Instead of these traditional labels, you might decide to use labels which would be more memorable and which would help the reader predict what each label designated. You might think of the following labels: "sluggers," "slims," and "slobs." Although these labels are both clear and memorable, they seem too cute for academic writing. Moreover, the term "slobs" might offend people who are somewhat overweight because it implies that such people are sloppy and careless. You need to be certain that your labels do not have associations that might offend readers. A sociologist who decides that welfare recipients fall into three groups, and who labels these three groups the "social misfits," the "unemployed proletariat," and the "abandoned dependents," runs the risk of offending at least two groups of people. By using the word "misfits" he may alienate those sympathetic to people receiving government assistance; by using "proletariat," a Marxist term, he may anger those who think only a Communist would use such a term. In academic writing it is usually better to choose more neutral terms for labels—but not terms so neutral they are useless as memory aids. The labels "category 1," "category 2," and "category 3" are neutral and wouldn't offend anyone, but they don't enable a reader to predict what the labels refer to.

Problem 2-6. The following passages contain labels for categories. Identify those labels that might offend some readers and explain why you think they would be offensive.

1. For the purpose of our economic analysis, we can divide the nations of the world as follows: backward, developing, and prosperous.

2. There is a considerable range in the attitudes of Americans regarding the use of forests. There are the Sierra Club fanatics who love trees more than people, the fence straddlers who want both conservation and development, and the "Let the Next Generation Be Damned" exploiters who don't care if a single tree is left standing as long as they turn a profit.

Problem 2-7. In this problem you are to provide a label to fit the information provided for the category. For some you will be able to use conventional labels; for other categories you will need to devise a label.

1. *a*) A person stands up and without preparation gives a speech.
   b) A person recites from memory a speech prepared in advance.
   c) A person reads a speech prepared in advance.
   d) A person carefully prepares a speech but delivers it without notes or text.
2. *a*) One threat to human life is posed by the nuclear bomb. It is possible that man could literally blow up the world.
   b) Another threat is posed by the high birth rate in many countries. If the number of mouths to feed becomes too large, the need for food may outstrip man's ability to feed himself.

    c) Another danger is the destruction of the environment through excessive industrialization, careless use of chemicals, or the ravenous mining of natural resources. Man could so desecrate the earth that it can no longer support life.

3. *a*) People who have learned a foreign language in the land in which it is spoken report that at first they suffer through a period in which they understand very little and speak even less. They are very self-conscious about their language skills and feel very uncomfortable at being unable to speak easily and at having to ask people to repeat what they have said to them.

    b) After suffering through this period, however, they become more proficient. Speaking and understanding are still difficult and require a great deal of concentration, but they manage to get along. They can even talk pleasantly with the corner grocer and sometimes share a joke with a neighbor. But if the conversation switches to an unfamiliar subject, the vocabulary for which they have not yet mastered, they are lost.

    c) Then, usually after several years in the country, there comes a day when they wake up and realize that language isn't a problem for them anymore. Their second language has ceased to be something to be learned and instead has become something to be used—used in the same way they were accustomed to using their first language.

4. *a*) One hypothesis concerning the origin of Black English emphasizes its similarities to African languages and to varieties of English called creoles spoken in the West Indies, to Gullah and Jamaican, for example. Advocates of this hypothesis maintain that the English spoken by black Americans evolved from a creole, from a language that was a mixture of African languages and standard English.

    b) Another hypothesis emphasizes how similar Black English is to so-called standard English, to the dialects of English spoken by white Americans. The undeniable differences between Black English and standard English are explained as cases of dialect divergence: blacks, removed physically and socially from whites, began to speak a dialect which diverged from that of whites. Advocates of this second hypothesis assert that Black English is simply another dialect of English.

Problem 2-8. Often you must categorize first—then label. Read the following information concerning the plight of a small town. How would you categorize the problems this small town is having? What labels could you use for these categories?

    1. Two plants north of town spew noxious clouds of pollution directly into the air.

2. Poor zoning regulations have resulted in overbuilding of the hillsides, resulting in erosion.
3. An overabundance of septic tanks in the north part of town has caused contamination of ground water supplies.
4. Overuse of fertilizers has caused excessive runoff of chemicals into the river that runs through town.
5. A potato factory near the center of town periodically dumps organic wastes into the river.
6. An inadequate landfill north of town is poorly managed by the city and the result has been blowing debris throughout the city, a continuous foul odor, and a serious health hazard to residents in the north part of town.
7. A small cattle feedlot a short distance upstream on the river has been improperly managed: too many cattle have been kept in the feed pens and the pens have been constructed too close to the river. The result has been seepage of animal wastes into the river, especially after heavy rains.
8. Joy riders on motorcycles during the summer and snowmobiles during the winter have stripped several surrounding hills of vegetation, causing serious problems with water runoff, especially in the spring.
9. The city council has consistently refused to push for major reforms that would curb industrial pollution. Members fear regulations would close plants, cause unemployment, and reduce the quality of life for citizens of the town.

Sequencing

Organizing ideas according to a sequence is usually not difficult. Many sequences involve chronology, or an ordering of events as they occur in time. The most common chronological sequence is from earliest to most recent event. Other sequences involve steps or stages in a process, and for these the simplest organization is from first to last.

Problem 2-9. Organize the following data into chronological order by numbering the items according to time of occurrence.

1. Roald Amundsen of Norway reached the South Pole with four men and a dog team on December 14, 1911.
2. The U.S. Navy's Operation Deep Freeze, led by Admiral Richard E. Byrd, was part of American scientific efforts in support of the International Geophysical Year. During the period 1955–57 it established five coastal stations and three interior stations.
3. In 1934–37, John Rymill led the British Graham Land expedition which discovered that the Palmer Peninsula is part of the Antarctic mainland.

4. Captain Robert F. Scott of Great Britain and four companions reached the South Pole from Ross Island on January 18, 1912. All five died in the undertaking.
5. In 1934–35, the American explorer Richard E. Byrd returned to the Antarctic and wintered alone at an advance weather station at 80° 08'.
6. The American explorer Richard E. Byrd established Little America on the Bay of Whales in 1929. He crossed the South Pole by airplane on November 29 and dropped a U.S. flag on the pole.
7. Hubert Willins of Britain was the first to use an airplane over the Antarctic region. He made his flight in 1928.

Often when you have many points to organize in a sequence it is best to group several points into a major step or stage in the overall sequence. If you were writing a paper on how to make bread, you might come up with a long list of things to do:

1. Put 2 cups warm water into a large mixing bowl.
2. Add two packages of dry yeast.
3. Add ¼ cup liquid shortening.
4. Add ¼ to ½ cup sweetening (honey, molasses, corn syrup, etc.).
5. Add ½ tsp. salt.
6. Let stand five minutes.
7. Add 1 cup rye flour.
8. Add 1 cup oatmeal.
9. Add ½ cup whole wheat flakes.
10. Add 3 cups whole wheat flour.
11. Mix well.
12. Let stand for fifteen minutes.
13. Add 4 cups flour (white or a white and whole wheat mixture).
14. Knead dough five minutes.
15. Let stand to rise to double original size.
16. Knead ½ minute.
17. Separate into three loaves.
18. Put in three greased one-pound loaf pans.
19. Let rise to double size.
20. Bake at 350° for forty minutes.

If you tried to write your paper from this list, you could find things getting boring: "first you . . . then you add . . . and then you add . . . and then you add. . . ." You could solve this problem by organizing the individual directions into larger units, or steps:

Step 1: Making a liquid base
Into a large mixing bowl put
2 cups water

2 packages active dry yeast
¼ cup oil
½ tsp. salt
¼ to ½ c. sweetening (honey, molasses, corn syrup, etc.)
Mix well and let stand five minutes.

Step 2: Adding dry ingredients
Add 1 cup rye flour
1 cup oatmeal
½ cup whole wheat flakes
3 cups whole wheat flour

Step 3: Kneading
Add 4 cups flour (white or a white and whole wheat mixture) or enough flour to make a mass that holds together and pulls away from sides.
Knead dough five minutes.

Step 4: Letting rise
Let rise to double size.
Knead dough ½ minute.
Divide dough into thirds.
Put in greased one-pound loaf pans.
Let rise to double size.

Step 5: Baking
Bake at 350° for forty minutes.

The advantage of using steps is that you are able to group ideas to show relationships between the items in each step. For example, when learning to make bread it is easier to consider five recognizable steps (each composed of related activities) than to study a long list of individual, unrelated activities.

Problem 2-10. Which of the following subjects could you break down into steps or stages?

1. how to solve a right triangle using trigonometric functions
2. your autobiography
3. a comparison of two methods of persuading an audience
4. the development of children's syntactic competence
5. major cities of the United States
6. the evolution of Dickens's prose style

Problem 2-11. Here is a list of the major events in the history of a fictional country, Eastendia. Put these events into chronological order, then break the chronological order into steps or stages.

March 16, 1930. President Albert Peachcraft plants a rutabaga as a sign of reconciliation with outlawed factions in the government.

September 1890. Five rutabaga barons file bankruptcy.

September 19, 1845. Eastendia gains independence from Fritzia.

July 1, 1845. Eastendian Revolutionary War begins.

February 6, 1890. Albert Crump is assassinated while making a speech denouncing the creeping threat of big business and "gross monopolies" in the rutabaga trade.

July 6, 1845. First major battle against Fritzia.

July 7, 1845. Albert Pomp, acting president of Fritzia, resigns.

March 3, 1890. Due to the sudden death of Albert Crump, there is widespread reaction against the "Rutabaga Barons of Big Business."

August 15, 1845. General Albert Crump rides nude through the city of Utlib yelling "The war is over! The war is over!"

March 10, 1890. Congress votes to outlaw rutabagas.

September 30, 1845. Albert Crump elected president by popular vote.

May 19, 1931. First exports of rutabagas made since 1890.

June 10, 1931. President Albert Peachcraft proclaims the success of "Rutabaga politics."

Comparing and Contrasting

When you compare or contrast two ideas, events, or processes you put them side by side and look for similarities or differences. In using this method you often first categorize to get some points of comparison. If you are writing a paper comparing the advantages of buying a home with those of renting a home you might begin by listing briefly the advantages of each.

Buying	Renting
freedom to redecorate house and yard	freedom from worry of repairs and maintenance
more storage space	no down payment needed
tax advantages	gain in mobility since no house to sell
investment potential	money saved on down payment can be invested
provides more privacy	
gives enhanced credit ratings	time saved on maintenance can be used for recreation
freedom for children and pets	good if have little furniture

These advantages must then be grouped to find major points of comparison. Some possible categories would be recreational opportunity, financial benefits, and personal freedoms. In developing your paper you would discuss the advantages of buying and renting under each of your categories, using specific examples from your list.

After you have points of comparison on your topic and know how you might develop each point with explanations or illustrations, there is one more problem that needs to be considered: How will you organize your presentation of the main points of comparison? Two patterns are commonly used, although there are a number of variations. Suppose that you were studying the metric system of measurement and wanted to compare it to the English system. You decide to use the following points of comparison:

	English System	*Metric System*
Point A: Vocabulary	uses separate words (inches, feet, yards, etc.)	uses standard system of prefixes (centi-, milli-, etc.)
Point B: Base	the base is inconsistent (12 inches in a foot, 3 feet in a yard, etc.)	the base is consistent (always 10)
Point C: Utilization	limited (primarily in U.S.)	broad (most countries use metric)

One way to compare the two systems is to discuss the English system first, covering each of the three points, and then the metric system, taking up the same points in the same order. The advantage of this approach is that you get a complete view of each system as a whole— you would present a good overview of the English system and then a good overview of the metric system. The disadvantage is that it is somewhat difficult to contrast specific points, such as Point A: Vocabulary. You might find yourself repeating some information about the vocabulary of the English system when you discuss the vocabulary of the metric system, in order to make the contrast clear. The second approach is to discuss one specific point at a time, comparing the two systems in terms of that one point. Thus, the first topic of the paper would be a discussion of vocabulary in the English and metric systems. The second topic would be a comparison of the bases in the two systems. The advantage of this approach is that the contrasts are clear. If you have many points of comparison, or if your supporting material includes complex facts or statistics, it's usually better to use this second approach. The disadvantage can be that an overview of each main topic is lacking.

Problem 2-12. Here are some facts that could be included in a paper comparing nuclear fission with nuclear fusion. Impose some order on them first by categorizing to find some points of comparison, and second by using one of the two patterns of presenting these points.

1. In nuclear fission, large atoms split into smaller ones.
2. In the 1940s, American scientists were attempting to produce the atomic bomb. They were responsible for the breakthroughs that led to the development of atomic fission as a source of energy.
3. In nuclear fusion, small atoms combine to form helium, a very safe substance. No radioactive atoms are released.
4. In nuclear fusion, small atoms are combined into larger ones.
5. Scientists have not been able to produce a controlled nuclear fusion reaction. The main problem is that atoms have to be heated to a temperature of millions of degrees before they will fuse.
6. Deuterium, an isotope of hydrogen, is used in nuclear fusion.
7. Isotopes of uranium and plutonium are used in nuclear fission.
8. Uranium and plutonium are rare metals; they are found in only a few places on the earth.
9. Nuclear fission was discovered in 1938 by Otto Hahn and Fritz Strassmann.
10. Scientists have known since the 1930s that nuclear fusion was the process used by the sun and stars to radiate energy, but they didn't know how to make it occur until the 1950s. The hydrogen bomb is produced by nuclear fusion.
11. Deuterium is found wherever there is water.
12. Atomic power stations with fission reactors are now being used extensively in the U.S. and Europe.
13. Scientists have not been able to build a fusion reactor because they haven't come up with a way of heating atoms to make them hot enough to fuse. They are experimenting with magnetic fields which they hope can be used to hold the atoms in place while they are heated.
14. Nuclear fusion requires only a small amount of deuterium.
15. In nuclear fission large quantities of uranium or plutonium must be used.
16. Nuclear fission reactors are potentially dangerous because radioactive atoms are produced in the process. If the cooling apparatus malfunctioned, the core of the reactor could melt, sink out of its protective shield, and release large quantities of radioactive substances into the atmosphere.

Finding Causes and Effects

When the topic for your paper involves causes and effects you often need to begin your thinking about the topic by categorizing—identifying and labeling several major causes and effects. Suppose you are attempting to write a paper exploring the causes and effects of political instability in Bolivia, a country which has had 189 coups in 155 years of independence. You might focus on several major categories of causes for instability, perhaps seeking these in Bolivia's political history, in the structure of its economy, in the ethnic mixture of its population, or in its relations to other countries. A useful way to display the relative importance of these causes of instability is to place each cause on a continuum such as the following:

political history	structure of the economy	relations to other countries	ethnic mixture of population

most important _____|_____|_____|_____|_____ least important
causes   causes

In making decisions about where each cause fits on the continuum, you will have to evaluate carefully the importance of each cause.

After you have these major categories you could explore each one in greater depth. For example, in working on your third category—relations to other countries—you might first discuss Bolivia's relations with her Latin American neighbors, then her relations to the U.S., emphasizing how these relations have failed to foster stability. In the process of gathering more detailed information on Bolivia you would probably reject some of your categories and add others. You might decide that Bolivia's relations with other countries have little to do with her instability. Eventually, however, you would have some possible causes that you could develop in your paper.

If you are interested in the effects, not the causes, of Bolivia's instability, you might concentrate on the way in which constant political instability has had particular economic repercussions—how it has affected development of the country's resources. Or you might explore the psychological and social effects: How deeply has this system of revolving-door government affected the people of Bolivia? Has it disturbed people in the countryside? Or has it only affected those who live in La Paz—the capital—and other large cities? Have people become cynical about the political process? The above effects could be grouped into the categories "political," "economic," "psychological," and "social."

Finally, we should mention one problem that is peculiar to cause/effect papers—the problem of simplistic causes. Often people make snap judgments, latching onto single causes when the situation is really much more complex. It is characteristic, for instance, for people to blame the state of the nation on the president, without looking carefully at the complex causes of such problems as inflation.

People seem to like simple explanations. Bad spelling is often blamed exclusively on weak training in phonics. We often hear that if you work hard, you will always succeed. Television is blamed for increased violence and the demise of the American family. But in academic writing you are committed to exploring a problem in its complexity, and thus you should avoid simplistic, singular causes.

Problem 2-13. For the following items, state some probable causes that might guide your further investigation.

1. The pressure to get high grades in college
2. The natural food movement
3. The gradual disappearance of movie theaters from the central business districts of many American cities
4. The near-extinction of the American bald eagle

Problem 2-14. State some possible effects of the following subjects.

1. The heavy emphasis placed on team athletics—particularly basketball and football—in high school
2. The development of the fast-food restaurant
3. The rapid and continuing development of the minicomputer
4. The rising cost of energy

The four methods of development discussed in this chapter are ways of thinking that are involved not only in academic writing, but also in many everyday situations. To decide which college to attend you might have used the *categories* of cost, location, size, and academic programs. Then you might have *compared* two or more colleges using these categories. Later, in explaining your reasons for deciding on one of the colleges, you might trace the steps that led you to your choice, using a *sequence* to organize your explanation. Even later in your life, you might try to find reasons or *causes* for your decision. Or perhaps you would see your college experience as a cause which produced important *effects*—it was at college that you gained self-confidence and discovered your major goals in life.

Although the four methods are used in common situations, they still must be practiced in the more specialized context of academic writing. The methods of development are tools of the academic trade, and to write well in college you need to be as familiar with them as a carpenter is with his tools. We have focused on each method separately in this chapter to give you practice with each. But, as with most strategies for writing, the methods need to be used in a flexible way. As you continue to practice and become more conscious of ways of developing academic papers, you will probably encounter other methods of development, often variations on the four we have concentrated on. You will also discover that writers often use combinations of these methods in developing academic papers. For example, a historical survey of the events leading to a crisis may precede an analysis of its causes. Or a comparison of two solutions to a problem may entail categorization—a grouping of specific recommendations under each proposal. Whether used singly or in combination, the four methods provide useful strategies for organizing and developing academic papers.

Example Paper 1

The following student paper illustrates several of the strategies discussed in this chapter. Although we can't know simply from reading the paper exactly what thinking processes the student used in working on the paper, it is fairly evident that she found categories useful in organizing her information. The student uses three categories to discuss alternative systems of hog production. She labels these operations as System 1, System 2, and System 3. While useful, these labels are not very descriptive. It might have been better to use labels such as Pasture System, Partial Confinement System, and Total Confinement System. Nevertheless, when the writer compares the three operations the labels are helpful: they provide a concise way to refer to the various operations. In the margins are additional comments pointing out how this student applied other strategies described in this chapter.

This student uses the endnote system of documentation, following the guidelines described in the *MLA Handbook for Writers of Research Papers, Theses, and Dissertations* (New York: Modern Language Association, 1977). Because this handbook and many other books cover the mechanics of documentation, we will not do so here, but a few comments are necessary. In the endnote system, the writer uses a raised number to indicate that the source of the previous statement is contained in a section called *Notes* which appears at the end of the paper. (Some teachers insist on footnotes—notes placed at the foot of the appropriate page—but most will allow you to use endnotes.) Here is a sentence from the student's paper and its corresponding note from the notes section:

> The farmer's income per litter would be higher than that of a litter produced in confinement, but he can't produce as many hogs.[4]
>
> [4]J. H. Herbst, *Farm Management, Principles, Budgets, Plans* (Champaign, Ill.: Stipes Publishing Company, 1976), p. 106.

You may have heard about bibliographies and may wonder why this student doesn't use one. A bibliography is a list of sources arranged alphabetically by the author's last name. Usually the bibliography includes only the sources acknowledged in the notes; sometimes it also includes sources the writer read but did not include in the notes. Although some teachers demand both endnotes and a bibliography, many teachers tell students that endnotes are sufficient. Apparently this student's teacher didn't insist on a bibliography and so she didn't include one.

Besides the endnote system there is also the reference list system of documentation. The writer of the paper "Conflicting Views on Black English" (reprinted at the end of chap. 3) uses this system. Here is a passage from that article:

> As J. L. Dillard (1972) summarizes, "Recent work makes it clear that there exists a dialect spoken almost exclusively by Blacks in the United States today" (p. 19).

Instead of a raised number the writer uses a date—1972—to indicate the source of the statement by Dillard. The date tells the reader that the work which includes this quotation was published in 1972; the page on which the quoted material occurs is placed within parentheses at the end of the sentence. To find out what this work is the reader turns to the *References* section at the end of the paper where all sources are listed alphabetically by last name of the author.

Notes are more common in the humanities—in history, English, art, and philosophy courses, for example; reference lists are more common in the social sciences—in psychology and linguistics, for instance. You should ask your teacher which system he or she prefers. The *MLA Handbook* previously mentioned contains all the information you'll need to use endnotes properly; the *Publication Manual of the American Psychological Association*, second edition, includes a clear and complete explanation of how to document a paper using the reference list system.

THREE SYSTEMS OF HOG PRODUCTION

Iowa is the leading state in hog production, and has been for many years. Because of this, Iowa farms are often thought to have hogs lying in a muddy pig pen and chickens running wild around the barnyard. This scene is changing rapidly, not only in Iowa, but in the entire corn belt. Hogs are being brought in out of the mud and put into confinements, thus causing big changes for the swine producers. With incorporated swine confinements, swine production can become a more stable and efficient component of our country's economy. But these changes aren't easy to make and are very costly, and producers often question whether the newer systems are worth the costs. Comparing three different types of hog housing systems—focusing on labor, facilities, and profits—makes it easier to evaluate alternative systems for swine production and to understand what effects the newer production systems will have on future hog operations.

> *Observe how the three methods of organization—categorization, comparison/contrast, and cause and effect—are being applied here. The writer has* categorized *her subject into three systems, which she will* compare and contrast *in order to understand the* effects *that new production techniques are having on the business of raising hogs. Note also that the writer has categorized to get her points of comparison—labor, facilities, and profits.*

In this paper I will compare the three major swine operations currently used by swine producers.

System 1: A *pasture* operation. In this operation the sows are given temporary farrowing and nursery houses, and the hogs are kept out in a completely open pasture the entire time.

System 2: A *partial confinement* operation. These usually include an open-front finishing unit, with concrete or partially slatted floors. This type of confinement has no automated feeding system.

System 3: A *total confinement* operation. In this operation the pigs are completely indoors. It has either partially or completely slatted floors, and usually has automatic feeders and waterers.

System 1

System 1 is the traditional type of hog production. This system is used when the producer has hogs as a secondary source of income. Only small groups of hogs are kept (150–300 head). If the farmer has more, he will usually go to some type of confinement system.[1] Farrowings are timed so that they will miss the peak labor period, which is during crop production. Many pasture systems are run on a six-month cycle, with farrowing in the late winter and late summer, so as to better utilize labor.[2] Pasture systems require hard physical labor, often referred to as "scoop-shovel" labor. The working conditions include mud, manure, and very often inclement weather. With this type of work, extra hands are hard to come by, and the farmer is limited to what he can do himself.

> *Observe that the student takes up each point of comparison in the same order she listed these points in her introduction: first labor, then facilities, then profits. These words become labels for her subpoints. By using a different label at the start of each of these paragraphs she helps the reader follow the argument.*

Facilities in an operation like this consist of little more than portable, individual farrowing houses. These houses are 6' × 8' with a solid floor.[3] Hog-tight fences are also needed. These should be made of woven wire, small enough that the young pigs can't squeeze through. Feed is stored in portable feeders, to help cut down on manual labor and to allow the pigs to self-feed.

Profits seem high with a system like this, because the farmer can use his own feed and because the building costs are minimal. The farmer's income per litter would be higher than that of a litter produced in confinement, but he can't produce as many hogs.[4] Therefore, the net income of this type of system would be less than that of a confinement, because fewer pigs are produced. A pasture system would work best for a large grain farm, where the surplus grain could be used for finishing the hogs before market. This wouldn't be a good setup for feeder pig production because of the variability of temperatures in an uncontrolled environment, which results in greater baby pig mortality. A hog production system of this type would be recommended for a producer who has little experience in working with hogs but has excess grain to feed out.

System 2

In System 2 the farrowing and nursery are in a confinement type setup, and the finishing hogs are in an open-front building. The farrowing house is often used for the nursery as well, but this is not to say that a different building can't be used. This system usually permits farrowing four times a year. This would mean a farrowing sequence of December and February, June and August.[5] During nonproductive periods, the sows are allowed to go out on pasture if the facilities are adequate.

> *Note that the student describes all the points—labor, facilities, and profits—for one system before moving on to the next system. She's smart to use this pattern of comparing/contrasting. If she talked about the labor requirements for all three systems, then the facilities required for all three, then the profits for all three, the contrasts between the three systems would be blurred: readers would perhaps be impressed with the problems of run-*

> *ning a successful hog operation but confused as to how one system differs from another.*

The labor requirements for System 2 are similar to System 1. The open-front finishing houses are usually made with solid concrete floors, making animal waste removal still necessary. In the farrowing and nursery, slatted floors can be used with a shallow manure pit to save on labor costs. This system also has a high demand for labor, in that the pigs need to be fed daily. Since the animals aren't on pasture the feeding must be monitored closely, to assure that cannibalism doesn't occur. Even with the labor required for cleaning animal waste, System 2 requires fewer manhours than System 1 because less time is spent handling the pigs. This is one of the advantages of a confinement system.

The facilities in System 2 are more extensive than those needed in System 1. The finishing house is an uninsulated building, approximately 112 × 32 feet. The building is divided into four pens. An apron—outdoor extension in front of the building—should extend 28 feet for each pen.[6] The hogs should be moved into the finishing pens at about 50–70 pounds, then moved through the four pens as they progress toward market weight. The farrowing house is equipped with farrowing crates and slotted floors for easy maintenance. Once the sows are brought into the house they do not leave until they are weaned.[7] The young pigs are usually weaned at four to six weeks. The farrowing house should be kept at about 70 to 80 degrees, so heaters are necessary, especially in cold weather. If a nursery is used it must have a controlled environment similar to that of the farrowing house. Totally slotted floors work well in keeping the pens clean. The pens should be about 10 by 10.5 feet in size, and accommodate four litters of pigs per pen.

> *In the first sentence of this paragraph the writer makes a skillful transition between two points of comparison—facilities and profits. The first clause—the part about equipment—harks back to the preceding paragraph; the second clause, which refers to profits, introduces this paragraph.*

Even with the extra costs for use and maintenance of equipment, this type of system still offers a fair amount of profit. This system is more expensive than pasture units, but you can raise more hogs per year with partial confinement. With more hogs raised, your net income will be greater than a producer with the pasture system. This type of system is one of the most popular of all hog operations.

Operators of System 2 type hog units have the advantage of being flexible concerning when to market their hogs. If the hog prices fall they can slow down their production and still have their grain crops to fall back on. This flexibility is a major concern of many hog producers because of the extreme variability of the market. Another advantage of System 2 is the better utilization of buildings and labor. Remodeling old chicken and horse barns increases the value of the farm, and helps avoid high building costs. Adding swine to a grain operation keeps the workers on a constant work flow, creating a more efficient labor program. A major disadvantage of System 2 is the loss of production in extreme cold. The open-front finishing house exposes the hogs to the cold, slowing their rate of gain.

System 3
Mass production of feeder pigs is the major goal of System 3. Such large scale operations usually have no less than 100 sows. Placing hogs in total confinement increases production, because of the controlled environment. The farrowing process becomes almost like a factory operation.[8] The sows are farrowed in groups, so that as soon as one group of sows has finished weaning, the next group is within one week of being ready to farrow. This continual cycle of production requires a high level of management skills to keep everything running smoothly. An operation of this size can produce over 4,800 pigs per year when running at full capacity.[9] The farrowing facilities are similar to those of System 2, since both use the farrowing crates. Twenty crates are used in the smaller systems and up to forty crates are used in the large-scale operations.

Observe that the writer does not repeat here the labor requirements of the other two systems; she expects her readers to remember them. Since her exposition is clear and not overly technical, readers should have no trouble. Repeating the labor requirements for Systems 1 and 2 here would make her discussion unnecessarily tedious.

The labor requirements in a system of this type are quite different than requirements in the other two systems. A large-scale operation makes it necessary to employ two or more men to insure large-volume production.[10] Moreover, these men need to have some technical training since the facilities are complex and almost totally automated. The operator must have good management skills to maintain an efficient production schedule with a large number of hogs.[11]

Facilities in a large-scale operation are designed to obtain maximum production in as small an area as possible. The entire operation from breeding to market is all done indoors. The floors are slotted for easy collection and removal of manure, which is collected in pits under the building. The temperature throughout the complex is 70 to 80 degrees, so the hogs remain in their comfort zone. The farrowing and nursery houses are set up and maintained much as they are in System 2. In many large scale operations, farmers will sell the feeder pigs just as they leave the nursery, instead of finishing them on a total confinement basis. This is done because the large scale operators don't have the grain surplus needed to feed the hogs out. There are many large scale systems that don't include a finishing house in their setup for this reason. Since System 3 involves primarily working with small pigs, nurseries and farrowing units are built with heated floors to cut down on mortality losses. This is especially useful when the pigs are first born. A good ventilation system is needed to keep the hog odors under control and to circulate in fresh air. These types of facilities should be set up for easy cleaning. After each farrowing, the entire farrowing house needs to be scrubbed and disinfected with hot water and iodine before the next group of sows can be brought in.

High maintenance, feed, and labor costs make producing hogs in a large scale operation cost more per hog than the other two systems. However, the larger number of litters produced can give the operator a higher net income than either of the other systems. This type of enterprise is only feasible when the facilities are utilized to capacity at all times. The high cost of owning an operation of this size continues whether or not the facilities are in use.

System 3 is set up for a producer who is totally committed to hog production; unlike operators in Systems 1 and 2, the operator of System 3 usually doesn't have a grain crop production to supplement his income. This is often considered to be a disadvantage for this producer. All the feed needed in his operation has to be purchased and added to the costs per pig, cutting into his profits. However, many pork producers feel the advantages of a large scale operation outweigh the disadvantages. One advantage is being able to make quick changes in feed and medication levels so that producers can better combat disease outbreaks. Another important advantage is being able to have multiple farrowing.

After categorizing and comparing, she now discusses the effects the discovery of new methods of raising hogs is having on the industry.

The trend in farming is toward large-scale operations. If hog operations are to become a more stable industry in the future, pork producers will have to become increasingly professional and committed to the industry.[12] This isn't to say that operations like

Systems 1 and 2 will be totally eliminated. For many farmers a combination of crop production and a swine operation is more efficient than a single commitment to one or the other. Large-scale swine operations are most common in the corn belt states, where large-scale feeder pig producers can work closely with the finishing pig producers, who have a large surplus of grain. This better utilizes both grain and labor. The hog industry has changed a lot in the last ten years, and the changes will continue. This change is a sign of a strong and versatile industry.

Notes

[1]Sydney James, John Miranowski, William Edwards, eds., *Selected Readings in Farm Management*, Course Readings for Economics 330 (Ames: Iowa State University, 1977), p. 188.

[2]David H. Bache, *Pork Production Systems with Business Analyses: Selecting the "Right" System*, Pamphlet of the National Pork Producers Council and Extension Service, U.S. Dept. of Agriculture (Washington, D.C.: GPO, 1976), p. 4.

[3]James, Miranowski, Edwards, p. 189.

[4]J. H. Herbst, *Farm Management Principles, Budgets, Plans*, 4th ed. (Champaign, Ill.: Stipes Publishing Company, 1976), p. 106.

[5]Bache, p. 4.

[6]Herbst, p. 107.

[7]Herbst, p. 106.

[8]Calvin Stemme, V. James Rhodes, Glenn Grimes, "Defining the Status of Large Hog Farms," *Hog Farm Management*, Dec. 1978, p. 55.

[9]James, Miranowski, Edwards, p. 189.

[10]Bache, p. 17.

[11]Gary Clark, "Farrow-to-Finisher: Changes Depend on Government Actions," *Hog Farm Management*, March 1978, p. 60.

[12]George Pettit, "The Farrower: Changes in the Marketing System," *Hog Farm Management*, March 1978, p. 62.

Example Paper 2

Here is another student paper. What methods of development does this writer use? Does she use them effectively? What are the major sections of the paper? How skillful is she at making transitions from one major section to another, and from one subsection to another?

SCHOOL VIOLENCE

Sending children into a danger zone is immoral—so is asking teachers to teach in one. Today's teachers have often been likened to "sitting ducks"—targets to be shot at, have their hair set on fire, their classrooms vandalized, or their families threatened. Yet in addition to the estimated 70,000 serious attacks made on teachers each year, hundreds of thousands more attacks are suffered by schoolchildren.[1] And annual costs of school vandalism and theft have exceeded $500 million since 1975.[2] Even schools in the suburbs, once the exception to the rule, are fast becoming equals in violence to the more infamous inner-city schools. The idealistic notion of the little red schoolhouse is dying fast. However, the purpose of this report is not to relate grim stories of school crime, but rather to look at ways in which professionals (psychologists, sociologists, school administrators, teachers, researchers, and statesmen) have attempted to interpret and deal with violent incidents, and in some cases, even prevent them from occurring.

Though some school crimes—especially those involving racial issues, such as busing—are sometimes thought to have been ignited by adult trespassers, most violent acts are committed by junior high or high school students. What motivates certain adolescents to commit violent acts? No one knows exactly, but researchers Sabatino, Heald, Rothman, and Miller have organized possible school crime motivating factors into six broad categories which I have listed as follows: (1) Drugs and rebellion: A student may break into a school building and steal equipment (to sell black market fashion) in order to support an expensive drug habit; on the other hand, a "high" and financially well-off student may vandalize and steal simply because he is confused or rebellious. (2) Hostility: An act of violence may be interpreted as a student's expression of hostility toward a school whose values he feels are in conflict with his own; this kind of student most likely feels alienated from the prescribed school curriculum and extracurricular activities. (3) Malicious play: This category includes violent acts such as setting the contents of a trash can on fire, and causing a worse fire on purpose, or simply by accident. (4) Adolescent emotional problems: The student deviates because of frustration in relating to others; he feels he has nothing but a formal relationship with the school staff and other students. (5) Poor grades: Delinquents almost always exhibit poor academic performance; therefore, school violence can be interpreted as either an expression of frustration about school failure, or an expression of resentment, which is directed toward more academically successful peers. (6) School gangs: The student joins a school gang, usually when he is unable to find another group to identify with, and commits deviant acts as a gang affiliate.[3]

Trying to identify the psychological factors underlying school crime is of course important, yet asking "Why are the schools and their students the way they are?" can be as fruitless as asking "Why is society the way it is?" Schoolhouse madness may not disappear entirely until we live in a utopian society, which is not likely to be soon, if ever. Practical prevention programs and crisis centers which treat the symptoms of school crime are more immediately necessary. Such programs include the use of sophisticated technological devices (to protect students, teachers, and buildings), crisis centers for battered teachers, psychological intervention for students "at risk," curriculum intervention, and most promising, the use of student committees to control and possibly prevent violence.

Sophisticated technological devices include the use of closed circuit televisions, radar alarm systems, and intercom receivers to monitor classrooms and hallways which are deserted during after-school hours. PASS (Private Alarm Signaling System) is a silent alarm resembling a fountain pen. If the teacher (or one of the students) is in danger, the teacher presses the alarm, alerting those in the main office to a need for immediate aid. The AAA (Automated Attendance Accounting), along with a minicomputer, can provide a minute by minute printout of school attendance and student location. Architects can help too, by using window substitutes of more resistant materials in their plans, as well as designing roofs without easy access, and hallways without hidden alcoves. There is also reason to believe that aesthetic buildings lead to school and community pride; students do not want to vandalize attractive buildings.[4]

UCLA psychiatrist Alfred M. Bloch, who conducted a five-year study of battered teachers ("Combat Neurosis in Inner-City Schools," 1978), found that the symptoms suffered by such teachers were similar to those suffered by war veterans: anxiety, insecurity, phobias, nightmares, hypochondriasis, and cognitive impairment. In drawing out the analogy between battered teachers and combat victims, Bloch insists upon the importance of group morale among teachers and soldiers. Battered teachers should not be ignored by school officials; violent incidents should not be glossed over. Bloch suggests a crisis center where teachers can receive aid and talk to other teachers about the trauma they have experienced. Teachers should also be psychologically prepared to deal with possible violent incidents in their classrooms. Before entering a stressful school, teachers should, in Bloch's words, "be taught to understand the language of the street as well as the games students play."[5] He also encourages the rotation of teachers from stressful to less stressful schools every two to three years, as well as not allowing violent students to return to the same school after suspension—they may be set up as a hero by other students for having beat the teacher.

Judith Ruchkin from the University of Maryland has explored different kinds of classroom programs, primarily for students "at risk" (chronic absentees, suspended students, pregnant teenagers, and "outsiders"—children who have been abused, rejected, or seem to belong nowhere).[6] Ruchkin notes the overcrowding as well as lack of verbal exchange in traditional classrooms. One of her proposals is the "mini-school" annex—a classroom with a few students—where children feel like more than "just a number." This kind of classroom allows for more personal interaction between teachers and students, and gives more explicit instruction to those who have missed a lot of school. Ruchkin also favors the alternative "parental classroom," where one male and one female teacher act as surrogate parents, combining this role with team teaching techniques. The improvement of attention spans, and thus more learning, is thought to take place in this situation. Furthermore, little-cared-for children thrive under the extra attention of the surrogate parents. Ruchkin feels it is up to educators, not policemen, to improve the schools. School should be a caring, nurturing place; in turn, this will help children later in life. Keeping "at risk" students from committing school crimes as children will prevent them from committing much more serious crimes as adults.

Curriculum intervention, a plan which supports the idea of "educating the whole child" as well as the placing of increased emphasis on vocational training, is another innovation. If, as part of the curriculum, educators work on instilling positive social behaviors and values from kindergarten on, children have a base to build on. This kind of curriculum is also more practical, introducing not just academic material, but career education and vocational training. Educators help the student to feel more a part of the school. With the addition of vocational training, the school becomes a worthwhile place for the adolescent to be—his education will be directly preparing him for later life. And hypothetically, the student will not want to destroy an institution which is there to help him.

Student committees have been most promising in the reduction and prevention of school crime. During adolescence, the values held by a student's peers become more important than values held by anyone else. The secret behind the success of the student committees lies in this fact of peer group pressure. Ideally, if the peer group can exert pressure on those involved in violent acts, students can influence the behavior of other students for the better. Inner-city high school committee members involved in a weekend workshop to improve conditions at their school concluded that emotional problems and frustration with school, parents, teachers, and peers motivated many incidents of school violence and vandalism.[7] Because of the greater trust between peers, troubled students are more likely to bring their problems to committee members rather than school staff. Serving on the student committee becomes a status symbol, and members include not only "traditional" leaders (students with leadership ability, good grades, and good citizenship records), but also "underground" leaders. Student committees track down rumors of planned violence, listen to student complaints, and try to work out problems between students; staff members are called in if the problem becomes too big for committee members to handle alone.

Good teachers, teachers who care, and students who are willing to change, help make teaching and going to school worthwhile. As long as there is something good about the institution of school, it will probably continue to exist. Schools do mirror our troubled society, yet while learning to deal with problems in school, students become better able to handle their difficulties in the outside world. Teachers are starting to "get tough" again; administrators are tightening up on unlimited student rights. For example, though students as citizens enjoy certain freedoms—including the freedom of speech—obscenity and disruption in the classroom are much less tolerated. And school pride, as well as student committees seem to be motivating factors in the reduction of school crime. The schools should be a place where students can grow emotionally as well as develop intellectual skills. Schools should adapt themselves to the society in which we live and try to give students the stability and vocational training they need to exist in our present society. Maybe we can't get back to the little red schoolhouse, where a respect for learning, teachers, and fellow students seemed to exist, but possibly through adaptation of new ideas and programs, something good can happen.

Notes

1"The Bad Ones," *Newsweek*, 30 June 1975, p. 62.
2"The Bad Ones," p. 62.

[3]David A. Sabatino, James E. Heald, Sharon G. Rothman, and Ted L. Miller, "Destructive Norm-Violating School Behavior Among Adolescents: A Review of Protective and Preventive Efforts," *Adolescence*, 8 (1978), 677–79.

[4]Sabatino et al., pp. 680–81.

[5]Alfred M. Bloch, "Combat Neurosis in Inner-City Schools," *American Journal of Psychiatry*, 135 (1978), 1192.

[6]Judith P. Ruchkin, "Does School Crime Need the Attention of Policemen or Educators?" *Teacher's College Record*, 79 (1977), 240–42.

[7]Robert Batchelder and Ted Urich, "Turning an Urban High School Around," *Phi Delta Kappan*, Nov. 1979, p. 208.

3 | Deciding on a Final Arrangement

Once you have developed your ideas for the body of the paper, you still must decide on a final arrangement for your main points. Your aim in most academic papers is to arrange your information so that a reader can understand it easily. If you order your major points according to a logical principle, your readers will usually find your ideas easy to follow. Your paper will seem clear and logical. Thus, the first topic of this chapter is how to arrange your information according to a principle.

In some cases choosing a logical principle is easy: only one principle seems to fit your material and so you use that one. In other cases, however, choosing a principle is difficult because it seems possible to arrange your material in many different ways. In such cases you need to assess which arrangement will achieve the effects you desire. The second part of this chapter explains how to do this assessing.

Arranging According to a Principle

Finding a principle for arranging your main points may be simple. The principle may be inherent in your subject matter. If, for an undirected assignment in a history course, you have decided to examine the rise of social Darwinism, chances are you've chosen an initial plan based on a sequence, and you've developed your material chronologically from early forms of social Darwinism to later forms. And that's probably a good order to use in your final paper. In a historical survey you often (though not always) follow a particular logical principle: starting with the early events and proceeding to recent events. In a paper explaining a procedure with clear steps—how to conduct an experiment in chemistry, for example—the order that makes most sense is to begin with steps that come first in the procedure and continue to discuss, in order, the steps that follow.

Although certain principles of arrangement may be inherent in your subject matter, more often you have to find a logical principle for arranging your main points. For example, if you are working on a paper on the effects of high gasoline prices, you may have decided that there are four main effects. But you will have to decide on a principle for arranging these effects in your final paper, perhaps from most predictable to least predictable, or from least damaging to the economy to most damaging to the economy.

Problem 3-1. In the following exercises you are given a series of main points that will be included in a paper. Arrange the points according to some principle and explain why you chose that arrangement. The first exercise is done for you.

1. *a*) One type of Vietnamese literature is oral literature—folk songs, proverbs, and fairy tales—that were handed down by word of mouth from one generation to the next.

   b) One type of Vietnamese literature is now written in the new Romanized script. This literature has been strongly influenced by Western, particularly French, writers.

   c) The earliest written Vietnamese literature was written by Vietnamese but in Chinese characters and clearly shows the influence of three great East Asian religions: Confucianism, Buddhism, and Taoism.

   d) One type of Vietnamese literature was written in Vietnamese characters, or demotic script. This demotic script is a modification of the Chinese way of writing but was used to write the Vietnamese, not the Chinese, language. Literature written in this script is freer from Chinese influences.

   Order: *a, c, d, b*

   Principle: from oldest form of producing literature to the newest.

2. *a*) According to the organismic model man's behavior is internally controlled.

   b) Organismic theories posit man as an active agent in the world.

   c) The mechanistic model views development as mostly determined by the quality of a person's environmental input.

   d) Mechanistic theories posit man as a passive entity in the world.

   e) The organismic model views development as mostly determined by the individual's structural organization.

   f) According to the mechanistic model man's behavior is externally controlled.

3. *a*) The individualized approach to reading has the advantage of adapting materials to each child's needs; however, the demands on the teacher are so great as to call into question the feasibility of this approach for most schools.

   b) The basal reader approach to reading instruction is severely limited because it is based on an inadequate definition of "readiness" and because the content of the readers is dull and lifeless.

   c) The language-experience approach to reading has all the advantages of individualization without its major problems.

4. *a*) The decimal numeration system is structured entirely around its base ten place value. It has ten digits and the placement of the digits determines their value. The symbol 0 is used to hold places. The numbers are written horizontally and the places increase in value from right to left. Thus the total value of a numeral is found by multiplying each digit by the appropriate place value and summing the results.

   b) The Egyptian numeration system was structured around base ten, but a different symbol was used for each power of ten. A symbol for one thousand was entirely different from a symbol for ten. For example, the number five hundred sixty-three would be represented by five of the one-hundred symbols, six of the ten symbols, and three of the one symbols. Obviously, the order in which the symbols were written was not significant.

   c) The Mayan numeration system was the first to utilize a symbol for "zero." This enabled the Mayans to use place value in writing their numerals. The symbols were written vertically with the places increasing by powers of twenty as they went from the bottom upward. The total value of each numeral was found by multiplying each digit by the appropriate place value and summing the results.

   d) The Roman numeration system utilizes symbols for powers of ten (I, X, C, M) and for half of these values (V, L, D). This system demonstrates limited place value. Since there is no "zero" to hold places, the values of the digits are usually simply added without regard to position. However, certain symbols (I, X, C) may be placed immediately preceding the symbols which represent five or ten times as much and in these cases (IV, IX, XL, XC, etc.) the smaller digit is to be subtracted from the larger.

One way to arrange your points according to a principle is to display them along a continuum: best to worst, simple to complex, low to high, old to new, and so forth. In the process of putting your points on a continuum you are forced to decide on an ordering principle. For example, suppose you are going to write a paper about proposed solutions to the water scarcity problem. You want to discuss what you know about three solutions:

1. One way to solve the problem is to learn how to make drinkable water from sea water.
2. One way to solve the problem is to use sewer water for irrigating crops.
3. One way to solve the problem is to recirculate water used for industrial purposes.

To order these solutions according to a principle, you can begin by considering several different continuums along which the solutions could be arranged:

simple ___2___3_____1_____ complex
principle: simplicity of proposal

very effective
in solving problem ____1_____2____3___ helpful, but
not effective
principle: effectiveness of proposal

most expensive ____1___3_____2_____ least expensive
principle: cost of proposal

Problem 3-2. In the following exercises you are given a number of different categories. Arrange them in some way (perhaps using a continuum) and explain the principle you used to order them the way you did. The first one is done for you.

1. *a*) four-lane highways
   b) single-lane paved roads
   c) single-lane dirt roads
   d) roads with two lanes (paved)
   e) roads with two lanes with passing lanes on hills (paved)
   Order: *a, e, d, b, c*
   Principle: the categories are arranged from best to worst roads.

   best _____ worst
       a   *e*   *d*   *b*   *c*

2. *a*) quadratic equations ($y = ax^2 + bx + c$)
   b) linear equations ($y = ax + b$)
   c) cubic equations ($y = ax^3 + bx^2 + cx + d$)
3. *a*) ambition for personal happiness
   b) ambition for fame
   c) ambition for money
   d) ambition for professional success
4. *a*) Individuals are responsible for their personal health care.
   b) The State Department of Health is responsible for state agencies.
   c) International agencies are responsible for international health problems.
   d) Federal Department of Health, Education and Welfare is concerned with problems on a national level.
   e) The County Health Boards manage disease prevention on a local level.

5. *a*) hard rock
   b) country and western
   c) bluegrass
   d) fifties rock and roll
   e) classical music
   f) jazz

Choosing among Equally Logical Arrangements

As we have mentioned, sometimes one arrangement seems clearly best for your material. Suppose your purpose is simply to tell someone how to change a tire. You would probably choose to arrange your information by steps:

Step 1. Jacking the car
    a) set the hand brake
    b) block the wheels
    c) put jack under car
    d) jack car up
Step 2. Removing the flat tire
    a) remove lug bolts
    b) take off flat tire
and so forth

This order seems best for a simple explanation of how to change a tire. Altering the order of these directions would probably result in confusion.

Sometimes, however, it's not so easy to determine the best arrangement. In these cases you have to assess which of several equally logical arrangements will be most effective for your readers. Suppose you are writing a paper on the disposal of toxic wastes for an Earth Science course. After getting this assignment, you decide to base your paper on three incidents involving the careless disposal of chemical wastes—one in New York, one in Michigan, and one in New Jersey. Which incident do you discuss first? In this case there are three equally logical ways to arrange the information in your paper: chronological, climax, and anticlimax order. Which arrangement you choose depends on the effect you want to achieve with your readers. If your aim is simply to offer some examples of the careless disposal of toxic wastes, it makes little difference which site you discuss first, which second, and which third. Arranging them chronologically, beginning with the site that was first identified, might be the most effective.

But suppose you wanted to convince your reader that the owners of companies that dump toxic wastes are morally responsible for the damage they do to the health of residents who live near the sites. If this is your aim you may want to arrange the incidents in a different order. Perhaps you'll want to begin with the incident in which the owners acted least negligently and end with the incident in which they acted most negligently. This is called *climax* order. Your strategy would be to build slowly up to the most extreme example of owner negligence. By the end of the paper, your reader would likely be left incensed by such blatant negligence.

Suppose, however, that you want to argue that the owners of chemical plants must be held responsible even when they have been only a little negligent in disposing of toxic wastes. If this is your purpose, it might be most effective to first shock your readers by mentioning clear cases of negligence, waking them up to the problem of toxic wastes, and then lead them gently to questionable cases. This is called *anticlimax* order.

There may be other cases in which neither climax nor anticlimax order seems appropriate. Sometimes a useful order to consider is *extremes first, middle ground last*. Assume that you are writing a paper for a course in urban problems. In your paper you plan to propose a solution to the problem of who is going to pay for the building and upkeep of a badly needed parking lot in the downtown area of the city in which you live. Your teacher has told you to play the role of an outside consultant, to imagine that your readers are the local taxpayers whom you are to persuade to adopt a proposal that you think is both feasible and good for the city.

After some research you come up with five possible solutions:

Label	Description of Solution
1. Federal Money Solution	Get money from the federal government for the project. (This is an excellent, desirable solution, but is unfortunately impossible.)
2. Businessmen-Pay Solution	Force downtown businessmen to pay for the upkeep, since they are the ones who are crying loudest for the parking facility. (This is another good but impossible solution.)
3. Penny-Pinching Solution	Try to get money by cutting back on other city projects (such as road repair and construction).
4. Borrow Now–Pay Later Solution	Get the city to borrow money to build the facility and then charge high fees to parkers to get the money back.
5. Taxation Solution	Raise local taxes immediately to raise money to build and maintain the parking lot.

One logical principle on which to arrange these solutions is from least irritating to most irritating to the public. You could arrange the solutions along the continuum:

	Federal Money	Business-men Pay	Penny-Pinching	Borrow Now–Pay Later	Taxation	
least irritating						most irritating

In this case, you could use either climax order (least to most irritating) or anticlimax order (most to least irritating). However, assume that you wish to argue for, and convince your readers to support, a combination of the Penny-Pinching and Borrow Now–Pay Later solutions, because these solutions are both feasible and acceptable to most citizens. One order you might use in this situation is the *extremes first, middle ground last* order. When you employ this strategy you mention the extremes first: Federal Money Solution (impossible), Businessmen-Pay Solution (irritating to the business community), and Taxation Solution (unacceptable to taxpayers). Then you discuss your proposal, a combination of Penny-Pinching and Borrow Now–Pay Later. The advantage of first giving the extremes is that anything presented after them emphasizes a nonextreme, middle-of-the-road approach.

Problem 3-3. In this exercise, you will be given a writing situation and a set of main points. You are to suggest a final arrangement for these points.

1. Situation: The writer is writing a paper for a public health course dealing with issues relating to health in large cities. The writer wishes to concentrate on city public health problems, but has found that city problems can't be separated from state, county, national, and international problems.

   Main Points: *a*) City problems
     b) County problems
     c) State problems
     d) National problems
     e) International problems

2. Situation: The writer wants to have his reader accept position *b*, the heredity/experience position. Position *a* and position *c* are generally considered extreme positions; position *b* is middle-of-the-road.

   Main Points: *a*) The heredity position: children are born with the ability to learn languages; they are programmed by heredity to learn to speak.
     b) The heredity/experience position: children in-

herit the ability to learn languages, but this ability can only be developed through experience. Heredity and experience are equally important.

c) The experience position: children learn languages through experience, by trying to speak to others who shape and reinforce their responses.

3. Situation: The writer wishes to concentrate his discussion on the large companies, and will mention smaller companies only as a contrast.

   Main Points: *a*) Companies with annual net profits of over $2,000,000

   b) Companies with annual net profits of over $500,000 (but not exceeding $2,000,000)

   c) Companies with annual net profits of over $100,000 (but not exceeding $500,000)

4. Situation: This writer wants to point out to his readers the virtues of owning a small pet (category *c*). His readers may or may not agree with him. He doesn't know.

   Main Points: *a*) Large pets (over 50 lbs.): the large pets that tend to eat you out of house and home, burn out your lawn, eat your furniture, and knock down your lamps.

   b) Medium sized pets (over 10 lbs., under 50 lbs.): these are OK for owners of large pieces of property.

   c) Small pets (over 3 lbs., under 10 lbs.): good companions for children.

   d) Very small pets (under 3 lbs.): the small, nervous kind of pet that you're likely to step on.

5. Situation: A student is writing a research paper on the topic: "The Food Chain in the Ocean."

   Main Points: *a*) drifting plant life in the sea (phytoplankton)

   b) microscopic creatures that eat the plant life (zooplankton)

   c) fish equipped with filter systems designed to capture phytoplankton and zooplankton

   d) meat-eating fish that feed on level *c* fish

   e) large meat-eating fish that eat level *d* fish

Problem 3-4. In a 1975 "State of the University" report, University of Michigan President Robben Fleming said that universities have less money for education of Ph.D.'s and that society probably won't need as many Ph.D.'s as in the past. The question to be answered then, according to President Fleming, was the following: Should every qualified student who wants to get a Ph.D. degree be allowed to get one? Fleming discussed four approaches to deal with these two related problems: the present money shortage and the projected Ph.D. surplus. Here are the four approaches in random order.

1. *Informed Consumer Approach.* In this approach the student who chooses to pursue doctoral studies is informed about the state of the job market by Ph.D.'s in his field, and then allowed to make a personal decision as to whether or not he or she will go for a Ph.D. degree.

2. *Optimum Consumer Approach.* In this approach the university administration "adds its best judgment to that of the informed student" as to the number of doctoral students accepted in a given field. In other words, in this approach not all qualified students who wanted to get a Ph.D. would be allowed to get one. University officials could say to the Ph.D. applicant in a field that no longer needed Ph.D.'s: "For your own good and the good of society, we will not allow you to study."

3. *Complete Laissez-faire ("leave it alone") Approach.* In this approach everything is left up to the student: if he or she wants to get a Ph.D., the university accepts him or her no matter what the state of the job market. The justification for this approach is that in a free society individuals ought to be able to make their own decisions regarding their future.

4. *National Planning Approach.* In this approach the central government (federal government in the U.S.) decides how many Ph.D.'s are needed in each field and tells the individual university administrations how many Ph.D. applicants they can accept. This is the approach used in socialist countries.

As mentioned above, these approaches are in random order. Organize them according to a specific principle and state the reason for this order.

Do you think President Fleming actually presented these approaches in the order you've arranged them in? Or is it likely that Fleming would have chosen an alternative arrangement? (Hint: President Fleming was advocating the "optimum consumer" approach.) Explain the reasons for an alternative arrangement.

In this chapter we have emphasized that the final arrangement for your paper should be both logical and effective. Papers are logical when the main points are organized according to a principle—low to high, first to last, and so forth. Sometimes the best organizing principle will be clear from your initial plan and your method of development. Thus, a "trace" assignment would lead you to organize and develop your ideas according to a sequence, and you could probably decide to arrange your points chronologically. Such an arrangement would probably seem logical and effective to your readers because chronology is usually associated with historical accounts. However, your method of development will not always point so clearly toward a final arrangement. You might develop your information around four solutions to a problem, but be able to conceive of several logical ways to arrange these solutions in your paper. In such cases, you are faced with a difficult decision—trying to decide which of the arrangements will best convey the solutions to your reader. You can consider a variety of arrangements, including three we have discussed—climax, anticlimax, and extremes first, middle ground last—but you can't always be certain that one arrangement is necessarily better than another. Ultimately, deciding among equally logical arrangements may be more a matter of relying on hunches than on clear-cut guidelines. This is what people mean when they say that writing is an art, rather than a science.

Example Paper 1

The author of the following student-written paper suggests three advantages to mandatory prison sentences: they will eliminate disparities of sentencing, preclude inconsistent parole and preterm release policies, and reduce crime. The order here is climax: from the least important advantage (reducing the unfairness of the present system) to the most important advantage (reducing crime—the real problem). The paper also illustrates an interesting problem: the problem of where to put "opposing views." In this case, the author waits till the end to point out two "drawbacks" to mandatory sentences (mandatory sentences can be circumvented by plea bargaining and are expensive). As you read the paper, you might ask yourself whether putting these drawbacks at the end is effective.

MANDATORY PRISON SENTENCES:
A PARTIAL SOLUTION TO CRIME

In recent years, crime in America has become a serious problem. Every current study supports the conclusion that the crime rate is escalating yearly. Since 1968, the amount of violent street crime in the United States has increased 57 percent.[1] Rising crime rates become increasingly disturbing when one considers the billions of dollars that have been spent, along with the immense amount of time that federal, state, and local police departments have devoted to combating crime. Obviously, our system is failing somewhere.

The fact is, most of the crime in our country goes unreported. Even when crimes are reported and the criminals arrested, a majority of the offenders avoid being sentenced to significantly long prison terms. During an eight-month period in 1973, a special Boston police anticrime unit made 636 arrests for violent street crimes. Yet only 7 percent of those arrested received a jail sentence of over one year.[2] The situation is similar in New York City where each year 97 percent of all adults arrested for felonies escape receiving a prison term.[3] In Senator Edward Kennedy's words, "Swift, certain punishment of the offender has all too often become the exception rather than the rule."[4] How can a justice system operate effectively when it imprisons only a small fraction of offenders? Moreover, how can a criminal justice system expect to deter criminal behavior when the criminal is aware that the chances of his arrest and the likelihood of his conviction, if arrested, are very slim? The answer, of course, is that such a system of justice simply cannot expect to deter criminal behavior.

The solution lies in the use of mandatory prison sentences for specified crimes. Federally predetermined lengths of prison sentences would assure the potential criminal that if he commits a crime and is subsequently convicted, he will serve time in prison. There are three advantages to mandatory prison sentences. First, the length of the prison term would be specified by law, thus eliminating the unequal sentences imposed by judges who sometimes use their discretion unfairly. Second, since mandatory sentences would be predetermined by law, they would also eliminate the need for parole or rehabilitative preterm release, both of which are ineffective in diminishing habitual criminal activity. Third, and most important, mandatory and more severe prison sentences have proven to be a significant factor in the lowering of crime rates.

The first advantage of mandatory sentences is that they would equalize the length of prison terms for specific crimes. Some supporters of our present criminal justice system have argued that sentencing disparities are justified. They contend that the nature and background of crimes must be considered along with guilt. However, sentences are unjustifiably disparate in various states. The "Federal Bureau of Prisons Statistical Report" illustrates this disparity.[5] The national average sentence for a narcotics violation in 1971 was 68.3 months, while the Eastern District of Ohio had an average of 180 months, and the Southern District of Illinois had an average of only 12 months during the same time period. Another illustration of this unwarranted disparity can be seen in the case of two men tried for embezzlement in the spring of 1971. The two men were convicted in the same courthouse during the same week but in different court rooms. There was little difference between the two cases; yet one defendant was given fifteen years in prison while the other was given only thirty days.[6]

Sentences are also not applied equally for all racial and social classes. The poor and members of some minority groups receive an unfair share of harsh sentences. The "Statistical Report of the Federal Bureau of Prisons" disclosed that for fiscal year 1969–70, of all prisoners sentenced to federal prisons, the average sentence for whites was 42.9 months, while for blacks it was 57.7 months.[7] The poor also are discriminated against by sentencing judges. Sentences are simply not handed out fairly in our justice system.

A second advantage of mandatory prison terms is that they would eliminate traditional forms of parole and preterm release which have been proven ineffective in curbing repeated offenses.[8] Some critics of mandatory sentences have maintained that the use of fixed prison sentences would affect rehabilitation since a prisoner with no hope of preterm release would have no incentive for rehabilitation. However, rehabilitation programs have not been the cure-all they were once thought to be. For example, a ten-year study in Georgia comparing inmates released under parole (carefully selected, counseled, and supervised) with inmates given unconditional releases (unselected, uncounseled, and unsupervised) showed no difference between the two groups in rate of repeated offenses.[9] Similarly disappointing results were obtained in a California study comparing rehabilitated parolees given extensive counseling to those given little counseling; both groups committed the same number of felonies. Finally, a comparative analysis of expenditures and manpower for rehabilitation, parole, and probation in all fifty states has revealed "the almost total absence of linkage between correction variables [rehabilitation] and recidivism."[10]

If rehabilitation doesn't deter crime, then what does? This is a difficult question to answer. First of all, a distinction must be made between deterrence and incapacity. Incapacity can be achieved by long terms of imprisonment, particularly for habitual offenders; the policy of "keeping criminals off the streets" does protect the public for a period of time, although it is done at a considerable cost ($15,000 to $20,000 per year per prisoner). On the other hand, the object of deterrence is to make the certainty and severity of punishment so great as to inhibit potential criminals from committing crimes. The third major advantage of implementing mandatory prison terms is that they reduce crime by providing more certain and slightly more severe (lengthy) sentences. For many years sociologists scorned the notion of deterrence, arguing that many crimes were committed without any consideration of consequences and that urbanization, population density, poverty, and other demographic factors had more to do with crime than did the severity of punishment. However, recent systematic studies have challenged this view. Sociologists Maynard L. Erickson and Jack P. Gibbs have analyzed criminal homicide rates and related them to the certainty and severity of imprisonment in the states.[11] The likelihood of imprisonment for criminal homicides ranged from 21 percent in Utah and South Carolina to 87 percent in South Dakota. The average number of months served for a criminal homicide ranged from a low of 24 in Nevada to a high of 132 in North Dakota. Erickson and Gibbs were able to analyze statistically these measures of certainty and severity in relation to homicide rates in the states. Their conclusions are as follows.

1. States above the medium-certainty and medium-severity rates have lower homicide rates than states below both mediums. In fact, the homicide rates for low-certainty-rate and low-severity-rate states were three times greater than the average rate for high-certainty and high-severity states.

2. Certainty of imprisonment may be more important than severity of punishment in determining homicide rates; but there is conflicting evidence on which of these variables is more influential.

3. Both certainty and severity reduce homicide rates even after controlling for all other demographic variables.

The implications of these results are far-reaching because mandatory prison sentences are by their very nature more certain and more severe than conventional sentencing practices. Mandatory sentences would not necessarily mean drastically longer prison terms, but rather, would ensure that convicted prisoners would spend a predetermined amount of time in prison.

A couple of drawbacks related to (but not caused by) mandatory prison terms could be acknowledged. First, mandatory penalties might be circumvented by plea bargaining. To the extent that prosecutors can set a defendant's charge on a range of degrees, prosecutors have considerable authority to decide the fate of a defendant. By plea bargaining, a defendant could conceivably circumvent a mandatory term. However, plea bargaining is not a problem unique to mandatory sentences; it is a problem in our present system as well.

A second drawback related to mandatory terms results from the increased costs of longer prison sentences. It costs taxpayers between $15,000 and $20,000 to incarcerate one prisoner for one year. If convicted criminals spend more years behind bars, our justice system will in turn cost proportionately more. However, crime also costs taxpayers a lot of money each year.

Often we hear such phrases as "everyone is treated equal under the law" and "crime doesn't pay." But can our justice system afford to make the drastic exceptions to these rules that it has made in the past? If ours is to be an adequately fair and unbiased system, then change is essential. Research has proven that very few criminals are actually apprehended and arrested. And of those arrested, fewer are convicted. Even of those convicted, only a minority serve prison terms of any duration. Moreover, those who are poor or minorities pay more heavily for the same crimes than those who are rich and white. Mandatory sentences will alleviate this, and, in addition, will deter crime. Thus, the solution to our crime problem is implementation of mandatory prison sentences for specified crimes.

Notes

[1] From a statement which Senator Edward Kennedy presented on the floor of the U.S. Senate, November 20, 1975. This statement is reprinted in "Is Expanded Use of Mandatory Prison Sentences a Sound Approach to Reducing Crime?" *Congressional Digest*, 55 (1976), 204, 206, 208.

[2] W. E. Hoffman, U.S. Cong., Senate, Committee of the Judiciary, Hearing before the Subcommittee on Criminal Law and Procedures, *Reform of the Federal Criminal Laws*, 93rd Cong., 1st sess., S. Rept. 1401 (Washington, D.C.: GPO, 1973), pp. 5358–64.

[3] Hoffman, p. 5360.

[4] Kennedy, p. 206.

[5] James R. Kapel, "A Plea for Appellate Review of Sentences," *Ohio State Law Journal*, 19 (1971), 412.

[6] Kapel, p. 402.

[7] Kapel, p. 411.

[8] Daniel Glaser, *The Effectiveness of a Prison and Parole System* (Indianapolis and New York: Bobbs-Merrill, 1964), p. 4.

[9] Frank K. Gibson, James E. Prather, and George A. Taylor, "A Path Analytic Treatment of Corrections Outputs," *Social Science Quarterly*, 54 (1973), 281–91.

[10] Gibson, p. 291.

[11] Maynard L. Erickson and Jack P. Gibbs, "The Deterrence Question," *Social Science Quarterly*, 54 (1973), 534–51.

Example Paper 2

The following paper deals with an issue in social foundations of education. The writer is interested in the problems which educators face in deciding what "expert opinion" to accept when dealing with nonstandard English spoken by minority groups. He is comparing various claims about two issues: where Black English originated and what educators should do about Black English in the classroom.

This paper follows the extremes first, middle ground last order for each of the two issues the writer discusses. For example, on the issue of where Black English originated, the writer first discusses the theory of American origins and then the theory of African origins; finally, the writer reports on a compromise position. Similarly, on the issue of what to do with Black English, the writer discusses three extreme positions, then a more moderate compromise.

Notice that the writer has used labeling: in discussing the first issue he uses the labels "dialectologists" and "creolists." The writer might also have designed labels for the three positions discussed in the second part of the paper. Can you think of appropriate labels to use for the proposals of how to deal with Black English?

Notice also that the writer uses the American Psychological Association (APA) reference system rather than the endnote system of documentation.

CONFLICTING VIEWS ON BLACK ENGLISH

Over the past several years many educators have been confused by the heated controversy over nonstandard English in the classroom. Much of the confusion is legitimate, stemming from the diversity of "expert opinion." For example, some authorities have wondered if Black English really exists at all, arguing that Negro speech differs little from the speech of some southern whites. But more recently, the majority of linguistic experts have acknowledged the existence of a Black English which differs from other varieties of American English. As J. L. Dillard (1972) summarizes, "Recent work makes it clear that there exists a dialect spoken almost exclusively by Blacks in the United States today" (p. 19).

But simply to agree that there is a Black English still leaves two broad areas of controversy: Where did Black English come from? and How should we deal with Black English in the classroom? These are the most significant questions for anyone concerned with nonstandard English. Our confusion comes from the fact that we frequently hear partial, inconclusive, or greatly divergent answers. My purpose here is not to give a final answer to these tough questions, but rather to organize the questions and some alternative solutions.

Although a historical account of Black English may seem simply academic, in fact historical theories can lead to practical consequences. It is significant whether we believe that Black English had its origin in America or Africa; there are social and cultural values at stake. The proponents of these two major theories of historical origins are the "dialectologists" and the "creolists."

The dialectologists see the differences between standard and nonstandard dialect as explainable through the established principles of linguistic change: when groups are divided, their dialects diverge. According to this theory, Black English, like other English dialects, is descended from an earlier form of English, but the development of the standard and nonstandard dialects has been different. Proponents of this view, while recognizing Black English as somehow separate, find rather superficial differences between Black English and standard English (Labov, 1969).

However this traditional view of dialectology has come under attack from the creolists, who see more fundamental differences between Black and standard English (Dillard, 1972). The creolists assert that Black English is derived not from the same ancestor as standard English, but rather from a pidgin language, possibly with origins in Africa. Because of the language mixing inherent in the slave trade in West Africa, the slaves were forced, both in African trade centers and in America, to communicate through a *lingua franca*. Pidgin English filled this function. The children of these slaves, born in America, spoke this simplified language natively, giving it the status of a creole. (A pidgin automatically becomes a creole when it has native speakers.) Of course as native speakers apply their language to new situations the vocabulary rapidly expands and the dialect soon becomes as complex as any other language. Thus, the creolist emphasizes the basic differences between Black English and standard white English: they have different sources.

For the nonlinguist, the existence of two schools of thought is confusing—both sound convincing, but the two are really quite opposed. Although both schools recognize the differences between black and white speech, they differ on the question of how the dialects differ. In essence, the fundamental question is whether the differences are simply on the level of "surface structure" or whether there are "deep structure" differences as well (see Robinson, 1973). Dialectologists for the most part see differences in the surface representation of identical deep (semantic) structures. On the other hand, some creolists posit deep structure differences—a natural enough conclusion if indeed the two are separate languages.

Professor Robbins Burling (1973) has taken a moderate position on this complex issue by stating: "Black English is too much like other English dialects to be simply dismissed as a Creole, but at the same time it is too much like the Creoles to be dismissed as a mere dialect" (p. 121). Burling explains this paradox through a theory of mutual influence: there probably was an early period of creolization, but it has been overlaid with extensive mutual borrowing among dialects. Although theories of language history seem to have educational consequences, Burling warns that we "should not exaggerate the relevance of historical arguments for present educational policy" (p. 126). Burling's position of mutual influence accounts for the data amassed by both sides and may be a practical stance for educators who are not professional linguists.

A more important concern for the educator is what to do about Black English. Convinced that Black English exists and that it differs in some ways from standard English, what might be the educator's response to the dilemma? There are essentially three proposals: (1) eradicate the black vernacular, (2) encourage bidialectalism, (3) accept Black English as a separate but equal language.

The first proposal, that Black English be eradicated, is probably a widely held position, stemming from the belief that Black English is "ungrammatical" and thus inferior for sophisticated use. Another supposition underlying eradication measures involves a historical interpretation: that Black English is derived from a debased language taught to slaves and therefore that it still carries connotations of slavery. Morse (1973) states this belief:

> Black English is demoralized language, an idiom of fettered minds, the shuffling speech of slavery. It served its bad purposes well. It cannot serve the purpose of free men and women. Those who would perpetuate it are romanticists clinging to corruption. (p. 839)

If the eradicationist position is the silent majority view, it is certainly not the position of the most outspoken linguists. The opponents of eradication are divided into two positions. The more popular of the two is bidialectalism. The term "bidialectalism" does not represent a unified approach to the problem; however, two assumptions are common and central: (1) a dialect is an adequate and useful aspect of a cultural minority; (2) in order to relate to a larger world, it is important to master the standard dialect. Because bidialectalists have some linguistic sophistication, they acknowledge the principle of linguistic relativity: all languages are equally functional. But they also claim practicality. Arthur (1973) acknowledges that "as this society currently operates, a student's future social and economic status may depend upon his ability to speak an 'acceptable' form of English" (p. 88). Shuy (1973) tested the hypothesis that speech was an important criterion in employability. He discovered that although employers consciously denied that speech was a consideration, in practice they were uniform: the "better jobs invariably went to the standard speakers" (p. 307).

However, other linguists have raised disturbing objections to bidialectalism. James Sledd (1969) has objected that bidialectalism cannot succeed. For one thing, the social pressures against the second dialect are simply overwhelming:

> The English teacher's forty-five minutes a day for five days in the week will never counteract the influence, and sometimes the hostility, of playmates and friends and family during much the larger part of the student's time. (p. 1313)

Second, Sledd (1972) argues that the best efforts of the bidialectalist have failed.

> In fact, the complete bi-dialectual, with undiminished control of his vernacular and a good mastery of the standard language, is apparently as mythical as the unicorn: no authenticated specimens have been reported. (p. 441)

If bidialectalism is impossible, why have the government and academic establishment spent such time and money on it? For Sledd the answer is obvious: white supremacy demands conformity. Sledd and his followers condemn bidialectalism as immoral because any effort to alter a student's language, despite protests of linguistic equality, must subtly condemn his vernacular (the language of his family and friends).

Once again, we are left with radically conflicting expert opinion. Robbins Burling (1973) tries to make sense of the differences by first acknowledging that "we seem to have a problem with nothing but poor solutions" (p. 136). But he takes another look at the problem, advocating a compromise between encouraging the use of nonstandard English and bidialectalism.

> We can begin to cut through our difficulties by recognizing that we are not really faced with so simple a question as whether or not to teach standard English. Instead, we have the far more complex question of what aspects of standard English to teach and of when in a child's education to present them. (p. 137)

Burling argues that since reading standard English is not dependent on speaking standard English, the major effort in primary education should be reading. The child should be permitted to use his nonstandard vernacular. Later, when a child is old enough to decide the matter, if he chooses to learn a prestige dialect the school should give him the best help it can.

The policy which Burling recommends seems to be a workable compromise. It will not, of course, satisfy all educators. As Burling recognizes, his plan gives a student the option of rejecting standard English: "It is the right of every American *not* to speak standard English if he does not want to" (p. 140).

References

Arthur, B. *Teaching English to speakers of English.* New York: Harcourt Brace Jovanovich, 1973.

Burling, R. *English in black and white.* New York: Holt, Rinehart and Winston, 1973.

Dillard, J. L. *Black English.* New York: Vintage, 1972.

Labov, W. The logic of nonstandard English. *Georgetown Monographs in Languages and Linguistics*, 1969, 22. (Reprinted in W. Labov. *Language in the inner city: Studies in the black English vernacular.* Philadelphia: University of Pennsylvania Press, 1972, pp. 201–240.)

Morse, J. M. The shuffling speech of slavery: Black English. *College English*, 1973, *34*, 834–839.

Robinson, J. L. The wall of Babel; Or, up against the language barrier. In R. W. Bailey & J. L. Robinson (Eds.) *Varieties of present-day English.* New York: Macmillan, 1973.

Shuy, R. W. Language and success: Who are the judges? In R. W. Bailey & J. W. Robinson (Eds.), *Varieties of present-day English.* New York: Macmillan, 1973.

Sledd, J. Bi-bidialectalism: The linguistics of white supremacy. *English Journal*, 1969, *58*, 1307–1315, 1329.

Sledd, J. Doublespeak: Dialectology in the service of big brother. *College English* 1972, *33*, 439–456.

4 | *Writing Introductions and Conclusions*

In the preceding chapters we have focused on the body of an academic paper. But a good piece of academic writing involves more than a well-organized body of information. It also includes a particular kind of introduction and conclusion. The introduction provides relevant background to the subject and forecasts the writer's main points. The conclusion provides a reminder of the writer's points and emphasizes their importance.

Introductions

Stated simply, the introduction to an academic paper should do two main things.

1. Provide *background*—general information on the subject and your particular perspective.
2. State the *thesis*—the most important ideas that you will deal with in your paper.

In certain types of writing—particularly writing intended for readers of popular magazines—another main goal of the introduction is to interest the reader in the topic. Thus, many journalists try to begin their essays with a startling statement or an intriguing incident which they hope will capture the reader's attention and "hook" him or her into reading further. Here is an example:

> A few months ago, on Friday the 13th of April, Bill Allen was strolling down the street on his way to work when all of a sudden he noticed he was about to commit the uncommittable, defy the undefiable. What he was about to do would jeopardize his mother's entire well being. As his foot angled down above the forbidden territory he sensed a responsibility for his mother's future. Then the back heel of his tennis shoe touched just short of the crack and his attempt to pivot off this fulcrum was futile, leaving him with a dreaded feeling of responsibility for his mother's almost certain misfortune. Like a growing number of individuals in our culture, Bill Allen was in the powerful grip of superstition, ruled over by a sense that "fate," "chance," or "luck" influenced the course of human affairs.

This introduction captures our interest by alluding to a well-known children's superstition: "Step on a crack, break your mother's back." The introduction is designed to make us want to read further to find out how an adult could be influenced by such superstitions. But this opening is probably too dramatic for an academic paper. In academic writing you can assume that your reader already has some interest in your topic, and it is therefore unnecessary to provide a "hook." You want to interest your reader not by being dramatic or shocking, but rather by sounding well-informed and reasonable. This is not, of course, to say that the opening of an academic paper must be dull. An interesting fact or brief story can provide an effective lead into the paper. In the following introduction to a paper on welfare fraud the student captures our interest with a reference to a specific case.

> Mary Smith may be Chicago's welfare queen. Indicted on 613 counts of theft from food stamps, Medicaid, and other public assistance programs, she is accused of using six aliases to receive more than $150,000 in illegal welfare payments.

While there is an element of shock in this account of possible fraud, it differs from the opening of the superstition paper. The welfare paper is more restrained, relying on the shock value of the allegations in the case rather than on exaggerated drama.

BACKGROUND

A good way to begin an academic paper is to provide general background information on the subject. The opening paragraph of the paper on welfare fraud is designed to provide background for the main point of the essay—what can be done to prevent such fraud. Here is the opening paragraph from the paper.

> Mary Smith may be Chicago's welfare queen. Indicted on 613 counts of theft from food stamps, Medicaid, and other public assistance programs, she is accused of using six aliases to receive more than $150,000 in illegal welfare payments.[1] Each year, thousands of Americans milk the government out of millions of dollars which they are not entitled to in public funds. Evidence of fraud is appearing extensively in every department of the government. Crooked employers file for thousands of wage dollars for nonexistent employees. Former Health, Education and Welfare Secretary Joseph Califano has estimated that his department's losses alone due to fraud exceeded 7 billion dollars for the last fiscal year.[2] In the past, the attitude towards those committing welfare frauds has been "hands off," but the taxpayers have become angry. They are the ones who are paying. They realize that something must be done.

By including background material you make the reader aware of the context surrounding your topic. For example, if you were writing a paper on Lincoln's Gettysburg Address, you might want to begin the paper by mentioning the background to that historic address. You could provide some information about the battle that took place at Gettysburg, and thereby help readers become more familiar with the context of the speech. Similarly, reports of psychological experiments usually begin with a discussion of past research related to the particular investigation reported. By mentioning these other studies, the writer presents a brief history of scientific activity in the field, thereby familiarizing the reader with the reason for the experiment and showing how it is related to preceding work.

Here is an introduction from a paper written for a course in literature.

> William Wordsworth's "A Slumber Did My Spirit Seal" is the cul-
> mination of a series of lyric poems, written in early 1799, known
> collectively as the "Lucy" poems. Critics have argued for nearly two
> centuries over different interpretations of the last poem of this group.
> Some interpret it as the poet's personal reminiscence of a secret
> lover; others regard it as a symbolic "killing off" of Wordsworth's
> sister, Dorothy, whom (some suppose) Wordsworth subconsciously
> desired incestuously. Many claim that the subject of this poem is the
> physical horror of death, with the recognition that Lucy (whomever
> she may represent) is dead. However, Wordsworth has insisted that
> the poet's business is to give pleasure. For Wordsworth, "pleasure
> has an absolute or mystical value, as a sign that our individual lives
> are rooted in a whole whose life is joy, are living branches of the tree
> of life, with its sap tingling in our veins." A proper understanding of
> Wordsworth's "A Slumber Did My Spirit Seal" enhances our chances
> of sharing in this pleasure, of feeling the "tingle" of life in our veins.

As background, the writer introduces the poem and the history of controversy concerning its interpretation. Moreover, because she is going to build her argument around a particular view of "pleasure," she must define this term. Her definition provides the background necessary to understand the main point of her argument: that a "proper understanding" of Wordsworth's poem "enhances our chances of sharing in this pleasure, of feeling the 'tingle' of life in our veins."

Sometimes inexperienced writers include background material in their introductions, but it is the wrong kind of material. Instead of telling readers what they need to know to understand the subject, writers describe their own struggles to understand it:

> When I first began to investigate the welfare system one of the most
> interesting aspects to come to my attention was the case of welfare

fraud. As a result of further investigation, I found that there were many types of such fraud—too many to include in a single paper. Therefore, I have decided to limit my discussion to a few of the more important types.

Such introductions are weak because readers don't want to hear about the history of your research; they want you to get to the point.

THESIS STATEMENT

The thesis statement tells your readers in brief what you are going to tell them at greater length in the body of your paper. The thesis statement directs the reader's attention to your major points. It is often the last statement in your introduction. The thesis statement from the paper on Wordsworth's poem reads:

> A proper understanding of Wordsworth's "A Slumber Did My Spirit Seal" enhances our chances of sharing in this pleasure, of feeling the "tingle" of life in our veins.

This statement forecasts the writer's main point: the writer is going to pursue the "proper understanding" of Wordsworth's poem. Once the writer explains the proper understanding, she will be able to clarify how this understanding helps the reader share in Words-worth's "pleasure."

Here is an introduction written for a paper in radiochemistry.

Background
Autoradiography is primarily a means of determining the localization of radioisotopes in a given tissue section, gross sample, or chromatogram. In autoradiography, a tissue section or other biological sample containing radioactive material is placed in close contact with a sensitive photographic emulsion. After a given period of exposure the film is developed and the precise localization of the radioactive matter in the sample may then be determined from the pattern of darkening on the film.

Thesis
This paper will discuss the characteristic interactions involved in the exposure of photographic emulsions to biological radioactive substances and the necessary conditions for high resolution of the autoradiograph.

This author begins with background—a definition of the term "autoradiography" and a general explanation of the autoradiographic process. The thesis statement indicates both the main point and the order in which major supporting points will be discussed.

So far, we have considered thesis statements that are one sentence long. If your paper is fairly short and direct, you might keep your thesis statement one sentence long. However, if your idea seems to be complex or your paper is long and involved, you might need to write a thesis statement that is longer than one sentence, as in the following introduction:

> Mobility is an essential and enduring characteristic of American life. The freedom to go where we will, how we will, has had a strong impact on the style and structure of this country. Perhaps the single most important contribution to this American ethos has been the private automobile. For many people, the automobile is a symbol of freedom, providing both status and autonomy. Unfortunately, our national love affair with the private automobile threatens to become a national disaster—producing air, water, and land pollution, consuming valuable and irreplaceable resources, destroying both city and countryside, and, ironically, denying freedom of movement to those unable, or unwilling, to drive.
>
> The purpose of this paper is to examine various aspects of transportation in the United States. The subject may be logically divided into several categories: the private automobile, alternatives to the private automobile, the feasibility of implementing those alternatives, and the economic and social implications of adopting them.

Thesis

In this case, the thesis statement takes two sentences: the first describes the writer's purpose; the second describes the points the writer will take up. In the following introduction, from a paper entitled "Buddhism and Change," the thesis statement is even longer.

> Buddhism has undergone many changes throughout the centuries. In part, its rapid spread was a result of its almost unlimited tolerance for change. Such tolerance has led to many splits in Buddhism; while there are only two main forms, Hinayana and Mahayana, there are countless sub-sects of each of these. There have been so many changes over the years that if Buddha were to come back and view modern Buddhism he would probably not be able to recognize a vestige of his original teachings.
>
> Most of the changes in Buddhism can be attributed to four factors: first, the lack of any documentation of Gautama Buddha's original teachings; second, the fact that Buddhism has spread throughout many countries all with a myriad of traditions; third, the inherent differences in man, every individual interpreting a certain teaching differently; and fourth, and perhaps most important, the changes that have come about through modernization. As many of the Buddhist countries become more Westernized, much of the old religion is being lost. These four factors have influenced the division of sects, especially the two major sects. An understanding of these four factors

Thesis

will clarify why it was inevitable that changes in Buddhism would take place.

The major purpose of the thesis statement is to help your reader recognize how you plan to develop your paper. The following thesis statement, taken from a paper written for a course in physical education, accomplishes this purpose well.

> In this paper two high jumping styles will be analyzed, the straddle and the flop. The purpose of both techniques is to get the athlete over the cross bar without dislodging it. In doing so, several things should be taken under consideration: the approach, takeoff, clearance, and landing of the athlete.

We know from this thesis statement that the writer is going to discuss two jumping styles, probably comparing them, and that he will discuss the two styles as sequences of steps: approach, takeoff, clearance, landing.

However, the following thesis statement is less effective in indicating the author's plan for the paper.

> Marriage should be done away with.

This statement is fine in some respects: it is direct and concise; it is also startling (most people accept marriage) and therefore should catch the reader's interest. But it offers no clue as to how the paper will be developed. The reader has no idea if the writer is going to attack marriage as unnecessary for people secure in their love, or tell a sad tale about a friend trapped in a disastrous marriage, or launch into a humorous account about how life for the writer has become complicated since he (or she) became married. The writer could improve this thesis statement by expanding it.

> Marriage should be done away with because it takes the excitement out of living together and binds people with legal ink instead of with love.

By adding information the writer forecasts what is to come. First the writer will attack marriage for taking the excitement out of living together, then he will develop the argument that it binds people with laws not with love.

Problem 4-1. Which statement in the following pairs of statements would best help the reader understand how the writer is going to develop the paper?

1. *a*) Rocks are commonly divided according to their origin.
   b) Rocks are commonly divided according to their origin into three major classes—igneous, sedimentary, and metamorphic.
2. *a*) Before any so-called Right to Die laws are enacted, many people should be consulted.
   b) Before any so-called Right to Die laws are enacted, representatives from the fields of law, medicine, and theology must be consulted.
3. *a*) Capital punishment should be abolished for both legal and moral reasons.
   b) One of the best things that can happen in the U.S. is the abolishment of capital punishment.
4. *a*) *The Godfather* is a dangerous film because it romanticizes violence and encourages people to think all Italians are gangsters.
   b) All in all, I believe *The Godfather* is a highly dangerous film.
5. *a*) The members of some fraternities are incredible conformists.
   b) The members of some fraternities are incredible conformists: they wear the same clothes, take the same courses, and have the same political beliefs.
6. *a*) Theodore Roosevelt raised the consciousness of Americans.
   b) Although he had his detractors, Theodore Roosevelt raised the consciousness of Americans regarding such issues as conservation and physical fitness.
7. *a*) Writing is a useful thing for educated people to know how to do.
   b) Writing is useful in clarifying your own thoughts and in communicating them to others.
8. *a*) School is a waste of time.
   b) For many children school is a waste of time because they get little attention, are made to feel inferior, and have few successes.

Problem 4-2. Rewrite each of the following statements to make thesis statements that will help readers make predictions about what the writer is going to write about in the body of the paper.

1. There should be laws to save whales from extinction.
2. Parents are too lenient (or strict) with their children.
3. Knowing something about art is important.
4. It is important to eat well.

Another function that a thesis statement can fulfill is to suggest that you are aware of different, possibly opposing, points of view. You may write a paper which presents a point of view which is different from that held by your readers. If they believe very strongly in their view, and if you don't mention it, you might easily be accused of faulty scholarship, ignorance, or foolishness. One way to avoid such a reaction is to acknowledge their point of view in your thesis statement. Consider the following thesis statement:

> Grades should be abolished because they produce anxiety and discourage a love of learning.

This is an adequate thesis statement. It directs the reader to ask specific questions. Do grades produce anxiety? Do they discourage a love of learning? On the other hand, if this paper were written for a professor who has outspokenly defended grades as the most efficient way to motivate students, this professor may expect the writer to say something about grades and student motivation. In fact, if the writer doesn't say something about the power of grades to motivate students, then the writer may actually insult that professor by ignoring his point of view.

The writer could recognize this opposing viewpoint in the following way:

> Although there might be some advantages to using letter grades, they still should be abolished because they produce anxiety and discourage a love of learning.

Here's another way a writer might acknowledge the professor's argument (especially if the writer doesn't want to commit himself to agreeing with the professor):

> Some might say that there are advantages in using letter grades, particuarly for motivation. However, grades still should be abolished because of the far greater harm they do in producing anxiety and discouraging a love of learning.

In either case, the writer will dismiss the opposing argument in the paragraph that immediately follows his introduction. But by acknowledging the professor's point of view right away in his thesis statement, he shows a willingness to be reasonable and to consider other people's points of view.

Problem 4-3. In the following exercise, you are given a thesis statement and a differing point of view. Rewrite the thesis statement to acknowledge the differing point of view. The first is done for you.

> 1. *Thesis*: Marijuana impairs a person's mental and physical health.
>   *Different point of view*: Three recent studies suggest that marijuana is not harmful to a person's mental and physical health. (Although a few studies suggest otherwise, eighty percent of the

doctors I interviewed said marijuana impairs a person's mental and physical health.)

2. *Thesis*: Women's athletic teams at the University of _____ _____ have been shabbily financed and shabbily coached for years.

Different point of view: The Office of Finances, in a recent memo, points out that money for women's athletics has doubled in the last two years.

3. *Thesis*: My high school teachers could have tried a little harder to provide their students with an interesting and practical education.

Different point of view: Two of my friends have said that the education that they got in high school was as good as they could expect.

4. *Thesis*: I am in favor of court-ordered busing because I think it is the only way to achieve peace and justice in this country.

Different point of view: Others feel that court-ordered busing is irresponsible because it is expensive, is unsafe, and takes students out of their own neighborhoods.

5. *Thesis*: Research proves that the threat of the electric chair does not stop people from committing crimes such as rape and murder.

Different point of view: Governor Johnston and members of the Council on Crime Deterrence have stated that rape and murder can be effectively controlled by strict and "meaningful" punishment: the electric chair.

Problem 4-4. Writing Thesis Statements. For each set of main points, write a thesis statement that could be used for the paper.

1. A student plans to write a paper comparing the advertising techniques used to promote Smirnoff Vodka in two advertisements. The following are the student's main points:
   a) The mood in both advertisements is similar.
   b) Both advertisements appeal to emotions in similar ways.
   c) Both advertisements limit their language to direct, simple statements.
   d) Both advertisements build on the good reputation of Smirnoff Vodka.

2. A student is writing a paper about the problems of running a fireworks stand for the Fourth of July. He lists three main problems:
   a) Government regulations
   b) Safety problems
   c) Problems of getting good, reliable help on a holiday.

3. A student is going to write a paper on building a compost heap. Here are his main points:
   a) A compost heap should be built at a distance from your garden.

 b) Many cities have ordinances against burying garbage in your yard.

 c) Many people are prejudiced against neighbors who bury garbage in their backyards.

 d) Compost heaps are useful because they help people to recycle organic material such as grass clippings and kitchen waste, and also help gardeners to improve their soil.

4. A student is going to write a paper on exercise. Here are his ideas:

 a) Many people like sports and feel that they should do some sort of exercise.

 b) Exercising is an important part of keeping healthy.

 c) In order to begin an exercise program, one should start out slowly.

 d) Many people should start out by walking.

 e) Once they are in better shape, people can begin to jog or run short distances.

 f) Once in better condition, people can explore a variety of exercises.

Problem 4-5. Recognizing the Parts of Introductions. This exercise presents several introductions to student papers. For each introduction identify the background and thesis statement. The first one is done for you.

1. ("I'm bald because my mother's father was" is a typical statement about how the baldness trait is acquired. People have perpetuated this homespun conclusion without much consideration for available information on the subject.) (An understanding of a simple genetic property—sex trait determination—yields a different answer to the question of baldness determination.)

Background
Thesis Statement

2. The shrill whistle and screeching brakes of the steam engine train echo through the narrow streets of the town as the locomotive chugs to a halt. Anxious observers crowd together on the wooden unloading platform, straining to glimpse a familiar face as the passengers disembark. The crowd moves into the depot, richly decorated with plush carpet, velvet upholstered chairs, sparkling mirrors, and glittering chandeliers. The men, wearing grey pinstriped suits and starched white collars, laugh and talk together, while the women gossip, straightening their hats and smoothing their long tight skirts. This scene depicts the heart of a community at the height of the railroad age—a scene which has faded with passing years. When trains began vanishing in America, people blithely assumed that the bus, the truck, the plane, and the automobile would perform all of the railroad's specialized functions, and could do a better job as well. Only recently have the results become evident: congested airports, stalled freeways, lethal smog,

and disastrous accidents—all warning of far more serious consequences in the future.

3. Each day enough sunlight falls on the United States to supply our nation's energy needs for two to three years, but finding efficient ways to harness this energy has been the major drawback in utilizing the sun. Agricultural production consumes 21 percent of our nation's total supply of energy, so all branches of agriculture are concerned with the problem of solar utility. Much research conducted by the USDA, state universities and labs, and private manufacturers has led to the development of solar equipment designed for farm use. These new implements have had mixed success, but one thing is certain from the latest research findings: every agricultural producer should now consider the applicability, efficiency, and economy of implementing solar devices.

4. Hyperkinetic syndrome in children is a kind of minimal brain dysfunction caused by genetic inheritance, biochemical imbalance in the central nervous system, brain damage resulting from lack of oxygen at birth, or allergic response to certain chemicals. It is characterized by irregular patterns of hunger, excretion and sleep, withdrawal from new objects or new persons, slow adaptation to changes in environment, isolated or nomadic play activities, and abnormal increase in motor activity with impulsive behavior at home and at school. Generally speaking, the drugs used for hyperkinetic syndrome are Dextroamphetamine and Methylphenidate. This paper will try to determine which of the two is the better choice, based upon their relative efficacy, potential side effects, and prospects for patient compliance.

5. Centuries separated the lives of the Hawaiians and visitors to the islands. The missionaries of the 1800s stepped into the past, a Stone Age compared to their modern Western civilization. The Hawaiians had been stranded in time, lost in a vast Pacific Ocean, an isolated population since A.D. 400 or 500. Though totally oblivious to Western civilization, the Hawaiians had developed a unique and complex civilization of their own. Today, no written record exists of their ancient history, but the ancient chants and hulas link Hawaii's past to its present. They should be preserved in their original forms, not only for their historical value, but for their linguistic, musical, and artistic values as well.

Conclusions

In some kinds of writing—for instance, a short story with a twist at the end, or a magazine article intended to keep the reader in suspense—it is important to hold back information, entice the reader, hint, until, at the end, the writer provides the snappy conclusion that ties things together. The conclusions of academic papers usually aren't so snappy. The writer forecasts in his introduction what information will be covered in the rest of the paper. Therefore nothing that is said in the conclusion comes as a complete surprise. Instead, the conclusion to an academic paper usually does one or both of the following:

> Summarizes the main points covered in a paper
> Answers the question "So What?"

SUMMARIZING IN THE CONCLUSION

One of the problems with conclusions is that they often are a waste of time. You write a perfectly clear two page paper and in your conclusion you repeat what you have just said. When your paper is short and your ideas so clear and direct, your conclusion can become overkill and your reader might go away insulted or bored. On the other hand, when you write a long paper or a paper with several scattered or complicated points, you may want to help your reader to put the parts together, to see things all at once. Consider the following conclusion.

> It is true, from the teacher's point of view, that letter grades have a certain amount of utility: they make it easier to keep concise records. But when we weigh this small advantage against the great disadvantages of grades, the argument for the utility of letter grades seems weak. Grades are, as we have seen, the greatest cause of anxiety among students. This anxiety disrupts both personal and academic development during the college years. Moreover, grades discourage a love of learning. By working for a grade rather than for knowledge, students learn to value the immediate rewards of a higher grade rather than to value the long-range goal of a love of learning. Thus, by using the antiquated system of letter grades, schools actually subvert the scholastic ideals which they proclaim.

If the paper were long, the writer would be justified in restating the main points. Doing so might help the reader put all the arguments together at one time. However, in a short paper, the writer might have been better off just saying, "Thus, by using the antiquated system of letter grades, schools actually subvert the scholastic ideals which they proclaim."

ANSWERING THE QUESTION "SO WHAT?"

Often you may want to conclude by considering the implications of the points you have discussed in the paper. For instance, in the previous section we gave you an example of one way to conclude a paper on "letter grades." That conclusion simply summarized the writer's thesis statement. Instead, a writer might have ended the paper differently.

> It is clear that grades should be abolished. While we continue to use this antiquated system to frustrate and misdirect our students, we are continuing a system that in the long run will hurt not only ourselves and our children, but also society in general.

Here, instead of directly restating the thesis, the writer points to implications.

In a paper on biorhythm theory, a student used the following thesis statement.

> As with most theories, the discovery, development, and practical use of biorhythm theory had its basis in mathematics.

His conclusion states:

> Like all scientific theories, biorhythm analysis had its origin and basis in mathematical theory. Its inductively reasoned discovery, its modeling upon the sinusoidal wave, and the statistical occurrence of critical days all had their origin in mathematical research. Biorhythms are now applied to such varied fields of human endeavor as aviation, industry, medicine, marriage counseling, and sports forecasting. Less cryptic than fate, fortune-telling, or predestination, perhaps the current state of biorhythm theory was best stated by research psychologist Douglas Neil: "Biorhythms are a small but significant piece of the puzzle of complex human behavior."

The student restates his thesis, summarizes his paper, and addresses implications by pointing out that biorhythms are useful in many different fields.

Finally, the following is the conclusion of a paper written for an upper division biology class. The title of the paper is "The Effects of *Artemisia tridentata* on Soils and Surrounding Vegetation."

> The results of this experiment show that *Artemisia tridentata* may have some rather unique method of effecting changes in the success of plants competing with it. Findings show a dramatic change in natural species composition as well as changes in soil organic matter. It should be noted that these results reflect data collected for only one sample (one sagebrush plant) and may well be an exception. However, it does indicate that further data should be collected, and procedural methods improved to establish any trend for certain.

Future research should include taking at least fifty random sage-brush as representative samples. Starting at the base of each plant, ten soil samples should be taken at 15 cm intervals for at least 150 cm moving in a straight line away from the sagebrush. These samples would then be potted and placed in the greenhouse for observation. The endogenous seeds would be allowed to germinate to establish any trends in mature vegetation. Also soil pH and organic matter content would be tested. The data from this experiment should be enough to determine whether or not there are effects produced by sagebrush. If it is determined that there are effects, the next step would be to determine what causes them and how they work (bio-chemical, competition for water, etc.). Once this is found, it would be possible to predict or experimentally determine the effect sage-brush has on grasses commonly used in reseeding projects.

This writer concludes her research study with a statement of the consequences that could result from further research. Such a conclusion is typical of papers that involve the explanation of an original research project.

Problem 4-6. How do the following conclusions deal with the question "So What?"

1. Here is a conclusion to a paper describing the history of and controversy surrounding the drug diethylstilbestrol (DES), a drug used to promote weight gain in cattle, but which seems to be linked to an increase in cancer.

   DES is clearly a controversial drug. Both sides of this nation-wide argument have valid, though conflicting, scientific cases. We must all realize that we are human and that this decision will affect the lives of our sons and daughters, if not ourselves. Is the 10–15 percent weight gain per head of cattle worth the 0.14 percent of cancer cases linked to DES? When this question can be answered to the satisfaction of both the FDA and the animal science industry, our dilemma will be resolved.

2. Here is the conclusion to a paper entitled "Rights of the Mentally Committed."

   People are becoming more aware of the absurdities of the mental health system. Organizations, such as the National Association for Mental Health, have worked hard to enlighten people about mental illness. But as a whole, the public still distrusts and fears ex-patients. The most efficient way to make sure the mentally ill receive the rights they deserve is through legislation. Mental health reform continues to confront us with the problem of balancing the parental and police functions of the government against the rights of the individuals. Criminals lose their freedom because of what they do, but the noncriminal mentally ill lose their rights and liberty because of what others think they are. In any case, the procedures for commitment must be picked apart and redeveloped. Potential patients should be represented by counsel and an in-depth, fair hearing ought to be provided for them. The mental health system also masks a number of other problems which imply the need for more and better facilities for the mentally ill. Greater public awareness as well as concrete steps taken by Congress, state legislatures, and state and federal courts can make changes that will give back rights taken away from the large group of the mentally ill.

3. Finally, here is the conclusion to a paper which has analyzed two styles of doing the high jump.

In conclusion, both the straddle and the flop require a great amount of technique. The high jump is an event which is successfully achieved by only a selected few. But of the two styles, the flop seems to be the more successful. This may be because the flop style of jumping allows the jumper a greater amount of velocity when approaching the bar, which in turn allows a greater jumping ability. The flop requires less body action than the straddle. The flop seems to allow more consistency in performance. If a jumper is running into a stiff head wind, the flop allows the athlete to perform closer to his ability under these conditions. Therefore, in training a young high jumper, it is best to start him out using the flop technique for better and more consistent performance.

Introductions and conclusions play an important role in helping the reader of an academic paper. From the reader's point of view, a good introduction is perhaps the single most helpful part of an academic paper because the introduction enables the reader to form initial ideas about the main topic of the paper. The more accurately he or she can form this prediction, the easier the reading will be. The paper will seem logical; it will "make sense." Therefore, one of your goals must be to make this prediction process easy—to give the reader a number of hints at the very outset about what the paper will be about. Thus introductions provide important background information and a guide to the main points that will be covered in the paper. The conclusion, because it is the last thing encountered, is likely to affect how your reader remembers the paper. Conclusions, therefore, play an important role in providing a reminder of your main points and a final statement of their implicatons.

5 | *Making Your Paper Coherent*

"Coherence" comes from a Latin word that means the quality of sticking together. In a good paper, all the parts stick together; there are no gaps that readers cannot bridge. In this chapter, we will first explore this notion of "coherence" more carefully and teach you to recognize what coherence gaps are. Then we will show you how to use your thesis statement, topic sentences, and some signaling devices to make your papers more coherent.

Understanding Coherence

The basic aim of coherence is to help your reader see how you are making connections between your major ideas. When connections aren't clear, there is a gap which you have to bridge. Some coherence gaps are fairly easy to recognize.

Problem 5-1. In which of the pairs of sentences is there a gap in coherence?

1. John went to the store. Elephants are supposed to have good memories.
2. John went to the store. He bought an apple and returned home.
3. Oil is one source of energy. Other sources are coal, the sun, and the wind.
4. I could not do the sixth problem. The painting of fire hydrants in different colors is a part of an attempt to beautify the environment.

You undoubtedly had little trouble distinguishing the coherent from the incoherent pairs. Probably no one would include pairs of sentences such as 1 and 4 in an academic paper. The gap separating the sentences in these pairs is so wide that only someone with an extremely fertile imagination could bridge it. But writers do sometimes write paragraphs that readers find incoherent. The incoherence is more subtle than that illustrated in problem 5-1, but still damaging to the quality of a paper. One nursing student, for example, began a paragraph of a paper on the care of geriatric patients like this:

> Baths are not needed so frequently by the older patient because of the decreased sweat secretion. This will help to preserve the major skin areas; however, special attention must be given to the perineum to prevent skin excoriation.

In this case, it is not really clear what will "help to preserve the major skins areas." What is needed is a bridge between ideas.

> Baths are not needed so frequently by the older patient because of the decreased sweat secretion. Less frequent bathing will help to preserve the major skin areas; however, special attention must be given to the perineum to prevent skin excoriation.

Coherence problems often stem from the fact that, as a writer, you know your subject so well that the connection between main points seems perfectly clear, perhaps even obvious. The writer of the paper on geriatric patients knew that the word "this" meant "less frequent bathing," and assumed that her readers would understand this meaning too. But readers usually don't know your subject in the same way you do, and so your task becomes one of trying to decide which gaps between points are bridgeable by which readers. Those readers who share your knowledge can make many pairs of sentences coherent that others would find perplexing.

Problem 5-2. What special information does the average American possess that would enable him to perceive the following pairs as coherent? Would a foreigner, a visitor from Burma, for example, find them coherent?

1. Mike's wallet was stolen. He had to get a new driver's license.
2. Mrs. Smith didn't go to work today. She was on jury duty.
3. Mary went to the corner drugstore often. She loved milk shakes.
4. Americans are devoted to McDonald's because of price, convenience, and uniformity. The golden arches are a familiar landmark in almost every part of the country.

The average American probably possesses the necessary knowledge to bridge the gaps in the above sentences. The problem is that you seldom write for the average American; usually you write for readers who make up a special subgroup in American society. The trick in writing coherent paragraphs then is to make sure that all gaps are bridgeable by the particular readers you are writing for.

Problem 5-3. The gaps between sentences in the passages below would be bridgeable by some readers, unbridgeable by others. Explain what readers could bridge the gaps.

1. Jim was like Hemingway in some ways and different from him in others.

   For example, he liked bull fights.

2. A bedridden patient must be made to lie in different positions.

   Since lung weakness could further complicate the patient's other health problems, it is very important that none develops.

3. The score was tied and time was running out. Tall Mike Fevine stood under the basket hoping to catch a rebound that he could slam dunk for two. "Whee" went the ref's whistle. "Three seconds!" he shouted.

   There went Canton's chance for a tourney bid and it was all Mike's fault.

The principle of bridging gaps is crucial when you put together the important points in your paper. The relationship between points may be clear to you, but not to someone else. Consider the following two paragraphs:

> The little old lady stood in a pink gingham dress with a fake antique necklace around her neck. T-shirted people walked by the table without giving a second look to the wares she was displaying. Quilted pillows, crocheted dogs, and quilts in numerous patterns and colors covered the table. To this woman, here lay her art. It might be true that she produced it only for commercial reasons (if you asked her), but nevertheless, she made it with her hands. It was the little old lady in the gingham dress who chose the materials for their quality and color, texture and contrast. She had learned quilting from her grandmother. Quilting is a craft. As a craft, it reflects the culture from which it came.
>
> Eskimos carve beautifully simplistic sculpture from stone, wood and bones during the long, cold days when it is almost impossible to go outdoors. They utilize the few poor materials found in their environment to create carvings which they value for their smoothness. Never outstanding in color or delicacy, Eskimo sculpture reveals the stark black and white nature the native finds himself in.

Although the writer wants to make a connection between the two paragraphs, the connection is not clear. By adding a sentence (italicized in the following example) the writer can make it more clear.

> . . . Quilting is a craft. As a craft, it reflects the culture from which it came.
>
> *Crafts are important in other cultures as well.* Eskimos carve beau-

tifully simplistic sculpture from stone, wood and bones during the long, cold days when it is almost impossible to go outdoors. They utilize the few poor materials found in their environment to create carvings which they value for their smoothness. Never outstanding in color or delicacy, Eskimo sculpture reveals the stark black and white nature the native finds himself in.

By constantly being aware of the necessity to bridge gaps—to make clear to others what is perfectly clear to you—you will be able to solve many of your coherence problems. In academic writing, however, there are also several specific devices you can use to ensure that your papers are coherent.

The Thesis Statement and Topic Statement

Good thesis statements and topic statements will help make your papers coherent. By using these devices you tell your reader where you're going and how you're going to get there. This helps the reader connect the points you make in the body of your paper.

Here is a thesis statement for a paper attacking letter grades.

> Although there are advantages to the present letter grade system, it still should be abolished because it produces anxiety and discourages a love of learning.

This thesis statement lets readers know what the author will argue: that the present grade system should be abolished. It also lets readers know how the writer will develop the points in the paper. First, the writer will argue that grades produce anxiety, and second, that they discourage a love of learning.

But, of course, a good thesis statement alone won't make your paper coherent. Your thesis statement may announce your plan, but if later in the body of your paper you don't follow this plan or appear not to follow this plan, your readers will find your paper incoherent. You have to do in the body of your paper what you announced you were going to do in your thesis statement. Moreover, you often need to make perfectly clear that you are following your thesis. Sometimes, when you are writing a paper that gets complicated and involved, your reader may have trouble keeping your thesis in mind. An author may write a long paragraph discussing how grades produce anxiety, but when the author comes to the second point—that grades discourage a love of learning—readers may have momentarily lost track of the overall concern: that grades should be abolished. To make sure readers won't lose track of the overall concern, the author may want to remind readers periodically of the main points. A good place to do this reminding is in a topic statement.

Topic statements are to the paragraphs of your paper what the thesis statement is to the whole paper: they announce what will be covered in a particular paragraph just as a thesis statement announces what will be covered in the paper as a whole. Moreover, if skillfully constructed, they can also remind readers of the thesis statement. The thesis statement is:

> Although there are advantages to the present letter grade system, it still should be abolished because it produces anxiety and discourages a love of learning.

Moving directly out of this statement, the writer introduces the first point with a clear topic statement.

> The present system does benefit the administration and the student in several ways.

In the next paragraph, the writer moves to a second point with another topic statement.

> But grades under the present system make students fear school.

Here, the writer hopes that readers will make the connection between "make students fear school" and what has been described in the thesis statement as "produces anxiety." Finally, the writer moves to the last point, introducing it with a final topic statement.

> Besides making students anxious, the present grading system has another serious disadvantage: it discourages a love of learning.

Here, the writer restates the preceding point—that grading makes students anxious—and then moves on to the last point: that grading discourages a love of learning. This statement echoes the writer's initial thesis statement: "the present letter grade system . . . should be abolished because it produces anxiety and discourages a love of learning."

Problem 5-4. One of the sentences in each of the following groups is a thesis statement and the others are topic statements. Decide which sentence should be the thesis statement and number the topic statements in the order you'd arrange them in your final paper (1 = the topic statement which would occur first.) Then explain briefly *why* you chose the order you did. The first group of sentences is done for you.

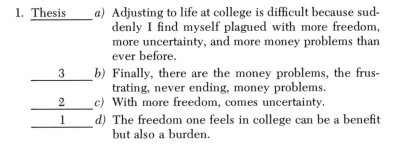

1. Thesis _____ *a)* Adjusting to life at college is difficult because suddenly I find myself plagued with more freedom, more uncertainty, and more money problems than ever before.

____3____ *b)* Finally, there are the money problems, the frustrating, never ending, money problems.

____2____ *c)* With more freedom, comes uncertainty.

____1____ *d)* The freedom one feels in college can be a benefit but also a burden.

Why this order? The thesis sentence indicates the order in which the topics will be discussed: freedom, uncertainty, money problems. Sentence *c* appears to be a transition from the topic of freedom to the topic of uncertainty. The signal word "finally" in sentence *b* shows that it introduces the last main topic.

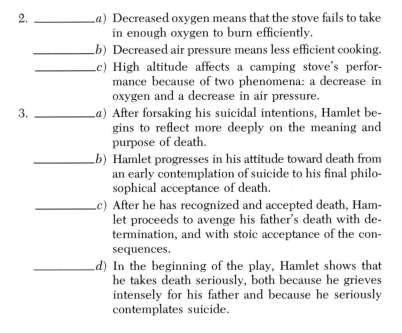

2. _____*a*) Decreased oxygen means that the stove fails to take in enough oxygen to burn efficiently.

_____*b*) Decreased air pressure means less efficient cooking.

_____*c*) High altitude affects a camping stove's performance because of two phenomena: a decrease in oxygen and a decrease in air pressure.

3. _____*a*) After forsaking his suicidal intentions, Hamlet begins to reflect more deeply on the meaning and purpose of death.

_____*b*) Hamlet progresses in his attitude toward death from an early contemplation of suicide to his final philosophical acceptance of death.

_____*c*) After he has recognized and accepted death, Hamlet proceeds to avenge his father's death with determination, and with stoic acceptance of the consequences.

_____*d*) In the beginning of the play, Hamlet shows that he takes death seriously, both because he grieves intensely for his father and because he seriously contemplates suicide.

The following exercise contains topic statements designed to do two things: provide a transition from the previous paragraph and introduce the paragraph coming up. You do not need to begin every paragraph with a topic statement that does both these things, but often topic statements that both summarize and introduce are useful. They help the reader follow the thread of your argument.

Problem 5-5. Read the following topic statements. Then answer two questions about each.

> Questions: *a*) What is the topic of the immediately preceding paragraph?
> *b*) What is the topic of the paragraph coming up?

1. Other regulatory agencies are bad not because they are inefficient but because the bureaucrats running them lack an understanding of the industries they are responsible for regulating.
2. Its lack of fairness is one problem with Jones's approach to prison reform; another problem is cost.
3. In addition to differences of territory, Sudanese political groups are also distinguished by religion.
4. The spirit of freedom and optimism that swept over Poland and East Germany after the signing of the Helsinki accords swept over Czechoslovakia as well.
5. Clearly the rights of adults are being violated; the situation concerning young people is worse.

Problem 5-6. In the following student essay, blanks have replaced the topic statements. Fill in the blanks with appropriate sentences or phrases.

> Alienation in contemporary society occurs for a number of reasons. A person is "alienated" when he possesses some characteristic that society cannot understand or accept. To avoid the frustration of coping with a person who is "different," society forms a stereotype, alienating the type of person in question. Alienation is a cruel process, isolating an individual for circumstances over which he has no control. The causes of alienation can be divided into four major categories: personal habits, disabilities, race, and beliefs and ideologies.
>
> _____. Poor hygiene, alcoholism, and drug abuse are justifiable causes for alienation. The individual, due to misplaced priorities, acquires a habit that society deems unacceptable. Since the individual should be capable of eliminating this habit, society does not feel compelled to tolerate this type of person. The individual possessing the undesirable habit is alienated from society until he chooses to conform to the social conventions.
>
> _____. These can be either physical or mental. Physical disabilities such as speech, hearing, and vision

impediments are common causes for alienation, creating extensive difficulties for the afflicted individual. Society often views the physically handicapped as a "nonperson," lacking feelings and rights. Therefore, the physically disabled individual finds the agony of alienation added to the inescapable burden of his handicap.

_____ are also a cause for alienation from society. Disabilities such as schizophrenia hinder the individual's ability to function within society. Society, in general, does not understand mental disabilities, failing to realize that the afflicted person requires understanding, compassion, and patience in order to recover. Instead, society often shuns the mentally disabled, adding further to their existing problems.

_____. Society stereotypes the various races on the assumption that undesirable personality traits are linked to a specific race. Since this ideology is totally illogical, the individual who is alienated for this reason is outraged by his or her predicament. Alienation because of race is very unjust, because an individual is condemned before he is even born.

_____. The beliefs held by the majority of the people are viewed as "correct" and "acceptable." Beliefs and ideas straying from this "social norm" are condemned. Therefore, individuals are often alienated for such reasons as religion, politics, and personal morality. Despite the belief in "freedom of choice for the individual," vast numbers of people are alienated from society on the basis of their beliefs and ideologies. This is very hypocritical, especially in America, where society supposedly believes in "freedom of the individual."

Alienation is obviously a serious problem in contemporary society. Innocent people are unjustly condemned for circumstances over which they have no control. Alienation is a cruel process, placing additional burdens on those individuals already experiencing difficulties in life.

Signals

In addition to using clear thesis statements and topic statements to make your paper more coherent, you can also use special signals to further stick your ideas together. Three of these signals are linking words, numbers, and repetitions of key terms.

LINKING WORDS

Of the signals that writers use to make the ideas in their papers cohere, linking words or phrases are probably the best known. These words can be grouped into four types according to the function they play in linking one idea to the next.

1. Making an additional (parallel) point: *moreover, furthermore, also, in addition, another.*
2. Giving an example: *to illustrate, for example, similarly, for instance, in other words.*
3. Making a contrasting point: *however, on the other hand, but, in spite of, on the contrary, yet, although.*
4. Providing results, summary, or a concluding point: *therefore, consequently, hence, thus, finally, in summary, in conclusion, as a result.*

In the following paragraph from a student paper, the linking words have been italicized.

Despite these problems, there are a number of advantages that

example favor the development of photovoltaics. *For instance,* photovoltaics attain the highest efficiency conversion of solar to electrical energy devices. Here, the efficiency is the percent of the incident light energy that is converted into electrical energy. Cells are now being

additional point produced that are about 30 percent efficient. *Another* advantage is the long life expectancy of solar cells. They can provide their rated output for perhaps a dozen years with virtually no maintenance re-

additional point quired. *Also* advantageous is their high power to weight ratio. This has made solar cells essential in the development of our space program and, in view of the probable need for large arrays as a means

concluding point of reducing cost, will allow practical construction of such arrays. *Finally,* photovoltaics have the advantage of being easy to apply. The proper combination of cells can provide any DC voltage and current which can power any intended load. Once activated, the installation can run unattended for a number of years.

Problem 5-7. Identify and underline the linking words in this paragraph from a student paper. How effective are these words in making the paragraph coherent?

However, the NOCSAE (National Operating Committee on Safety in Athletics) has no power to force the manufacturers of football helmets to comply with the standard. The manufacturers may voluntarily produce helmets which meet this standard, but no one can force them. On the other hand, test results immediately stimulated the manufacturers to improve their helmets in order to compete with other types and brands. Consequently, the safety of football helmets has steadily improved. During the period from 1971 to 1976, when the NOCSAE played a major role in helmet safety, a 55 percent reduction was made in the annual football fatality rate compared with the six-year period prior to 1971. As a result of this reduction, a new NCAA rule in 1978 required all student athletes to wear an NOCSAE approved helmet.

NUMBERS

Another common device for providing coherence is to number (or letter) separate points. The numbers serve two useful functions. They can serve as signals that the writer is beginning to discuss another major point. They are also useful in permitting the writer to refer back to a previously numbered idea by using the number only: "the second point is most important." There are several devices for using numbers—one device is to use words such as "first," "second," or "one," "another," "still another." Another device is to use arabic numerals or lowercase letters enclosed in parentheses: (1), (2), (3), or (a), (b), (c).

In the following example note the use of words to signal the main points: "first," "next," and "finally." Notice how the writer can use the word "first" in the last sentence to provide a clear link to the initial stage in the argument.

> There are three stages to Sir Charles's argument: first, he proposes that there is a mutual failure of contact and comprehension between scientists and nonscientists. Next, he suggests that this failure is at least unfortunate, and probably dangerous. Finally, he claims that it is possible to find ways to close the gap between the two groups. The first of these propositions cannot be seriously doubted.

The next paragraph illustrates use of numbers to keep references to major points clear.

> Three court cases are of importance because they represent key decisions in this area. (1) In one of the earliest cases, *Engel* v. *Vitale*, a New York school board required that a prayer be recited aloud each morning in the presence of a teacher. The Supreme Court ruled that this requirement constituted a violation of the establishment clause of the first amendment. (2) In *School District of Abington Township* v. *Schenepp et al.*, a Pennsylvania statute required that at least ten verses from the Bible be read at the opening of classes each school day. (3) In *Murray* v. *Curlett*, the Baltimore school board required Bible reading and/or recitation of the Lord's prayer. These last two cases are so similar that they may be considered together. In both cases, the laws required religious exercises which were in direct violation of the rights of those who brought suit. The point made in

each of these three cases is that Bible reading and/or recitation of the Lord's prayer, when required by school authorities, is in violation of the first amendment of the Constitution.

The next paragraph provides another illustration of use of numbers to identify key ideas. Notice how the use of the numbers enables the writer to refer quite simply but clearly to "the second area" later in the paragraph.

There have been several major theories advanced concerning alternative authors of the plays traditionally attributed to Shakespeare. Four areas which are usually discussed in the development of these theories are: (1) arguments for the rejection of William Shakespeare as author; (2) arguments for the rejection of some other candidate as author; (3) reasons for the long concealment of the identity of the proposed author; and (4) reasons the authorship was formerly attributed to William Shakespeare. The theories differ most drastically in the second area, while the arguments for the other points are often nearly identical.

REPETITION OF KEY TERMS (OR SYNONYMS)

Finally, writers achieve coherence by repeating the key terms often enough to keep the topic that is being discussed clear for the reader. In the following example from a student paper, the key terms have been italicized.

Closely aligned with the value of innocence in American culture is the value of *hopefulness*. From the beginning, Americans have been people of *hope*. The Puritans were innocent concerning what they would find in the new world, but they were *hopeful* of the success of their venture. Later immigrants also came with high *hopes* for success. To everyone, America seemed a land of opportunities. The revolution in the colonies reflects the *hopefulness* of America at that time. If Americans had not been *optimistic* about success they probably would not have started the revolution. In the nineteenth century there was also a rise in immigration, another reflection of the *hopefulness* in America. Just as earlier immigrants, they viewed America as a land of *hope* and opportunity.

Notice how this student repeats the key word *hopefulness* (or one of its forms: *hope, hopeful*) enough times to keep the topic of the paragraph constantly in mind.

The following paragraph is another in which terms are repeated to make it clear what the writer is discussing. In this example, the writer uses slightly different (but synonymous) terms to achieve a bit of variety. This variety can be useful in a paper because repeating the same term too many times can become monotonous.

> In theory, there are many remedial steps that can be taken to stop *illegal spending of public funds*. The hiring of auditors to keep an eye on departmental spending and the close surveillance of government employees seem to be appropriate deterrents, but for the most part, these have been unsuccessful. The White House has not yet launched a full-scale campaign to stop *illegal spending* throughout all government agencies, so each department must set its individual policies. Most agencies will make little effort to detect or prevent *improper activities*, but instead, take action only after reports of *unlawful activity* have been received. In addition, directors of departments short of auditors and investigative staff often believe that hiring additional employees would be costly and fairly ineffective. The basic underlying problem is that while the government continues to spend money, "no attention is given to protecting programs from *abuse*."

Problem 5-8. This paragraph is from a paper written for an economics class. Underline the key terms which are repeated. How effective are the coherence devices in the passage?

> Historically, labor unions have tended to advocate quotas and tarrifs on U.S. imports. Their assumption is that foreign imports cut into the profits of American companies and drive down American employment. It is questionable, however, whether limitations on foreign trade would, indeed, benefit American workers as a whole. It is true that some industries and, hence, some employees, benefit from barriers to trade. Such industries are those where productivity is below average and wages are the lowest. But other workers in industries may not benefit. If the U.S. increases its trade barriers, the probability is that other countries would increase their own trade barriers. The net result could be an increase in the number of jobs for the lowest-paid, import-oriented sector of the economy and a decrease in the number of jobs in the higher-paid, export-oriented sector—although some laborers could be better off, there could be a substantial lowering in the average wage of the laborer. Moreover, although some laborers might appear to be better off, the prices of goods would also go up, and the goods most likely affected would be those purchased by consumers with the lowest incomes. Thus, while individuals may receive increases in money income, their real wages may or may not increase.

In addition to repeating the key terms, you can also use pronouns which clearly refer back to the key term. Pronouns help to achieve variety and thus function much like synonymous terms. But using pronouns introduces a potential problem: sometimes it is not clear which key term the pronoun refers to. Clarity is more important than variety. If there is any doubt about whether the pronoun will be clear or not, then repeat the term instead of using the pronoun.

One group of useful pronouns refers to people: *he, she, him, her, they, them.* Using these pronouns presents no problem when only one person is being discussed. But when more than one person is discussed, a pronoun usually refers to the closest previously mentioned name of a person. The paragraph below mentions two women, Iolani and Keahi. Thus the writer must be careful about how she uses the pronoun *she.*

> One legendary figure stands above all others during the 1900s. In 1915, at six months of age, Iolani Luahine was chosen to live with her auntie, Juliet "Keahi" Luahine, court dancer for King Kalakaua. Iolani became part of the life of Keahi Luahine, who was her *kahu hanai*, her foster mother and her teacher, the woman responsible for everything Iolani was to learn about the sacred ancient dances and chants. She studied hula unceasingly, living in two worlds, the ancient and the modern. The Luahine eminence in the dance was established in the years following Keahi's death in 1937. By the mid-1950s, Iolani had become what she is today: a legend associated with historic places. She had been curator at Iolani Palace, the Royal Mausoleum, and, most recently, Hulihee Palace.

Whenever the writer uses "she" the reference is clear: the intended person is always Iolani, and the name "Iolani" is always the closest previously mentioned name.

A second group of useful pronouns refers to things, ideas, or concepts: *it, this, these.* As with the previously discussed set of pronouns, there is always a potential for ambiguity when you use these pronouns. The best advice is to use pronouns cautiously, re-reading passages to see if your reader will understand exactly what the pronoun refers to. The following example uses "these" and "this" to refer to previously mentioned key terms: "stocks" and "International Business Machines."

> There are stocks which might fit neatly into both capital gains and dividend areas. One example of these is International Business Machines, which pays a dividend and is well known as a growth stock. This and similar stocks are the exceptions rather than the rule. Individuals will be attracted to invest in these stocks, but as more and more do so the prices will rise.

Problem 5-9. The writers of the following paragraphs use both repetition of terms and pronouns. Identify these devices and decide whether they are used effectively.

1. There has been one treatment that has been successful in some of these cancer cases. This is the use of natural progesterone. It has been developed only in the past three years; therefore, there is little evidence available on the treatment's effectiveness. One fact is known, however: the treatment does cause regression of the cancers in some females. Doctors hope that with further research they can develop it so that it will cause regression in a higher percentage of women.

2. Both Dextroamphetamine and Methylphenidate are central nervous system stimulants. They act by stimulating the nerve fibers in a certain area of the brain called the brainstem. The efficacy of both drugs was compared in an experiment conducted by Weiss et al. (1978). They found that both drugs reduced hyperactivity, distractibility, aggressiveness, and excitability, and that they produced more goal-oriented behavior. However, they also found that Methylphenidate was clinically more effective than Dextroamphetamine in calming and quieting hyperactive behavior, in stabilizing and settling down the children, in allowing more efficient social and play relationships, and in improving their speech and handwriting.

One way to check your paper for coherence is to examine carefully the links between the sentences in a paragraph, paying special attention to places where key terms are repeated and how pronouns are used to refer to previous terms or concepts. By drawing lines that connect the terms you will be even better able to visualize the links. The following paragraph illustrates how to draw these lines.

Buses also lend themselves well to more ingenious and innovative *strategies* for mobility. One such *strategy* is the concept of *demand-responsive transportation systems.* These *systems,* composed most commonly of a fleet of small buses, may complement fixed-route systems or *they* may serve all the transit demands in communities with no other transit service. *Demand-responsive systems* are intrinsically suited to low-to-medium-density communities with low demand densities and widely dispersed origins and destinations. These *systems* have proven attractive because *they* are flexible and accommodate the realities of modern communities.

Problem 5-10. Try drawing lines connecting key terms and pronouns in the following paragraph.

> Since 1955 the South African government has not participated in General Assembly debate on the subject of apartheid. The government rejects United Nations discussions of what it considers its domestic prerogatives. However, reasonable and rational people could not regard the Pretoria regime as legitimate. It derives its authority only from the transfer of power by the colonial rulers to a minority, without regard to the right of all people to self-determination. The United Nations General Assembly has even declared the Pretoria government to be "illegitimate" and the liberation groups to be the authentic representatives of the South African people.

Recognizing and achieving coherence is crucial in academic writing. In an academic paper you are usually dealing with a large number of facts or with complex ideas or theories. This complexity means that the reader can easily get lost, failing to see the connection between particular facts or concepts. We have presented two strategies for achieving coherence: writing clear thesis and topic statements, and using signals such as linking words, numbers, or repetition of key words (or synonyms and pronouns). You need to be aware that coherence is often a problem in academic papers and you must constantly try to recognize potential problems in your own writing.

Problem 5-11. In the following paper, see if you can isolate the coherence devices the writer uses to clarify concepts and link ideas to ideas. Look for all of the devices mentioned in this chapter.

THE DEVELOPMENT OF THINKING:
PIAGET'S THEORY OF STAGES

People's ideas about children's thinking have changed substantially since earlier times. In the middle ages the common conception was that children were simply "little adults." If you look at medieval paintings you will notice that the children are just adults painted
5   smaller—the children's features are still adult. This idea that children are essentially the same as adults, only smaller, still exists today, even in theories of children's mental processes. Some psychologists believe that children's thinking is basically the same as adults in *quality* (in mechanisms of thought), but that there are differences in
10   *quantity* of knowledge. A child simply needs to learn more to become an adult. However, one contemporary psychologist has argued strongly for the opposite view: that children's thinking differs from adults in quality. The Swiss psychologist, Jean Piaget, believes that in their mental development children pass through four distinctly

15 different modes of thought. Piaget's theory has been very influential, and most authorities on child development now appear to view children's thinking as qualitatively distinct from that of adults. This paper will briefly examine each of Piaget's four stages: the sensorimotor period, the preoperational period, the concrete operational period,
20 and the formal operational period.

At the beginning of the sensorimotor period the infant makes no distinction between himself and the outside world—everything is bound together in an undifferentiated whole. The main achievement of this first period is for a child to become able to explore the world
25 and thus establish it as an objective reality distinct from himself. The young child develops simple systems for interacting with his world: sucking, looking, listening, grasping. These simple systems combine, so that the child is able both to look at an object and to grasp it. This coordination makes the child interested in the consequences of his
30 actions and leads to further exploration of the world.

In the next stage, the preoperational period (roughly from age two to age seven), children develop the ability to think symbolically— they have mental images of things in the environment. But children in this period have difficulty focusing on two aspects of a situation
35 or problem at the same time. For example, they have difficulty seeing another person's point of view at the same time as their own. Piaget did an interesting experiment to illustrate this inability to see from other perspectives. He showed children a scale model of three mountains placed on a table. These mountains were different colors and
40 sizes, and had distinguishing features like a stream or a path. After walking around the display, each child sat on one side of the table. He was shown a series of pictures depicting the mountains from various perspectives. (Obviously, the mountains would look different from various sides of the table.) Then a doll was placed on different
45 sides of the table and the child was asked, "Pick the picture that shows what the doll would see from here." Children in the preoperational period always picked the picture showing their own view (what they saw when they looked at the mountains). The explanation for this is that preoperational children cannot focus on two dimen-
50 sions, both their own view and another, and so they pick the picture showing the most vivid perspective—their own.

If the preoperational child is characterized by focusing on one specific aspect or dimension of a situation, the concrete operational child (about age seven to twelve) is characterized by the ability to
55 focus on several aspects of a situation at a time. This is an advance in thinking, and permits the child to solve new problems. One of Piaget's most famous experiments illustrates this difference. In this experiment, the child is presented with two identical glasses filled with equal quantities of liquid. Then the content of one glass is
60 poured into a third glass of a different shape—for example, shorter and wider. Then the child is asked again whether the two glasses

contain the same amount of liquid. A preoperational child will claim that the quantities are not equal, often that the taller, thinner glass has more. The concrete operational child, on the other hand, consis-
65 tently says that the quantities are the same, despite the transfer to a differently shaped glass. The concrete operational period marks the beginning of logic in children's thinking. And yet the child's thinking remains "concrete," limited to tangible, material objects.

In the final stage, the formal operational period (beginning at about
70 age twelve), children develop the ability to move beyond things or events in the immediate present. Thinking is applied to hypotheses—not only to the real, but also to the realm of the possible. The kind of thought characteristic of this stage resembles the kind of reasoning a scientist often uses. By adolescence most children are
75 able to gather and organize data, explore all possible variables, and come to a conclusion based on logical proof. This kind of intellectual power is a great advance over the thinking of early childhood.

Piaget's studies give us a picture of children advancing through four qualitatively different kinds of thought. At each new stage chil-
80 dren can solve problems that they could not manage during earlier periods. Thus, Piaget's account of the development of children's thinking challenges the idea that children are simply "little adults," using the same kinds of thinking as adults. If children have distinctive ways of thinking at various ages, then our interaction with them—
85 and, most importantly, our educational programs for them—need to be geared to their own individual modes of thought.

Problem 5-12. Fill in the numbered blanks in the following paper, using some of the coherence devices discussed in this chapter: linking words, numbers, and repetition of key words. The blanks are numbered so that you can easily refer to the devices used by the author (listed in the "Answers to Selected Problems" section).

SUN POWER COMES TO AGRICULTURE

Each day enough sunlight falls on the United States to supply our nation's energy needs for two to three years, but finding efficient ways to harness this energy has been the major drawback in utilizing the sun. Agricultural production consumes 21 percent of our nation's total supply of energy, so all branches of agriculture are concerned with the problem of solar utilization. Much research conducted by the USDA, state universities and labs, and private manufacturers has led to the development of solar equipment designed for farm use. These new (1)_____ have had mixed success, but one thing is certain from the latest research findings: every agricultural producer should now consider the applicability, efficiency, and economy of implementing (2)_____ _____.

The (3)_____ consideration should be whether or not solar equipment can be (4)_____ successfully to an individual's farming practices. Farmers have been using solar energy in a number of ways. A Nebraska farmer has already pumped thousands of gallons of water to fields for the irrigation of soybeans, and also plans to grind feed, ventilate livestock buildings, charge batteries, and perform other various functions—all from energy captured from a single solar apparatus.[1] An Illinois farmer uses solar energy to warm his swine building when it is cold, and then uses the same sunpower to charge a generator, which can reverse the air flow and blow cooler outside air in on the hogs when it is hot.[2] The Dairy Industry has been successful in heating the large amounts of water necessary for commercial milk production with solar energy.[3]

(5)_____ _____ use of solar implements is in grain drying. In a year with normal rainfall, more energy is consumed in (6)_____ _____ than is used in planting and harvesting the entire crop. Because of this, much research has centered on an effective way to (7) _____ _____ with solar energy. In Illinois, a large farm using only solar equipment to (8)_____ _____ _____ produces marketable grain moisture readings. Other farmers have had similar success utilizing solar energy for the same purpose.[4]

But there are problems with solar grain drying. (9)_____ _____ is that grain moisture readings above 22 percent cannot be dried with solar collectors. At high moisture levels, heat generated by solar equipment causes mold to multiply in grain bins. Cooler, faster moving air produced by conventional dryers is necessary for efficient drying in cases of wet grain. A (10)_____ _____ of solar drying is that it is not useful in all regions of the country. High humidity regions, such as Iowa and Missouri, have very high moisture content in their grains, even in relatively low rainfall seasons. Commercial dryers must be used in these areas.

Overall, however, solar equipment applicability has been expanded successfully into many farm operations. Over 200 manufacturers currently produce solar devices and General Motors, Exxon, General Electric, Alcoa, and other large firms are eyeing the potential.[5] These manufacturers insure that a large selection of commercial collectors will be available for agricultural uses in the future.

In addition to (11)_____, (12)_____ is the second aspect of solar energy requiring consideration, with many types of collectors, representing various degrees of efficiency. Using only dark colored metal plates on the roofs of farm buildings, it is possible to convert sunlight to electricity with 50 percent efficiency. More sophisticated black absorber plates covered with clear fiberglass siding operate at 70 percent efficiency. Both of these two types have been easily incorporated into existing buildings.

More advanced solar equipment requires building preparations, but utilizes energy more effectively. L. Whitt Brantley of the National Aeronautics and Space Administration Marshall Flight Center has developed a spheroidal collector that can be incorporated into plans for new buildings.[6] This collector can generate the equivalent of 29,520 gallons of propane gas and 198,066 kilowatts of electricity in one year. With this system, it is conceivable that excess solar energy, that not required for the farm's electrical load, could be converted to a transportable state, reversed through the electrical meter, and then sold back to the power company.

Generally, buildings with solar collectors are more energy efficient than those buildings without. Although certain climatic conditions, such as snow and rain, can seriously reduce a collector's efficiency, most solar devices provide for large stored reserves of energy, which can be utilized whenever they are needed; in this way, solar devices are energy efficient.

The (13)_____ major consideration is the (14)_____ of solar equipment. Commercial collectors are now being produced at a cost of from three to twelve dollars per square foot. The breakeven point has been calculated by experimental results and computer analysis as being between fifty cents and a dollar per square foot. Most solar devices are not yet economically feasible, but there are a couple of reasons to believe that solar feasibility will change. (15)_____ _____ is that conventional energy costs have been rising at a tremendous rate for over a decade. Forecasted consumer trends in energy use indicate that these costs are likely to continue rising in the immediate future.

Comparison of current costs of production with and without a solar apparatus illustrates a (16)_____ _____ why solar energy is becoming more feasible. Vance Morley, a University of Minnesota agricultural engineer, has calculated the justifiable collector costs of grain drying near three midwestern cities: St. Cloud, Indianapolis, and Des Moines. Indianapolis has the highest justifiable cost of forty-nine cents per square foot. This is below most solar construction costs; thus solar apparatus could prove to be a profitable investment in Indianapolis. Des Moines, however, had only a fifteen cents per square foot figure.[7]

The U.S. government is aiding farmers in bridging the gap between conventional and solar energy by implementing various programs. The Department of Energy has a goal of reducing the cost of producing a watt of solar electricity by 3000 percent by 1986. If this goal can be reached, the cost of solar energy will probably be lower than that of conventional forms, given the conventional's rising cost trends. Subsidies provided by the government to farmers building solar equipment and to state labs and universities conducting research are accelerating the progress of solar utilization. An energy conscious national policy could also help speed agricultural energy transition.

Generally, the outlook seems good for the increased use of solar materials. Their wide applications have provided researchers and innovative farmers with a promise that solar energy is a legitimate source of energy for most farming needs. The efficiency of solar energy production exceeds that of (17)_____ _____ sources, with capabilities above those considered possible before, such as in selling excess energy back to a utility company. Economically, much progress is still in the formative stages. Solar implements aren't financially sound for all farm needs, but they have been applied to many kinds of farm practices with success. Considering the rising prices of (18)_____ _____ sources and the projected lowering of solar energy prices, it seems likely that energy from the sun will soon supply more of our nation's energy needs. An awareness of potential solar uses available for farming operations is now necessary in making energy choices in agriculture.

Notes

[1]"A Solar System for Swine House Heating, Cooling," *Agricultural Engineering*, Jan. 1978, p. 24.

[2]Larry Reichenberger, "A Little Light on the Solar Question," *Successful Farming*, Oct. 1978, p. 27.

[3]William Fairbank, "California's Dairy Energy Committee," *Agricultural Engineering*, Jan. 1978, p. 20.

[4]L. Whitt Brantley, "Selling Solar Energy as a Cash Crop," *Agricultural Engineering*, March 1978, pp. 12–16.

[5]"Solar Energy; Now, Later, or Never?" *Farm Industry News*, March 1978, p. 50.

[6]Brantley, pp. 12–16.

[7]Reichenberger, p. 32.

Example Paper

The author of the following paper uses a number of different coherence devices. As you read, you might especially consider the author's thesis statement, topic sentences, and use of linking words.

ANOREXIA NERVOSA

Anorexia nervosa, a disease of uncontrollable dieting, strikes young women, usually between the ages of sixteen and eighteen years. The victims have a tremendous obsession with becoming fat. Although the first documented case of anorexia nervosa was reported in 1689 by an English doctor, little is yet known about the disease. No one is absolutely certain how this disease gets started, but doctors suspect it is a combination of physical and mental illness, with most experts emphasizing the psychological causes of the disease. Anorexia nervosa is a difficult disease to treat successfully. It can, in fact, be fatal. My aim in this paper is to consider some of the symptoms, causes, and treatments of this disease which threatens many young women in our society. Perhaps the best introduction to the subject is to relate the story of an anorexic I met in one of my college classes.

Susan: An Anorexic Victim

I met Susan in zoology lab. We walked home from class a few times and discovered we had a lot in common. We started studying together and after a few weeks she asked me to proofread one of her English papers. The paper described her struggle with the disease anorexia nervosa. Before that day, we had never talked about her excessive thinness, but I had a strong suspicion that something was wrong with her. Letting me read her paper was a way of saying she wanted to talk. As we talked, I learned a number of things about Susan's past.

During her childhood, Susan's brother always received the most attention from her parents. He was the first son—the perfect child—and spoiled. Susan's parents stressed the importance of good grades to their children because they felt that without good grades no one can get far in life. Susan strived for her parents' attention by getting excellent grades, but her brother always managed to top any of her achievements. Susan attended a small farm school until ninth grade, when she then went to a larger community school, and it was hard for her to adjust to the large school and the new surroundings. She felt very lost and alone. This lack of self-confidence is typical of anorexics. Her grades were still good, but this did not give her the attention and the recognition that she craved. She just wanted to be noticed. Many of her classmates were going on diets—it was the popular thing to do—and she thought if she lost a few pounds she'd then be noticed. Susan is 5 feet 4 inches tall and her weight before she started to diet was 120 pounds. She has not been able to stop dieting since, and that was five years ago. She now weighs a little over 80 pounds.

After a year of Susan's continual dieting, her parents admitted her to the hospital for testing. Susan knew, at least subconsciously, that she was very sick, but she still protested strongly against going to the hospital. Yet, if it weren't for her parents' intervention, Susan would probably be dead now. Upon admission she weighed 79 pounds, a loss of almost 35 percent of her original body weight. During her five-day hospital stay the doctors gave her high calorie meals, most of which she would flush down the toilet when they weren't looking.

Common Symptoms

Susan's story is a fairly typical case of how anorexia develops. Victims of anorexia nervosa are usually teenage girls from white, well-educated, middle-class families. The disease occurs only rarely in males, nonwhites, or persons from lower socioeconomic classes.[1] Traditionally, anorexics have been described as intelligent students, but their high grades are usually the result of intense, hard work rather than exceptional brilliance.

One physical symptom of anorexia is the sensation of coldness. Anorexics often wear numerous layers of sweaters and pants in an effort to keep warm, because their body temperature frequently hovers around 96°F. Hypothermia is the term used to describe body temperature below normal and it has been suggested that this hypothermic action by the body is an attempt to conserve some of its energy. In extreme cases, the victims lack the physical energy to pull themselves out of bed in the morning. They can only huddle under the covers. Other physical symptoms include frenzied overactivity, chronic constipation, and amennorrhea (cessation of menstruation).[2]

Anorexia also affects the victim's personality. Anorexics are generally depressed, teary, and moody. They feel very ineffective. They don't feel they have any control over their lives and believe they are acting in the way that others expect them to.[3] Because they have no positive self-identity and view themselves as "nobodies" they have trouble adjusting to new situations. Anorexics develop great pride in each pound they lose and they are happy about each new bone that shows. Through their slimness they feel they will gain some control over their lives, and will no longer have to remain a nobody.

Anorexics' adamancy against eating gives them some feeling

of control, yet their major fear is that they won't have enough control to stop eating and thus become inconceivably fat. They feel guilty about eating, even if they are hungry and are merely trying to satisfy the physical feeling of hunger. They will complain that they are full, even after only one or two bites. However, they may gorge themselves before going to bed because they can then go to sleep and not have to feel guilty about eating.

Causes of Anorexia Nervosa

Despite mutual efforts of psychologists and medical doctors, no specific causes of anorexia have yet been uncovered. For a time, anorexia was thought to be primarily a medical problem, resulting from a pituitary or hypothalamic dysfunction.[4] But now these metabolic and endocrine disturbances are considered to be secondary effects due to the malnourished state of the body. Anorexia is now being attributed primarily to psychological causes.

Some experts attribute anorexia to a maturational conflict between the family and the adolescent, a conflict which the adolescent interprets in terms of body weight and shape. Problems concerning maturation may be rooted in such matters as gender identity, individuation, threatened family breakups, or an impending separation such as going away to college.[5] Anorexia seems to reflect an intense fear of inadequacy about meeting new demands imposed by approaching maturity and new situations. The anorexic dreads womanhood and may stop eating in an effort to retain a childlike body, which in her mind will forestall growing up. She sees maturity as unavoidable and feels she's losing control of her life. So she turns to dieting in an effort to exert control over some aspect of her life, in this case her body, the only thing left that she has complete control over.

Dr. Hilde Bruch, professor of psychology at Baylor College of Medicine, postulates that the anorexic suffers from a fear of not being good enough and of not accomplishing what is expected of her.[6] She may have great concern over her grades in school and work exceptionally hard to achieve high marks. This drive for achievement represents an attempt to compensate for a lack of autonomy and to establish self-identity. This phase usually precedes dieting. If her goals aren't reached, the anorexic feels she hasn't succeeded in pleasing her parents and teachers, so she turns to dieting to assure herself that she is in control of her life. Added to this is the stress of growing up and coping with new sexual urges, and she soon becomes obsessed with dieting and achievement.

Dr. Bruch identifies three kinds of disordered psychological functioning present in the anorexic.[7] First of all, the anorexic has a disturbance in her perception of her body image. She doesn't see her true proportions. She sees herself as fat, even when quite emaciated. Second, the anorexic has a misperception of bodily functions. Awareness of hunger seems to be absent. Perhaps the anorexic never learned to correctly interpret bodily cues. Third, she haş an overwhelming sense of personal ineffectiveness. Though usually an outstandingly good child, her perfect and over-conforming behavior is a camouflage for self-doubt. Control of her body represents accomplishment in her mind, and she doesn't see her emaciation as sick or ugly.

Treatment of Anorexia Nervosa

Until recently, treatment of anorexia nervosa varied from doctor to doctor. The usual practice was to hospitalize the patient and force-feed her, or feed her intravenously, until she reached normal weight. However, after she was discharged from the hospital, often the anorexic returned to dieting and soon lost all the weight she had gained. Now, anorexia is recognized as serious and in need of prompt attention. Perhaps most important is early diagnosis. The earlier anorexia is recognized, the easier it is to treat, and the more successful the treatment is likely to be. There are two basic approaches used today in the treatment of anorexia nervosa.

Many experts advocate treatment based on principles of behavior modification. With this approach, the patient is hospitalized and placed in a room containing only the bare essentials— bed, closet, and restroom facilities. She is not allowed any privileges; she may not watch television, talk on the phone, or have visitors. She is told that restoration of privileges is contingent upon weight gain, and as target weight is reached, her privileges are gradually restored. Dr. Bruch disagrees with this method. She says that patients who are "tricked" into gaining weight will lose it all again after leaving the hospital.[8] In fact, behavior therapy may even be harmful for victims of anorexia, since "this method undermines the last vestiges of self-esteem and destroys the crucial hope of ever achieving autonomy and self-determination."[9]

Instead of behavior modification, many doctors advocate a combined approach: psychotherapy along with a weight gain program.[10] It seems to be very important to determine the psychological causes underlying a patient's anorexia, along with encouraging her to gain weight. Hospitalization in an atmosphere conducive to eating and free from decision making seems to be effective.[11] The doctor goes so far as to choose all the patient's meals for her, making sure they are high in protein and calories, so as to leave the patient free to concentrate completely on therapy. It is important to involve the family in therapy so that they understand anorexia thoroughly. Most important of all is to determine the psychological causes leading to the development of anorexia nervosa, and to help the patient and her family realize what led to this particular case of the disease. Then steps can be taken to solve the basic problems.

Even after "recovery," anorexics have been found to be low in self-esteem and inhibited in social interaction.[12] Perhaps the anorexic is never completely cured. Roughly two-thirds of anorexics recover sufficiently. But 15 to 20 percent die from the disease.[13]

Conclusion

Since death accounts for so many victims of the disease, it is important for teenage girls to be well-informed on the dangers of anorexia nervosa. Susan, my anorexic acquaintance, makes an effort to talk to anyone whom she suspects of having anorexia. She feels that she must warn the possible victims of the suffering and agony she has endured during the past five years. She wants to tell them that anorexia is like cancer: it keeps eating away at you. One voice in your brain tells you to eat, but you can only listen to the voice that tells you not to eat.

Susan is still too thin, but she is starting to feel more sure about herself now. Psychiatric counseling has helped. She feels her life is beginning to take some shape and direction. Her outstanding grades have finally paid off because she has been accepted into pharmacy school. She is beginning to be happy with herself and with the path her life is taking.

Notes

[1]Robert A. Vigersky, Arnold E. Andersen, Ronald H. Thompson, and D. Lynn Loriaux, "Hypothalmic Dysfunction in Secondary Amenorrhea Associated with Simple Weight Loss," *New England Journal of Medicine*, 297 (1977), 1143–44.

[2]Hilde Bruch, "Anorexia Nervosa," in *Nutrition and the Brain*, ed. Richard J. Wurtman and Judith J. Wurtman (New York: Raven Press, 1979), III, p. 105.

[3]Bruch, p. 106.

[4]Marie V. Krause and L. Kathleen Mahan, *Food, Nutrition, and Diet Therapy*, 6th ed. (Philadelphia: W. B. Saunders and Co., 1979), p. 662.

[5]M. Pillay and A. H. Crisp, "Some Psychological Characteristics of Patients with Anorexia Nervosa Whose Weight Has Been Recently Restored," *British Journal of Medical Psychology*, 50 (1977), 375.

[6]"The Self-Starvers," *Time*, July 28, 1975, p. 50.

[7]Bruch, pp. 103–6; see also Richard Ashley, "Anorexia Nervosa: The Self-Starvation Disease," *Harper's Bazaar*, June 1976, pp. 68, 114C.

[8]Jean A. Seligmann, "The Starvation Disease," *Newsweek*, Sept. 9, 1974, p. 56.

[9]Hilde Bruch, "Perils of Behavior Modification in Treatment of Anorexia Nervosa," *JAMA*, 230 (1974), 1421.

[10]Pillay and Crisp, p. 376.

[11]Krause and Mahan, p. 663.

[12]Pillay and Crisp, p. 379.

[13]Krause and Mahan, p. 664.

6 | *Putting It All Together*

In the preceding chapters we have presented a number of strategies for writing an academic paper. We have focused on those elements of writing that all good writers know how to use—devising an initial plan, using the methods of development, arranging the main points in the final paper, writing introductions and conclusions, and making the paper coherent. Our aim has been to teach you strategies that will help you do these things well. However, by focusing on these strategies one at a time in separate chapters, we may have given the impression that writing is a linear process. When talking about different aspects of writing it is difficult to avoid giving this impression. But most writers don't gather all their information and only then start to organize and develop it. Usually they do some organizing as they are collecting their information. And good writers never completely forget their reader while they are working on a paper; they think about the reader often, not just at set times during their work. Moreover, writers eventually develop their own strategies which may be a bit different from those we recommend. In sum, you have to be flexible in applying our strategies.

Our aim in this final chapter is to provide a concrete example of how the various strategies we have discussed could fit together when you actually write a paper for a college course. To do so we present a situation in which a student, whom we'll call Lisa, is required to write a paper for a course in American Studies. We will trace Lisa's approach to her essay from receipt of her assignment to the completion of her paper. You'll find her completed paper at the end of the chapter and the articles she used to write it in the appendix. Don't read this account with the expectation that you should be able to imitate every move of Lisa's mind when you write your next paper. Instead, read it to see how the strategies we recommend, if flexibly applied, can make your writing better.

Devising an Initial Plan

Lisa's first problem is to understand her assignment and develop an initial plan. Her assignment is as follows:

There are many issues in American society that are complex and hard to resolve because they involve a clash of values. For example, such familiar issues as gun control, capital punishment, and abortion persist because people approach them from different perspectives—political, legal, medical, and ethical. Find an incident in which the values of diverse interest groups are involved and must be reconciled. Describe the incident and the issues and values that underlie the debate concerning it.

Key words in this assignment are "incident," "issues," and "values," and the directives are "find" and "describe." It is fairly clear that an "incident" means a specific confrontation between groups with different values. What are the definitions of "issue" and "values"? Fortunately, these vague terms are clarified somewhat by the examples given earlier in the assignment: "issues" are such controversial problems as gun control and capital punishment, and "values" seem to be the beliefs of people with a special perspective on the issue, such as individuals who share a particular political persuasion or people who hold certain ethical or religious convictions. Still, the term "values" might be troublesome and may need further clarification. The directives in the assignment are vague and not very helpful. The term "find" implies, however, that Lisa should seek an incident involving some issue other than those listed in the assignment—perhaps a less familiar issue than those worn out topics. The term "describe" means simply that the various aspects of the incident and the underlying issues and values are to be presented in some detail. The assignment does not suggest a particular organizational scheme.

A major task for this assignment is to "find" an appropriate topic—an incident which involves a clash of values. How will Lisa discover such an incident? There is no easy answer. A remark in class, a passage in the textbook, a TV show, a news item, a discussion with the teacher or classmates—any of these might produce an idea. With luck, Lisa will be able to come up with several possibilities, and she will then need to select one incident to pursue. This incident should be one on which sufficient material is available, one that does not involve overworked issues, and, most importantly, one that Lisa finds interesting.

We'll assume that Lisa recalls a newspaper article concerning a fairly recent conflict between environmentalists and politicians over the building of a dam in Tennessee. Lisa remembers the incident because she has had a continuing interest in environmental concerns, sparked originally by a biology teacher in high school. She recalls that the courts decided the dam couldn't be used because it would destroy the river where a small fish, an endangered species, lived. Although the environmental issue is familiar, this particular incident is not, she thinks. Are there enough materials? Lisa consults a librarian, who refers her to the *Reader's Guide to Periodical Literature*. She looks under the subject heading "Endangered Species" and is referred to "Rare Animals," where she finds a number of recent articles on the snail darter, the name of that small fish the dam allegedly would destroy. The topic seems worth pursuing.

Gathering Information

In the next stage of her writing, Lisa begins reading the articles listed in the *Reader's Guide*. Sometimes the footnotes in these articles lead her to other useful articles. An article by Ross Sandler ("Overview"), for example, contains a footnote to the text of the Supreme Court's decision in the snail darter case. She doesn't understand what the numbers and letters in the footnote refer to, so she asks the reference librarian; he steers her to a section of the *United States Law Week* which contains, in addition to the affirmative and dissenting opinions of the Court, a syllabus, or summary, of the key events in the case. This proves to be a valuable source.

At first her reading is fairly undirected: she tries to get an overview of what transpired in the conflict over building the dam. It turns out that the incident Lisa has selected—the controversy surrounding the building of the Tellico Dam—has a long and complex history. Lisa has to read a number of articles before she understands the facts in the case.

Organizing and Developing Information

Soon Lisa's reading becomes more directed. She decides that the best way to understand the case is to list the main events in chronological order. In constructing her list she relies primarily on the syllabus section of the *Law Week* entry on the case, the article by Ross Sandler in *Environment*, and the first part of James Kilpatrick's editorial "Lessons to be Learned from a Bad Law." Her list begins as follows:

1. 1967:	Tennessee Valley Authority begins construction on Tellico Dam and Reservoir Project.
2. Summer, 1973:	University of Tennessee icthyologist discovers previously unknown species of fish—the snail darter.

3. December, 1973:   U.S. Congress passes the Endangered Species
Act to protect plants and animals in danger of
becoming extinct.

She continues to list the remaining key events, ending with the
closing of the dam's gates in December, 1979. It's not easy for her
to reconstruct the chronology. At first she can't keep the three decisions of the different courts straight. She is also puzzled until she
realizes that the same committee is variously referred to as "the
cabinet-level review committee," the "interagency-review committee," and the "Endangered Species Committee." Eventually, however, she has enough information to complete her chronology. At the
start she felt discouraged, overwhelmed by facts—facts about the
dam, about the fish, about the laws. Arranging these facts in chronological order has given her confidence; she feels that she is gaining
mastery over her subject.

She looks back at her assignment. "Describe the incident," the
assignment reads, "and the issues and values that underlie the debate concerning it." The best way to describe the incident, she concludes, is to provide the reader with a chronological sketch of key
events. That will be easy, she decides; all she'll have to do is flesh
out the list of key events she compiled for herself. But how should
she describe the underlying issues and values? What are the key
issues? There are many of them, she knows—so many that they are
all jumbled up in her mind. Lisa decides that the best way to un-
jumble them is to categorize them. Looking back at the assignment,
she reads her teacher's list of perspectives—political, legal, medical,
ethical—from which Americans approach complex problems. She
wonders if people have approached the snail darter controversy from
these perspectives. Could she use any of them as labels for her categories? She decides that the legal, political, and ethical perspectives are important in the snail darter case. But she's not completely
pleased with these labels. After more thinking she decides on the
following labels for her categories: environmental, legal, cultural,
and economic. Under *environmental* she puts down some facts about
the snail darter and the arguments for and against preserving such
small and exotic species. Under *legal* she notes the arguments pro
and con on the question: Is the Endangered Species Act a good law?
She also makes some notes on Sandler's argument that in its decision
in the snail darter case the Supreme Court signals that it will not
play an active role in environmental law. Under the headings *cultural* and *economic* she makes a note of the most important aspects
of these issues.

Lisa is encouraged by the progress she has made. She knows now that the snail darter controversy is without doubt "an incident in which the values of diverse interest groups are involved." She's convinced that she's chosen a good incident, one that holds her interest and also is the type of incident her teacher wants students to choose. At this point in her work she also begins to arrive at some conclusions regarding the snail darter case. She decides that even if there were no controversy over the snail darter's fate, the dam shouldn't have been built because it is unnecessary and probably will be unprofitable.

Deciding on a Final Arrangement

Now Lisa begins to think less about how to organize the information for herself and more about how to arrange it for her reader. She knows that to understand this complicated case the reader will need a chronological summary of key events. The assignment also instructs her to describe the incident. She decides that by placing her chronological sketch after her introduction she'll be both making her paper readable and fulfilling the demands of the assignment.

Then she considers her four perspectives and wonders if it makes any difference how they are ordered. She examines them more closely, looking to see if they fall along a continuum. Are some perspectives clearly more important than others in understanding the snail darter case? No, she decides; each perspective is equally important. "Least important to most important" is therefore not a possible continuum. Do those who approach the case from one perspective provide information that is simpler and less arguable than those who approach it from other perspectives? No, she decides; the information produced by all perspectives is complex and controversial. Thus "simple to complex" and "least arguable to most arguable" are ruled out.

She thinks some more and concludes that the perspectives could be usefully placed along a continuum ranging from questions of fact to questions of value. Those who approach the problem from an economic perspective deal for the most part with facts and figures, with how many megawatts of electricity the dam would contribute, with how many dollars of net profit the dam or the free-flowing river would bring to the area. Those who adopt the legal perspective also deal mostly with questions of fact: According to the language of the Endangered Species Act, is the snail darter an endangered species? Would the dam destroy its habitat? Did members of Congress intend to exempt the Tellico Dam from the Endangered Species Act by appropriating funds to build the dam after they knew about the snail darter? Lisa remembers reading Justice Berger's statement that it is not the court's job to settle issues of value, to decide on priorities; that's Congress's job. This statement of Chief Justice Berger strengthens her conviction that those who adopt the legal perspective are interested primarily in questions of fact.

Those who adopt the cultural and environmental perspectives, however, deal with questions of value. They don't, for example, dispute whether the valley that will be flooded includes the sites of ancient Cherokee towns; they know that's not at issue. Instead they ask: Which has a higher value, ancient Indian sites or opportunities for flatwater recreation and a slight increase in the supply of electricity? Those who adopt the evironmental perspective ask: Which should be given higher priority, the preserving of species for future generations to admire and perhaps use for food and medicine, or the building of dams to provide electricity and flatwater recreation?

Lisa knows that her continuum won't survive intense scrutiny. She knows, for example, that questions of fact are important to those who adopt the environmental perspective, particularly the question "Does the survival of the human race depend on preserving small and exotic species like the snail darter?" She therefore decides that she won't make her continuum explicit in her paper; in other words, she won't include transitional sentences like "Unlike the economic and legal issues, which involve questions of fact, the cultural issue involves questions of value." But she will discuss the four issues in her paper in the order that she has arranged them on her continuum, thinking that this progression from questions of fact to questions of value is better than a random arrangement. Although she elects not to emphasize this continuum, in the process of constructing it she has learned a lot about her subject.

Writing the Introduction and Conclusion

Lisa is now ready to write a rough draft. Although she knows some writers prefer to write the introduction last, she likes to write it first. She knows she can always change it later. Because she's planning to provide a chronological sketch of the case in the body of her paper, she decides to provide only a little background information in her introduction—just enough to identify her subject. She experiments with a more general thesis statement but finally decides to make it specific by including the labels for her four issues—economic, legal, cultural, and environmental. To complete her thesis statement and provide a transition to the next section, her chronological account, she explains that to understand these issues one must understand the history of the case.

Lisa starts work on the body of the paper next, working on it in two-hour stretches. Since she has other courses to prepare for, writing the rough draft takes three or four days. Because she has already organized her notes, the writing goes quite easily. Her sketch of the history of the case is an expansion of her list of key events. When this is done, she takes up the issues one by one. In discussing three of the issues she presents first one view of the issue, then the opposing view. In discussing the legal issue, for example, she first describes the view of those who think the Endangered Species Act is a bad law, then the views of those who admire the law. In discussing the cultural issue, however, she gives only the views of those who think the sacred Indian sites should not be flooded, assuming that the opposing view—that the sites aren't valuable enough to halt the dam—would be obvious to her reader.

The conclusion gives Lisa the most trouble. She decides against a summary conclusion. Reviewing the main events of the case and reiterating the four issues would make her paper repetitive and boring, she decides. Concentrating on answering the question "So what?" strikes her as more appropriate. She reads through her rough draft and thinks again about the lessons of the snail darter case. One lesson, she believes, is that the case is multifaceted—it has economic, legal, cultural, and environmental ramifications. She knows this is not an astounding insight, that her teacher has told her in his assignment that "diverse interests" underlie most complex problems, but she still thinks it's an important enough point to emphasize in her conclusion. If nothing else, by stating it she will emphasize that the incident she has chosen to write about is the kind of incident she is supposed to write about.

She thinks about the case some more. There's no avoiding the conclusion, she decides, that the dam shouldn't have been built—not because it would kill the snail darter (she's not absolutely sure construction should be stopped on its account), but because the dam wasn't needed and would flood the sacred land of the Cherokee. She decides that is the point she wants to emphasize in her conclusion—the bitter irony of destroying Indian lands and the snail darter for no good reason. So she ends with this idea, adding the point that if the issues surrounding the dam had been aired more completely before construction began, it might never have been built.

Documenting the Paper

Documenting her paper takes time. The task is not too difficult, however, because she has carefully recorded all the information she needs—name of journal, volume number, date of publication, etc. If the article was short, she photocopied it and wrote this information on the copy; if the article was long, she took notes on it, not forgetting to include the information she will need to document the paper. She follows the MLA system, as outlined in the *MLA Handbook for Writers of Research Papers, Theses, and Dissertations* (New York: Modern Language Association, 1977).

She is troubled by one problem: what form to use in listing laws and government documents. She consults her *MLA Handbook*, which has sections on how to cite "Legal References" and "Government Publications." These sections are helpful, but she's not sure she gets notes 5, 7, 8, and 26 exactly right.

Revising the Rough Draft

Lisa doesn't edit the rough draft as soon as she finishes it because she's afraid she is too close to her words and ideas to edit objectively. To distance herself from her paper, she puts it in her desk drawer, gets a good night's sleep, and looks at it the following morning. Then she reads it through, trying to react to her writing in the way she imagines her teacher will react to it.

She checks it for coherence and decides it holds together quite well. The thesis statement clearly forecasts her plan of development and she follows this plan in the body of her paper. Chronological order holds her background sections together and her labels—economic, legal, cultural, and environmental—help guide her reader through the section on the four issues. Deciding that the transition at the start of paragraph 11 ("The snail darter controversy has also raised legal issues.") is too abrupt, she reworks her first sentence, turning it into a topic statement that summarizes the previous discussion and also introduces the new topic:

> The legal issues raised by the snail darter controversy have proved to be as divisive as the economic issues.

She also decides that the two main sections of her paper—the one on background and the one on the four issues—are not clearly related. So she adds a new paragraph—paragraph 7—to provide a bridge between sections. Then she improves the phrasing of some sentences, checks the spelling of some proper nouns like Fort Loudon and Hiwassee, and types her paper. After proofreading it carefully, the paper is ready to be turned in to her instructor.

THE SNAIL DARTER AND THE DAM

In December, 1979, the gates closed on the Tellico Dam, flooding the rich land along the banks of the Lower Tennessee River and destroying the habitat of the snail darter, a three-inch-long fish of the perch family. It remains to be seen whether the closing of the dam's gates will close the controversy between proponents of the dam and supporters of the snail darter. This controversy has raged for nearly a decade, highlighting in the process some important economic, legal, cultural, and environmental issues. I will discuss these issues, but first it is necessary to review the political and legal battles that occurred before the gates of the dam were finally closed.

At the heart of the controversy is the undramatic snail darter, who wasn't known to exist before a University of Tennessee ichthyologist found it above the dam site in the summer of 1973. The discovery would not have been notable except that in December of the same year Congress passed the Endangered Species Act, a tough piece of environmental legislation. The purpose of the act is to prevent the extinction of threatened flora and fauna. According to the statute, anyone can ask the Office of Endangered Species to review an animal or plant to determine whether it is endangered. In November, 1975, an association of biological scientists, a conservation group, and other interested parties petitioned to have the snail darter added to the endangered list. These groups were motivated by other things besides a concern for the snail darter. The dam would destroy one of the best trout streams in the area and some excellent land that could be used for farming and recreation. It would also destroy the burial grounds and some ancient town sites of the Cherokees, including the former capital of the Cherokee Nation and the site of Tennasee, from which the name for the state derives.[1] The petitioners wanted to save the snail darter but they also wanted to use the little fish to save these other things they valued.

The Office of Endangered Species agreed with the petitioners that the snail darter was an endangered species. According to Section 7 of the Endangered Species Act, federal projects must not "jeopardize the continued existence of . . . endangered species . . . or result in the destruction or modification of habitats of such species which is determined . . . to be critical."[2] Deciding that the snail darter was endangered, and that the Lower Tennessee was its "critical habitat," the Office put the darter on their list. The dam builders became worried that their dam was doomed.

At first, their concern seemed unjustified. When opponents of the dam went to District Court to request an injunction to stop work on the dam, the judge concluded that it made no sense to let a little fish halt a project that had already consumed 58 to 78 million dollars of the taxpayers' money. On January 31, 1977, however, the Sixth District Court of Appeals reversed the District Court's ruling, arguing that the courts could not allow construction of the dam unless Congress exempted the Tellico Project from the restrictions of the Endangered Species Act or the Secretary of the Interior removed the snail darter from the list of endangered species. The Appeals Court also rejected the argument that the law didn't apply to dams that were near completion: "Whether a dam is 50 percent or 90 percent complete is irrelevant," the Appeals Court said, "in calculating the social and scientific costs attributable to the disappearance of a unique form of life."[3]

The case went eventually to the Supreme Court of the United States, which announced on June 15, 1978, that by completing the Tellico Dam the Tennessee Valley Authority would violate the provisions of the Endangered Species Act. The snail darter seemed to be off death row, but its security was shortlived; others were plotting its destruction. Senator Howard Baker of Tennessee, one of the original sponsors of the Endangered Species Act, became concerned that the act was too inflexible. He sponsored an amendment to establish an Endangered Species Committee with the power to grant exceptions in cases of irreconcilable conflict, so that the government could finish its public works projects like the Tellico Dam.[4] The amendment was passed,[5] but this plan to save the dam failed when the committee created by the amendment refused, in its first formal decision, to exempt the Tellico Project. When on May 9, 1979, the Senate Environment and Public Works Committee approved a bill to extend the Endangered Species Act for two and a half more years, the prodarter, antidam forces took heart.

Their hopes were dashed, however, in October, 1979. When the committee Senator Baker was instrumental in establishing failed to exempt the Tellico Dam, Baker adopted another strategy: he attached an exemption provision to a 10.8 billion dollar energy and water appropriations bill. President Carter didn't like the dam, but Baker's bill preserved the president's Water Resources Council, which would have the power to rule on future projects. In addition, when the bill came up, the president was trying to obtain congressional support for the Panama Treaty and a Department of Education bill. In the view of environmentalists, Carter traded his support for the dam for assistance on these other issues which he thought were of higher priority. So he signed the bill—with great reluctance. "I accept, with regret," the President said, "this action as expressing the will of Congress."[6] With all obstacles removed, the gates of the dam were closed and water pushed out from the banks of the Little Tennessee, filling up the valley. As for the snail darter, some were transported to a new habitat, the nearby Hiwassee River, and scientists are watching to see if they'll survive in this new home.

Clearly those who have struggled with this case as it has developed during the past seven years have had to deal simultaneously with a host of different issues and do research in a variety of fields. The footnotes of Chief Justice Burger's majority opinion on the case, for example, include references not only to previous court decisions but also to books on Cherokee myths, technical articles in biology journals, and government documents on a variety of topics.[7] The issues are separated here for convenience; I don't mean to suggest that the case can be resolved by adopting only one perspective.

One of the issues is economic: would the Little Tennessee River produce more profits for residents of the area if it were dammed up or if it were left alone? At first, the TVA insisted that the dam would bring great economic benefits. It was supposed to promote development of the region while also providing "flatwater" recreation and flood control. In addition, according to some reports, the dam was supposed to generate enough electricity to heat 20,000 homes.[8] But during the first meeting of the Endangered Species Committee, Cecil Andrus, Secretary of the Interior and Chairman of the Committee, reported that according to his figures the river with no dam would produce an annual net profit 0.6 million dollars higher than that which would be earned if the river had a dam on it. This figure did not include the value of the sacred Indian grounds and historic sites and the wildlife habitats that would be destroyed by the dam.[9] The General Accounting Office also studied the project and reached the same conclusion as Secretary Andrus: leaving the Little Tennessee alone was more profitable than damming her up.[10]

TVA's projections for the electrical output of the dam appear to have been off base. According to members of the Tennessee Endangered Species Committee, the TVA, trying to capitalize on fears concerning the energy crisis, overemphasized the capacity of the dam to produce electricity. The committee pointed out that the dam would have no generators; water from the Tellico dam would flow through a canal to another reservoir where there were generators. The dam would increase the present supply of current by only 0.1 percent, the committee members argued.[11] According to Zygmunt Plater, the dam wasn't built to produce electricity. It was part of a grandiose project involving sixty-eight dams; its purpose was "to create subsidized lakefront industrial sites and a final flatwater recreation lake."[12] Plater rejects TVA's claim that annual revenues of $1.4 million can be derived from the Tellico Reservoir by capitalizing on its recreation potential. This is unrealistic, he says, because there are already twenty-two other reservoirs close by and the dam would destroy one of the best trout streams in the country.

In short, the antidam advocates seem to have won the economic argument. *Time* magazine reports that now even the TVA admits that the dam won't provide any electric power.[13] The dam appears to have been a typical pork barrel effort, a patronage project designed by politicians to please their constituents.

The legal issues raised by the snail darter controversy have proved to be as divisive as the economic issues. Some think the Endangered Species Act is a fine law, a tough piece of environmental legislation that has been attacked only because it has put some obstacles in the way of the pet projects of selfish politicians seeking reelection. Others, such as James Kilpatrick, agree with the purpose of the law but object to the law itself because it is too sweeping and uncompromising. Kilpatrick points out that there are 1.4 million species of animals and 600,000 species of plants. He wonders if the law should protect them all.[14] The law's definition of species *is* very inclusive: it includes everything except those members of the Class Insecta that have been determined to be pests. Many people are wondering if any public works project can be completed without trampling on an endangered species or its habitat. Some are willing to accept sacrifices to save the whooping crane and the bald eagle, but wonder if the species *Homo sapiens* and their needs shouldn't take precedence over the Indiana bat and the Furbish lousewort (a plant of the snapdragon family)—two species that have delayed other federal projects.

Justice Powell criticizes the law in his dissenting opinion to the Supreme Court's decision in the snail darter case. According to Justice Powell, the purpose of the Act is "admirable," but its language is flawed. It's "a textbook example of fuzzy language," he says, "which can be read according to the 'eye of the beholder'."[15] He argues that the framers of the law intended it to apply only to prospective projects and that an analysis of the wording of the Act supports this conclusion. Section 7 of the law reads that all federal agencies must do whatever is necessary to "insure that actions authorized, funded, or carried out by them do not jeopardize species" or destroy critical habitats. According to Justice Powell, by "actions authorized," which he admits is a vague phrase, the legislators meant "actions that the agency is deciding whether to authorize," i.e., future actions, not dams almost completed.[16]

The law has its supporters, however, the most influential being

Chief Justice Burger, who wrote the affirmative opinion in the Court's decision on the darter and the dam case. He objects to Justice Powell's view that the language is fuzzy. "One would be hard pressed," he says, "to find a statutory provision whose terms were any plainer than those in Section 7 of the Endangered Species Act."[17] He argues that when the legislators wrote "actions authorized, funded, or carried out," they could not have meant only future actions, as Justice Powell argues. If they meant this, he says, they wouldn't have included the phrase "or carried out," a phrase which, Burger argues, clearly suggests actions already completed—like the Tellico Dam.[18]

Other supporters of the law point out that there have been only a few lawsuits to halt federal projects. Often the matter has been settled by making only a slight change in the plan. For example, in Mississippi an interstate highway was rerouted to protect the habitat of the sandhill crane.[19] Although the law *is* rather uncompromising, it probably has to be tough to defend plants and animals endangered by politicians and developers, two groups that won't be stopped by only token resistance. At least the snail darter case proves that, tough as the law is, there *are* legislative means of circumventing it. It should also be remembered that the amendment sponsored by Senators Baker and Culver makes the original act more flexible. This amendment provides for the creation of an Endangered Species Committee with the power to grant exemptions in cases of "irresolvable conflict" between an "agency action" and the conserving of an endangered species. If those in favor of a federal project can prove that the project is clearly in the public interest, it now can be approved even if the project could destroy a species or its habitat.[20]

Further court decisions may clarify how the law is to be interpreted, but according to Ross Sandler we shouldn't expect the courts to set environmental policy. He thinks that the Supreme Court's decision in the snail darter case "signals a pulling back of federal court action in environmental law."[21] The court justices saw the snail darter case as a constitutional issue involving separation of powers, he argues, and they used it to make the point that Congress must set the priorities—must decide, for example, if the darter is worth more than the dam. The job of the courts is simply to enforce the law.

The cultural issues in the snail darter controversy can be fairly simply stated: which has a higher value, completion of a major public works project or the preservation of sacred Indian grounds and historical sites? Peter Matthiessen urges us to recognize the cultural value of the Indian sites. He visited the valley just before the water rose and talked to an eighty-year-old Cherokee medicine man named Lloyd Sequoyah, who told him, "If the homeland of our fathers is covered with this water, it will cover the medicine and spiritual strengths of our people because this is the place from which the Cherokee people come. When this place is destroyed, the Cherokee people cease to exist . . . then all the peoples of the earth cease to exist."[22] Matthiessen also quotes a report prepared by Department of Interior archaeologists which ascribes "worldwide significance" to the Indian sites in the valley. The report declares that "the physical records of American prehistory present in Tellico cannot be matched in any other area this size in the continent."[23] People opposed to the dam point out that the valley that would be flooded has been inhabited by man for 10,000 years.

The rising waters would destroy non-Indian as well as Indian historical sites—Fort Loudon, for example, the oldest British fort west of the Appalachians, and the McClung McGhee Mansion, an impressive antebellum house.[24]

The environmental issue raised by the darter and the dam saga is the most difficult to evaluate because no one, not even the experts, can answer a crucial question: How many species can be eradicated before ecological systems are destroyed? The key issue, says Constance Holden, is whether "sustaining diversity of species equates with sustaining life in general."[25] What precisely is the value of small, little known species? According to a congressional report, their value is "incalculable" because they are a "potential resource" which may provide "keys to puzzles which we cannot solve" and "answers to questions which we have not yet learned to ask." The report mentions that a chemical used to control ovulation in humans was discovered in a common plant.[26]

According to Stanford biologist Paul Ehrlich, man's fate is bound up with that of the lousewort and other rare species: destroying them is like removing, one by one, the rivets from an airplane wing; eventually the plane will crash.[27] Others make fun of those who fuss over mud turtles and louseworts. In their view, people like Ehrlich who suggest that killing a snail darter will doom the planet are being melodramatic and overcautious. There's no satisfactory resolution of this debate in sight, though Ehrlich is convincing when he points out that it is insanity to keep eradicating species to discover how many we can live without.

What can we learn from the snail darter case? For one thing, it illustrates that most controversial and persistent issues are multifaceted. We may speak of economic issues, legal issues, and environmental issues, but these terms, while convenient, are misleading: issues like abortion, and capital punishment, and the protection of endangered species can't be settled by those who represent only one perspective on the problem. All factions must be heard and then we have to trust the political process to produce a satisfactory solution. In the case of the snail darter the evidence suggests that a bad decision was reached—the decision to build a dam that wasn't needed, wouldn't significantly enhance economic development, but *would* destroy valuable land and historical sites. If a species, even one as mundane as the snail darter, is to be sacrificed, it should be sacrificed for a worthwhile goal.

But no one should blame the political process for the bad result in the Tellico Dam case. Indeed, if there had been as much careful debate in the political arena on the dam before it was built as there was after it was nearly done, it probably would never have been built. Residents of the area would have been spared much anguish. And the innocent snail darter would still be swimming happily in the waters of the Little Tennessee.

Notes

[1]Sara Grigsby Cook, Chuck Cook, and Doris Gove, "What They Didn't Tell You About the Snail Darter and the Dam," *National Parks & Conservation Magazine*, May 1977, p. 12.

[2]Public Law 93-205, Section 7.

[3]Quoted by Constance Holden, "Endangered Species: Review of Law Triggered by Tellico Impasse," *Science*, 196 (1977), 1426–27.

[4]John Walsh, "Endangered Review Body Seems to be in the Clear," *Science*, 204 (1979), 815.

[5]Public Law 95-632. For a summary of the major provisions of this amendment, see *Digest of Public General Bills and Resolutions*, 95th Cong., 2nd Sess. (Washington, D.C.: Congressional Research Services, 1978), pp. 255–56.

[6]"Tellico Triumph," *Time*, 8 Oct. 1979, p. 105; see also Robert Cahn, "Perspective: The Triumph of Wrong," *Audubon*, Nov. 1979, p. 9.

[7]Chief Justice Burger, "Tennessee Valley Authority v. Hiram G. Hill, Jr.," *The United States Law Week*, 46, (1978), 4673–84.

[8]These reasons for building the dam were cited in testimony before a Subcommittee of the House Committee on Appropriations, 94th Cong., 2nd Sess. They are summarized by Burger (see note 7).

[9]"Snail Darter vs. Dam: 'Pork Barrelers' Win," *Science News*, 6 October 1979, p. 230.

[10]Zygmunt J. B. Plater, "Fish in a Porkbarrel," *The New Republic*, 8 Apr. 1978, pp. 15–16.

[11]Cook et al., p. 11.

[12]Plater, p. 15.

[13]"Tellico Triumph," p. 105.

[14]James J. Kilpatrick, "Lessons to be Learned From a Bad Law," *Nation's Business*, Aug. 1978, pp. 11–12.

[15]Justice J. Powell, "Tennessee Valley Authority v. Hiram G. Hill, Jr.," *The United States Law Week*, 46 (1978), p. 4686.

[16]Powell, p. 4687.

[17]Burger, p. 4678.

[18]Burger, footnote 18, p. 4679.

[19]Holden, p. 1426.

[20]See note 5.

[21]Ross Sandler, "Overview-Law: The Tellico Dam Case," *Environment*, July/Aug. 1978, p. 5.

[22]Peter Matthiessen, "The Price of Tellico," *Newsweek*, 17 Dec. 1979, p. 21.

[23]Quoted by Matthiessen, p. 21.

[24]Cook, et al., p. 12.

[25]Holden, p. 1428.

[26]U.S. Cong., House, *Report of House Committee on Merchant Marine and Fisheries on H.R. 37*, 93rd Cong., 1st Sess., H. Report 93-412. Excerpts from this report are quoted by Chief Justice Burger (see note 7).

[27]"Endangered Species May Determine Man's Fate," *USA Today*, June 1979, p. 15.

Appendix: Articles on the Snail Darter Controversy

WHAT THEY DIDN'T TELL YOU ABOUT THE SNAIL DARTER AND THE DAM

by Sara Grigsby Cook, Chuck Cook, and Doris Gove

So far, the Endangered Species Act is being implemented at a snail's pace," Jimmy Carter observed during the 1976 presidential campaign. A snail's pace is too slow for most animals and plants in need of protection, but the snail darter (*Percina tanasi*), a hunter of snails, may win its race against time.

This tiny fish of the perch family was discovered and named in 1973 by Dr. David Etnier, an ichthyologist at the University of Tennessee. That same year an overwhelming majority of Congress passed the Endangered Species Act, which may protect the snail darter from extinction—if the Act itself does not become endangered.

Not long ago, few people outside Tennessee had ever heard about the snail darter. Then news media across the nation picked up a story of a three-inch-long fish that had halted construction of a multimillion-dollar dam near completion by the Tennessee Valley Authority (TVA). Suddenly the snail darter was famous, and the Endangered Species Act seemed unnecessarily obstructive to many people. But few people have been informed about the most surprising facts in this controversy. Not only have reports given false impressions that the effort to stop the dam consisted of a last-minute lawsuit and that this lawsuit could cause the irretrievable loss of $101 million, but the *economic* facts alone tilt the scales heavily in favor

of halting the dam and thus protecting the snail darter.

Why is this fish so important anyway?" many people argue. Others lament the fact that an obscure species that elicits little admiration from most casual observers is involved in an important test case for the Endangered Species Act. But the snail darter has had its defenders for several years—people who believe a little fish deserves as much concern as more familiar and dramatic endangered animals—and they watched in dismay as TVA accelerated construction of the dam to try to avoid compliance with the Endangered Species Act.

In truth, this small fish represents a major public principle. Referring to endangered species, candidate Jimmy Carter said, "Abundant and diverse fish, wildlife, and plant species are essential to our enjoyment of the natural world, as well as our own survival. Each species is unique and plays a significant role in the earth's ecosystem. Our fish, wildlife, and plant resources act as an *indicator* of the health of our environment. I believe that when they have trouble surviving, we should seriously examine the quality of our environment."

However, implementation of the Act is difficult. Critical habitat requirements of most species have not been identified, leaving them without sufficient protection

Sara Grigsby Cook, Chuck Cook, and Doris Gove, "What They Didn't Tell You about the Snail Darter and the Dam," *National Parks & Conservation Magazine*, May 1977, pp. 10–13. Text and artwork reprinted by permission from *National Parks & Conservation Magazine*, May, 1977. Copyright © 1977 by National Parks & Conservation Association.

129

from destructive development projects—especially those that are already underway.

Luckily for the snail darter, however, its "critical habitat" under the Endangered Species Act has been officially designated by the Department of Interior as the lower sixteen miles of the Little Tennessee River in east Tennessee. Here the darters occupy a specialized niche—only portions of clean gravel shoals with cool, swift, low-turbidity water. They feed almost exclusively on snails abundant on these shoals.

Unluckily, this high-quality habitat lies directly in the path of TVA's Tellico project, which would eliminate the last remaining major stretch of free-flowing water in the Tennessee River system.

Under Section 7 of the Act, all federal departments and agencies, including TVA, must ensure that actions authorized, funded, or carried out by them do not jeopardize the continued existence of the snail darter and other species listed under the Act and do not result in the "destruction or modification" of habitat determined by the Secretary of the Interior to be "critical." Biologists theorize that the snail darter once inhabited several hundred miles of the Tennessee River and its tributaries. But since man has impounded virtually all of the Tennessee River system, the snail darter has been backed into its last corner—this last free portion of the Little Tennessee.

As Dr. Etnier explains, the ecosystems disappearing most rapidly in this country are the big river ecosystems. The signifi-

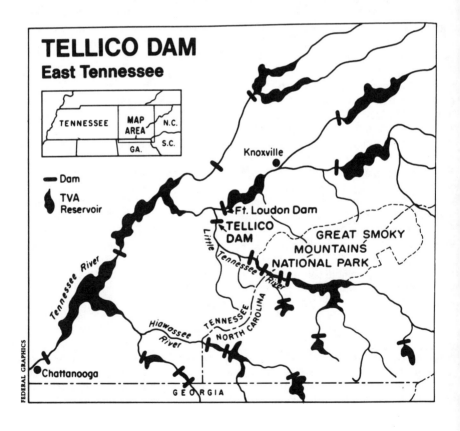

cance of the last existing populations of snail darters lies in the fact that big river habitats that had supported the species throughout the area are now destroyed. We are recognizing more and more that we are dependent on interrelationships of environmental factors and that destruction of these factors inevitably leads to a decrease in diversity and quality of life.

The Tennessee Valley Authority has nearly completed the Tellico Dam, which would inundate the last thirty-three miles of the Little Tennessee River valley and render the snail darter extinct. On January 31, 1977, the Sixth District Court of Appeals in Cincinnati ruled unanimously to halt construction on the dam and to permanently enjoin its closing.

The TVA has had a tremendous advantage in the conflict and with the publicity it released after the court decision: It spent taxpayers' money on the Tellico Project. No taxpayer wants to see money wasted, and no representative elected by taxpayers wants to admit that money has been wasted. This is why most pork-barrel projects succeed. When completed and working, they represent money "well spent" by definition, even if the costs so far exceed the benefits that the finished project would be better abandoned. TVA is using this advantage fully, claiming that $101 million will be "lost" if the project is not completed. A closer look at the project costs, however, does not substantiate this claim.

The Agency condemned and acquired 38,000 acres of land in the Little Tennessee River valley at a cost of $26 million. The only conceivable way for this public money to be lost is to flood the land. Fifteen million dollars have been spent on wages for labor on the project. This money already has had a beneficial effect on the local employment situation and the economy. An additional $34 million has been spent on "reservoir adjustments," which include new highways, a highway bridge, and a railway bridge—all of which were needed even without the dam. These benefits are not contingent on the existence of a reservoir, and are compatible with alternate uses.

Irretrievable costs include $14.8 million for the earthen and concrete dam structures and $6 million for a canal. (But half of these amounts were wages.) The larger point, however, is that $80 million of the project money has bought land, roads, and other improvements that have since increased in value far beyond the project's costs.

TVA has told the courts and legislators, in effect, "Look at how much money we have spent; you cannot stop the project now." However, inspection of the agency's figures shows that more than half the money was spent after TVA was well aware that it was violating the Endangered Species Act!

In response to the court injunction, TVA has initiated a massive public relations campaign, using the 1976–77 natural gas shortfall to magnify the dam's electrical generating significance. But the Tellico Dam has *no generators*. The reservoir will be connected by a canal to the nearby Fort Loudon reservoir; and Tellico water, when available, will flow over the Loudon generators, expanding the system capacity by only 0.1 percent.

Electricity is needed, of course; but such a small amount, at a cost several times more per kilowatt than that produced elsewhere in the TVA system, does not justify the dam. Furthermore, industry simply is not expanding in the Tennessee Valley as it used to. TVA's most recently completed reservoirs have not fulfilled their promises, and large tracts of land set aside for industry lie unused. There is no reason to believe that yet another reservoir will reverse this trend. Thus, opposition to this dam is based on several considerations in addition to the snail darter and is not a last-minute effort. In fact, Congress had approved construction of the Tellico Dam in 1966, and it was already half completed before the snail darter was discovered in late 1973. Yet hundreds of citizens have been working for more than ten years toward halting this dam project, which is unjustified on grounds other than the Endangered Species Act.

Much more beneficial use could be made of the project land than a lake in an area where almost every river has already been impounded. In February 1977 the Little Tennessee River Alliance, a group of six conservation organizations, called on Congress to authorize a study of the numerous alternative land uses for the Tellico Project area. They proposed that a study be conducted jointly by all agencies with jurisdiction over the area—TVA, the departments of Interior and Agriculture, and the state of Tennessee. All the land uses should be judged for economic soundness and compatibility with the maintenance of a river environment. The most promising alternatives are the return of the rich farmland in the area to agricultural production and the development of the area as a recreational resource sufficiently attractive to relieve visitation pressures on nearby Great Smoky Mountains National Park.

Approximately 15,500 acres of prime river bottom land would be permanently flooded by the Tellico Dam. Considering a threat of world food crisis and the relatively small amount of electricity that would be added to the Loudon system, burying such a valuable resource under fifty feet of water seems foolhardy. Intensive agriculture on this land not only would create 300 to 350 jobs, but would generate an estimated $27 million in revenue annually. The portion of the project site that would not be flooded also contains 10,000 acres of valuable agricultural land, which could also be returned to agriculture. Agricultural development would also involve resettlement of landholders displaced by the Tellico Project.

Agricultural values alone probably provide enough reason to maintain the Tellico area as a river valley. However, the recreational values also are considerable. With twenty-two reservoirs already within a fifty-mile radius of the proposed Tellico reservoir, a free-flowing diversified stretch of river is an important recreational attraction. The Little Tennessee River is one of the best trout rivers in the Southeast that consistently produces record-sized brown trout. The river is ideal for family canoeing, and it is clean and cold, supporting many species of vertebrate and invertebrate life.

The river flows through a valley that has been inhabited by man for ten thousand years. Along the river lies the birthplace of the Cherokee Nation, evidenced by ancient burial grounds and former town sites such as Tennasee (from which the fish, the river, the state, and TVA derive their names); Citico; Coytee; Tuskegee; and Chota, the capital of the Cherokee Nation in recorded times. Artifacts reveal the existence of a highly organized agrarian society dating back to 7500 B.C. at the Icehouse Bottoms site.

Historical sites include Fort Loudon, the oldest British outpost west of the Appalachians; Coytee Springs, the site of the first treaty between white men and the Cherokee Nation; and the McClung McGhee Mansion, an impressive antebellum structure listed on the National Register of Historical Monuments.

All these historical, archeological, scenic, and recreational attributes are located in a valley less than twenty miles from the overcrowded and fragile Great Smoky Mountains National Park. This park is the most heavily visited park in the United States, with more than eight million visitors annually. The park is severely overused, and a study is being conducted now to determine ways to reduce damage to the Smokies. The appealing qualities of the Little Tennessee River as a trout stream and canoeing area could attract many of the tourists, both relieving the pressure on the park and providing economic benefits for the valley.

The recent precedent-setting decision of the Appeals Court in Cincinnati gives the snail darter's friends good reason for celebration. The opinion reads in part as follows:

> Whether a dam is 50 percent or 90 percent complete is irrelevant in calculating the social and scientific costs attributable to the disappearance of a unique form of life. . . . The complexity of the ecological sciences suggests that the detrimental impact of a project upon an endangered species may not always be clearly perceived before construction is well underway. In effect, such was the case here. For Congress or the Secretary of the Interior to be able to make meaningful decisions in the furtherance of the Act, the opportunity to choose must be preserved. Once a living species has been eradicated, discretion loses its significance. (U.S. Court of Appeals No. 76-2116, Hill et al. vs. TVA.)

The Endangered Species Act specifically states that a species *and* its critical habitat must be preserved. In 1976 construction on the dam progressed to the point where snail darters could not go upstream during their spawning cycle because of a strong current flowing through the structure's pipes. TVA has attempted to confuse the critical habitat issue with a snail darter transplant program from the Little Tennessee to the nearby Hiwassee River, which seems to have only a small percentage of habitat suitable for the fish. The Appeals Court addressed this issue:

> We recognize that TVA has completed an experimental transplant of some 700 snail darter specimens from the Little Tennessee to the Hiwassee River, which is of similar physical character. While we share the hope that conclusive evidence, not yet available, will confirm that the displaced population is thriving and reproducing, even if that evidence were properly before us, it would not alter our decision to enjoin further Tellico Dam construction. It is not the courts but the Secretary of the Interior who bears the responsibility for maintaining the Endangered Species list and designating the critical habitats of listed species. The fact that both of these determinations are accomplished by rulemaking rather than by adjudication confirms the public importance of the issues at stake. Nowhere in the Act are courts authorized to override the Secretary by arbitrarily "reading" species out of the endangered species list or by redefining the boundaries of existing critical habitats on a case-by-case basis.

However, TVA is not an agency amenable to suggestions or court rulings, even if they are in that same public interest that TVA was set up to serve. Conservationists have won a battle, but the war continues in Washington. TVA plans a dual appeal to the Supreme Court and to the Congress. Court procedures take time, so efforts are being concentrated on the Senate and the House of Representatives. TVA hopes to convince Congress either to exempt the Tellico Project from the Endangered Species Act or to amend the Act itself. Proposed amendments may attack Section 7 or exempt projects that are already under way.

Even though the snail darter and the Little Tennessee River seem more vulnerable out in the political arena—where pork-barrel projects get funded as favors or because no one questions them—this turn of events allows all interested citizens, organizations, and political figures to express their opinions.

As President Carter's recent proposal to review thirty-five federal water projects indicates, inefficient use of our environment can no longer be tolerated, because our quality of life and very existence are at stake. The snail darter case provides an opportunity to look objectively at costs and benefits of the Tellico Project. Costs and benefits for all such projects should be examined *before* millions of dollars are spent.

The injunction against the Tellico Dam has national implications for its precedent-setting use of the Endangered Species Act, but another aspect of this decision is also important. If the injunction on the Tellico Dam remains in effect, perhaps agencies' strategy of accelerating spending on a project to avoid the law will not be used so frequently, and they will be held responsible for money that they spend after their projects come into conflict with environmental laws. But without public support, Congress may weaken the Endangered Species Act, and the strong judicial decision in favor of the environment will be lost.

The outcome of this controversy will have a far-reaching effect on all endangered species.

Sara Grigsby Cook is president of the Tennessee Endangered Species Committee, the citizens group that has raised some $15,000 to support the Tellico legal battle and has served as the educational and public information arm of this movement. She has been involved since late 1974 acting as the group's partial coordinator of activities, media liaison, and artist.

Committee member Chuck Cook, who has also been involved in the battle for more than two years, recently received a Master's Degree in Agricultural Biology with emphasis on Entomology and a minor in Ecology.

Doris Gove, treasurer of the committee, has a Master's Degree in Animal Behavior and Ecology and is presently working on a Ph.D. studying reptile behavior.

Acknowledgment is made to the members of the Tennessee Endangered Species Committee who researched the background information for this article.

ENDANGERED SPECIES
Review of Law Triggered by Tellico Impasse

Constance Holden

To condense the evolution of life on Earth . . . suppose the whole history of the planet is contained within a single year. The conditions suitable for life do not develop until late June. The oldest known fossils are living creatures around mid-October, and life is abundant . . . by the end of that month. In mid-December, dinosaurs and other reptiles dominate the scene. Mammals . . . appear in large numbers only a little before Christmas. On New Year's Eve, at about five minutes to midnight, man emerges. . . . The period since 1600 A.D., when man-induced extinction began to increase rapidly, amounts to three seconds, and the quarter century just begun, when the disappearance of species may be on the scale of all the mass extinctions of the past put together, will take another sixth of a second— a twinkling of an eye in evolutionary time.
—Norman Myers, in *Natural Resources Defense Council Newsletter*

The Endangered Species Act of 1973, designed as it were to extend that twinkling by a millisecond or two, seems a pathetic instrument indeed to slow the rushing forces of species extinction. But judging from some of the rumblings in Congress, one might think it was intended to cast humankind back to the dark ages. The Tennessee delegation in particular is abuzz over the prospect that the Tennessee Valley Authority's almost-complete Tellico Dam will end up not as a focal point for new industrial development but as a vast, silent concrete monument to the tiny inhabitant of the Little Tennessee River known as the snail darter.

Last January, a federal appeals court ordered work on the dam halted, saying that it would destroy the only known habitat of the 3-inch snail-eating fish and, therefore, it was in violation of the Endangered Species Act.

The TVA, with $103 million sunk into the project, is predictably unwilling to let the matter rest. So, environmentalists and many others now fear that the Tellico controversy will trigger a congressional reassessment that could culminate in a drastic weakening of section 7, the most potent segment of the act, which prohibits federal agencies from jeopardizing endangered species or habitats that have been designated as "critical." Specifically, this section says projects carried out by federal departments and agencies must not "jeopardize the continued existence of . . . endangered species and threatened species or result in the destruction or modification of habitat of such species which is determined . . . to be critical."

Section 7, with its unqualified admonition, has proved to be a remarkably powerful, and therefore controversial, component of the Endangered Species Act. Since the act's passage, there have been many hundreds of consultations between federal construction and land management agencies and the Department of the Interior's U.S. Fish and Wildlife Service, where the Office of Endangered Species (OES) is located. In the vast majority of cases it has been determined that

Constance Holden, "Endangered Species: Review of Law Triggered by Tellico Impasse," *Science*, 196 (1977), 1426–28. Copyright 1977 by the American Association for the Advancement of Science.

no endangered species are jeopardized. Indeed, in fewer than 100 projects has it been necessary to make alterations in the plans to accommodate the law. And, despite the fact that the only way to compel an agency to abide by section 7 is to bring a case to court, there have thus far been only three lawsuits. One was over Missouri's proposed $100 million Meramec Park dam, in which the Sierra Club sued in order to save the Indiana bat and an endangered pearly mussel. (The court ruled in favor of the dam on the grounds there was insufficient evidence to do otherwise, but the project is in trouble now for other reasons.) Another suit, brought by the National Wildlife Federation, claimed the habitat of the Mississippi sandhill crane would be ruined by completion of Interstate Highway I-10. The court ordered modifications in the route. The last suit was Tellico.

Most of the serious conflicts between public works projects and endangered species appear to be posed by dams, which tend to be all-or-nothing affairs, not amenable to much modification or relocation, and extraordinarily disruptive of ecosystems both aquatic and terrestial. Dams are also big money and therefore intensely political projects. The only other project about which a suit is imminently threatened is another dam—the Columbia Dam on Tennessee's Duck River, whose construction threatens some endangered snails (the Environmental Defense Fund has served notice to the TVA that it intends to move on this one).

The Tellico case is unusual in that it is an example of agency noncooperation—"the bad faith example that proves the rule," according to Tellico plaintiff Zygmunt Plater. The TVA has known about the snail darter since 1973 when it was discovered by a TVA zoologist. (It was officially put on the endangered species list in 1975.) The agency has expressed willingness to do anything to mitigate the situation—including relocating the darter to another river—except stop construction. Apparently it was confident it would win in a court confrontation, and indeed the first court ruling on the case last year was in TVA's favor. The appeals court, however, was not about to read equivocation into the act where it did not exist. The TVA was gambling that the advanced stage of the project would render it immune from tampering. But the court said: "Whether a dam is 50 percent or 90 percent completed is irrelevant in calculating the social and scientific costs attributable to the disappearance of a unique form of life. Courts are ill-equipped to calculate how many dollars must be invested before the value of a dam exceeds that of the endangered species."

Some congressmen just cannot get used to the idea that a tiny little creature could stop a big important dam.

"Are you going to do anything to get the snail darter off our backs?" cried an Alabama congressman to Interior Secretary Cecil D. Andrus at House appropriations hearings earlier this year. As Andrus replied, he could do nothing—Congress's only recourse was to change the law. A number of amendments are already brewing. One, introduced by Representative John J. Duncan (R-Tenn.) would exempt Tellico from the act. Another, by Representative Robin L. Beard (R-Tenn.) would exempt Tellico, Columbia, and the problem-ridden Tennessee-Tombigbee waterway, as well as any federal water project that had been authorized before passage of the Endangered Species Act. There has also been talk of an amendment that would give the Interior Secretary authority to exempt a project from the act. Representative Robert L. Leggett (D-Calif.), chairman of the fish and wildlife subcommittee of the House Merchant Marine and Fisheries committee, has asked the General Accounting Office to report on the costs and benefits of the Tellico Dam before it takes any action on proposed amendments.

Meanwhile, of immediate interest are July hearings on the Tellico problem planned by the Senate Environment and Public Works Committee. Committee member Howard Baker (D-Tenn.), who is also minority leader of the Senate, is said to be particularly concerned about the turn events have taken. One of the original sponsors of the endangered species act, he apparently is now having second thoughts and wants to look into ways in which it can be made more "flexible," says a staffer. The staffer insists that Baker has an open mind about the project, but other observers are convinced that he wants to weaken section 7, perhaps by giving decision-makers more discretion to weigh the benefits of a project against the benefits of saving a particular species.

One thing that's certain is that, as the Baker aide says, "the endangered species Act has turned out to be more of a surprise" to Congress than most other pieces of environmental legislation. "I don't think Congress when they passed the bill realized its potential scope or breadth," he adds. Undoubtedly many members of Congress were thinking thoughts of brown-eyed creatures and soaring winged things when they cast their vote, and are now finding themselves confronted with a Pandora's box containing infinite numbers of creeping things they never dreamed existed.

At any rate, this summer should be a showdown for the act, and conservationists are hoping that if all goes well (for diversity of species) both Congress and the public will arrive at a deeper understanding of what the act is all about. It has recently been subjected to some frivolous attacks, notably in the case of the Dickey-Lincoln project, a proposed dam on the St. John River in Maine, to be constructed by the Corps of Engineers. Dickey-Lincoln is still in the environmental impact statement stage, a stage not due to be completed till the end of next year. But already there has been a hue and cry about the possibility that a humble plant, a member of the snapdragon family named the Furbish lousewort, will bring the project to its knees. This project is opposed for a number of reasons, and environmentalists do not want to bring suit to halt the dam on the basis of the Furbish lousewort, but some environmentalists say the Corps has been "crying wolf" over the plant (which is to be included in the first listing of endangered plants) in an attempt to cast ridicule on the act.

The essential issue raised by the fuss over the act is: How far did Congress intend to go in protecting endangered species? The act as written is open-ended. It was clearly not intended to protect microorganisms whose populations and range would be impossible to measure fully, but since the law defines "species" as including subspecies, lesser taxa, and unique endemic populations, any organism for which it is possible to gather meaningful data (with the exception of "injurious" insects such as boll weevils) qualify for protection.

To some scientists, there is no place to draw the line on what merits protection. Endangered species are almost always part of a "remnant ecosystem," says Marc Imlay, an OES malacologist. Species put on the endangered list are really "marker" organisms that signal the existence of an entire ecosystem that inevitably contains other equally rare organisms. Endangered species, says Wayne Grimm of the National Museum of Canada, "are the key to the evolutionary process of all living things in an area, they demonstrate the process of isolation, genetic drift, the emergence of hybrids. . . ." No compromises are possible, says Grimm, when the problem is stated in terms of the question: "Do organisms have the right to exist?"—which, logically extended, means: "Does life on earth have a right to exist?"

Yes, but . . .

It would be hard for Congress to answer "no" to that, but it might choose to change the question to "does the right of an organism to exist always supersede the right of people to have a dam they want?" If the existence of an unprepossessing organism is the only thing that appears to be at stake, it is difficult to imagine Congress choosing principles over practicalities. But the Endangered Species Act is part of a constellation of legislation, starting with the National Environmental Policy Act, that is forcing project designers to put unquantifiable or intangible benefits into their cost-benefit equations. Rare is the case where threats to the existence of an endangered species comprise the only major disbenefit of a project—although in some instances, like the Tellico case, the act may prove to be the most useful lever for mounting opposition. As Jim Williams of the OES points out. "This is not a 3-inch fish stopping a dam, this is a 3-inch fish that may be saving a river valley" with fertile farmland, good fishing, rich archeological sites, and prime recreational areas.

Many opponents of Tellico therefore welcome the forthcoming Senate airing of the project, not so much in confidence that the value of species diversity will be affirmed but because they believe a thorough review of the facts will demonstrate the dam is not worth having by any standards.

The Tellico conflict is just what could be expected under the act, involving as it does the Southeast, dams, and aquatic life. According to fish and wildlife experts, there is an exceptional amount of variety in this part of the United States owing to the fact that it was not glaciated, and many pockets of unusual ecology remain. It has a lot of rivers and much rainfall, and is still underdeveloped compared to the rest of the country, so many aquatic organisms flourish there that may be threatened in the future by industrialization.

The Office of Endangered Species is engaged in a very real race against time to get endangered or threatened plants and animals listed in time to stabilize their conditions. The OES staff of specialists is far smaller than what biologists believe necessary, consisting of eight or ten experts in the fields of ichthyology, mammology, malacology, ornithology, herpetology, entomology, and botany. Evidence is gathered through contracts with universities and through petitions submitted by groups around the country as well as by research by staff scientists. Several thousand dollars' worth of work goes into the gathering of data for every species that finally makes the list. Half those under consideration fall by the wayside, says Imlay, as they "turn out to be already extinct, widespread, or invalid taxonomically."

A colossal amount of work remains to be done. Williams, an ichthyologist, estimates it will be 3 to 5 years before the office has succeeded in listing a substantial majority of all the fish in the country that are deemed endangered or threatened; there is no telling when the bulk of other animals and plants will achieve protected status—or when endangered populations will have been restored to the extent they can be taken off the list, which is the ultimate goal. One cannot list a species until detailed evidence of its rarity is gathered, remarks Williams, because "for every listing you have to think of yourself in a courtroom." The process can take years. Grimm says "it took 7 years to get one population with a 40-square-yard range on the list." He was referring to *Succinea chittenangoensis*, a Pleistocene relic land snail that used to be found in a range from Iowa to Southern Ontario, and which now hangs onto one niche under the spray of the Chittenango Falls in Madison County, New York.

Obtaining a "critical habitat" listing is even more difficult, because intricate knowledge of a species' life history and habits is required. At latest count, there were 38 mammals, 67 birds, 34 fish, 22 molluscs, and some reptiles and butterflies officially listed as either endangered or threatened in this country. Fourteen plants will soon join the list. Thousands more of everything are under consideration. Only six critical habitats have so far been listed, including miles 0.5 through 17 of the Little Tennessee River, home of the snail darter. Thirty-nine more are proposed.

Act Ahead of Its Time?

The Endangered Species Act is international in scope, requiring the listing of endangered species worldwide. But for this country, section 7 is the part that really shows. It's "the heart of the act ... the real teeth of the act," says Keith Schreiner, associate director of the Fish and Wildlife Service. And it embodies sophisticated, far-seeing ecological goals that run smack in the face of the concerns that traditionally impel the reelection-oriented congressman—federal money and the promise of contracts and jobs.

This summer will give some indication of how deeply the populace, through their elected representatives, have absorbed the concept that sustaining diversity of species equates with sustaining life in general. The House Appropriations Committee has not figured things out yet, judging from their decision to appropriate $9 million, in a public works bill, for the purpose of relocating endangered species that lie in the path of several projects now under development. (Variously labeled "outrageous" and "ridiculous" by an Interior official and a congressional staffer, the concept, as any ecologist knows, is at best naive.)

Howard Baker's call for more "flexibility" in the act is looked on askance by government officials who believe the record of accommodations made so far shows the act is already flexible. Conservationists and others hope that if an amendment is passed, it will be one that makes a single exception for Tellico rather than one that weakens the act as a whole. The President, in his environmental message of 23 May, indicated the former approach was preferable: "Major projects now under way that are found to pose a serious threat to endangered species should be reassessed on a case-by-case basis," he said.

FISH IN A PORKBARREL

Zygmunt J. B. Plater

The little snail darter that stopped the Tellico Dam, one of last year's more whimsical news stories, turns out to have known wherein it swam. The three-inch-long endangered species, newspapers reported last year, had halted a "$100 million hydroelectric dam" at the "eleventh hour" in a "classic confrontation between energy needs and the environment." The Endangered Species Act itself was soon endangered because of the backlash against what was called "statutory extremism" in the Tellico case. The congressional hearings and investigations that followed the fish's victory in the courts, however, have told a different story.

Shortly after the Sixth Circuit Court of Appeals enjoined the Tellico Dam for violating the Act, the General Accounting Office analyzed the TVA project. That study showed that deferring to the snail darter by *not* filling the reservoir can, even now, be more profitable to all concerned than closing the dam gates.

The dam, it turned out, was never intended to generate electricity. Rather, it was merely one component of a TVA regional economic development project that has dammed the river system in 68 successive lakes, 22 within 60 miles of Tellico. This last dam was planned only to create subsidized lakefront industrial sites and a final flatwater recreation lake, objectives which the General Accounting Office did not find particularly useful. The dam itself, which TVA rushed to near-completion after the discovery of the snail darter, is only a minor part of the project: $5 million worth of concrete and labor

and $17 million of earthworks, out of the project's total cost of $120 million. Most of the project's budget was spent to buy the valley's fertile farmlands and to improve roads and bridges in the area, assets that are valuable without the reservoir.

The GAO report found that TVA's benefit claims for the Tellico project were completely unreliable. The value of added flatwater recreation facilities, for instance, was projected at $1.4 million annually, almost half of total project benefits. This was unrealistic, given the existence of 22 nearby reservoirs, and considering that the dam would eliminate the finest remaining trout fishing water in the southeast.

The interests of the snail darter, it turns out, coincide with those of other species around Tellico, including human beings. Local citizens have been fighting the dam for 16 years, through lawsuits, petitions and, in several cases, shotgun threats to avoid being driven from their land. The little fish requires cool, clean flowing big river water, with shallow cobbled shoals for spawning. It used to live throughout the eastern portion of the Tennessee river system, but after the construction of 68 reservoirs in the valley, its remaining population now survives in the region's last such stretch of clear flowing river. After TVA's dam-building boom, the surrounding river valley also is unique. It contains 25,000 acres of prime agricultural land, as rich as the Mississippi Delta. A dozen major Cherokee historic sites line the riverbank, including Tuskegee, the village where the great Chief Sequoyah was born;

Zygmunt J. B. Plater, "Fish in a Porkbarrel," *New Republic*, 8 April 1978, pp. 15–16. Reprinted by permission of The New Republic, © 1978 The New Republic, Inc.

the Echota religious capital; and Tenassee, which gave its name to the river and the state. Colonial Fort Loudon is on the riverbank, and near there in 1975 archaeologists discovered two of the oldest sites of continuous human settlement in America, a record of 10,000 years of valley occupation. All these assets—the river, farmlands, and historic sites—would have been buried under about 20 feet of mud and water if the dam were closed.

Development of the river valley without a reservoir, thus saving the snail darter, appears to be a profitable alternative even today with the dam virtually complete. TVA is moving into land development ventures, now that it has run out of places to build dams, and the GAO study observed that the unflooded Tellico project is admirably suited for such development. In addition to river recreation and farming—which could yield twice as much yearly revenue as the entire reservoir project—the GAO noted the valley's tourist potential. Its historic sites along the river form a path connecting the adjoining Smoky Mountains National Park (with 10 million visitors a year) with the major north-south interstate highway, I-75. Carefully developing the valley instead of flooding it would relieve pressures on the park itself and add a valuable tourist route for the local economy. An extra two square miles of potential industrial lands also exist in the unflooded valley, adjoining major railroad lines and arterial highways.

So the snail darter may have saved a fertile river valley threatened by a marginal federal project. It also has shown us that the bloom is off the New Deal's sweetest smelling rose. No longer a model of state enterprise, the Tennessee Valley Authority has become a somewhat obstinate utility company—the largest in the nation—wielding extraordinary political power in its six-state region. Perhaps the Tellico snail darter case will remind it of its public-spirited origins.

Zygmunt J. B. Plater teaches law at Wayne State University.

OVERVIEW—LAW
The Tellico Dam Case

Ross Sandler

One June 15, 1978, the Supreme Court announced its decision in the Tellico Dam case.[1] The Court held that the Tennessee Valley Authority would violate the Endangered Species Act of 1973 (16 U.S.C. § 1531 et seq.), if it completed the Tellico Dam and operated it and that an injunction against the TVA was appropriate. The decision secures for the moment the critical habitat of a small member of the perch family, the snail darter. But for environmental law the case signals much more.

The Tellico Dam case involved the construction of a dam on the Little Tennessee River as a multi-purpose regional development project. The dam was designed to stimulate shoreline development, generate sufficient electric current to heat 20,000 homes, provide flatwater recreation and flood control, and improve economic conditions in the region. In 1973 a University of Tennessee ichthyologist identified a previously unknown species of fish, the snail darter, in the Little Tennessee above the dam site. The fish was found to live only in well-oxygenated, fast moving water. Food for the snail darter is almost exclusively snails which require a clear gravel substrate for their survival. Impoundment of water behind the Tellico Dam would destroy the entire known habitat of the snail darter.

In January 1975 a regional association of biological scientists, a conservation group and others petitioned the Secretary of the Interior to list the snail darter as an endangered species under the federal statute. The Secretary granted the peti-tion in November 1975 and declared the area of the Little Tennessee that would be affected by the dam to be a critical habitat within the meaning of the statute. The Secretary, based upon these determinations and in accordance with the statute, declared that "all federal agencies must take such action as is necessary to insure that actions authorized, funded, or carried out by them do not result in the destruction or modification of this critical habitat area." As the Supreme Court noted, this notice was pointedly directed at the TVA and was clearly aimed at halting completion or operation of the dam.

The TVA refused to halt construction, arguing that the Endangered Species Act did not apply to a dam which was 50 percent complete when the Act was passed and 70 to 80 percent complete when the snail darter was officially listed as endangered. The biological scientists and conservationists went to court against TVA. After a hearing, the trial judge found that the reservoir behind the dam would probably result in the complete destruction of the snail darter's habitat, although recent experiments show there is a possibility of successfully reestablishing the species elsewhere, making it highly probable that the continued existence of the species would be jeopardized. But the judge refused to enjoin the nearly complete dam because he saw no alternative to scrapping the entire project. The judge emphasized the loss of $58 to $78 million of public money if the injunction were issued and concluded that under the cir-

Ross Sandler, "Overview—Law: The Tellico Dam Case," *Environment*, July-August 1978, pp. 4–5, 42–43. Reprinted by permission of the author.

142

cumstances of the nearly completed project it would be unreasonable to apply the statute to protect the snail darter.

The court of appeals reversed the district court and enjoined the construction and operation of the dam until such time as Congress exempted the Tellico project from the Act or the snail darter had been deleted from the list of endangered species. The court rejected the TVA's attempt to distinguish its nearly completed project from the requirements of the Act. More importantly, the appellate court also rejected the attempt of the lower court to balance the worth of an endangered species against the value of an ongoing public works project. The appellate judges reasoned that courts are ill-equipped to calculate how many dollars must be invested before the value of a dam exceeds the value of an endangered species. A court's role, it held, was to preserve the status quo, thereby guaranteeing the legislative or executive branches time to resolve the issue.

The Supreme Court upheld the injunction. The Court reviewed at length the legislative history of the Endangered Species Act and prior legislation, as well as the history of the Tellico project, concluding that the TVA would be in violation of the Act if it completed or operated the Tellico Dam as planned. Under the statute and the ruling by the Secretary of the Interior, the TVA must insure that its actions do not jeopardize the continued existence of the snail darter or result in destruction or the modification of the fish's habitat.

The Supreme Court then held that a court had no authority to hold back from issuing an injunction. The district judge had ruled that it would be unreasonable to issue an injunction, but the Supreme Court thought differently. Once Congress has set priorities in a given area, it is for the executive to administer the laws, and for the courts to enforce them when en-

forcement is sought. The Supreme Court saw this as a constitutional issue involving separation of powers. The executive branch, through the Secretary of the Interior, had pursuant to statute made the requisite findings concerning critical habitat, and Congress had set priorities which struck a balance in favor of conserving endangered species and their habitats. The Supreme Court held that it would violate constitutional principles if a court could find in a particular case that it would be unreasonable to follow the balance struck by Congress within its delegated powers.

While the Supreme Court's opinion is a victory for environmental values, the opinion signals a pulling back of federal court activism in environmental law. Over the past decade the courts have played a dominant role in the development of environmental law. But the Supreme Court in this and other cases has made it clear that it is Congress that primarily formulates policies, mandates programs and projects, and establishes their relative priorities for the nation. In the Tellico Dam case this resulted in a ruling favorable to conservation values. But that was because Congress had placed the value of endangered species over another authorized federal action—public works construction.

But Congress rarely makes such a final decision in the environmental area. The Refuse Act of 1899 prohibited the discharge of any pollutant into the navigable waters of the United States. But once the full impact of that absolute prohibition was felt, Congress established a vastly different and less absolute program in the Water Pollution Control Act of 1972. The Delaney Amendment of the Food, Drug, and Cosmetic Act currently prohibits without exception the use of any food additive which has been shown to cause cancer in man or animal. It was this flat prohibition which caused the storm over saccharin when saccharin was shown to cause cancer in test animals. Congress promptly passed legislation to soften the impact of the Delaney Amendment on saccharin and continues to consider alternatives to the flat prohibition.

Absolute statutes are not typical of environmental legislation. The more typical statutes require the executive or administrative agency to balance environmental concerns against social and economic goals. NEPA is such a statute. The Supreme Court has ruled under NEPA that once the executive agency has followed the procedures of NEPA and has taken a hard look at the environmental consequences of its decision, then there remains no room for a court to overturn the substantive decision. The court can act only to prevent wholly arbitrary and capricious agency action, a rare occurrence.

From the point of view of people seeking conservation or environmental values, the Supreme Court's decisions mean that battles will be won or lost in the legislature, the Congress, and the agencies, and not the courts. Issues of toxic chemicals, discharge of pollution in the rivers, reduction of air pollution, and the like all depend on agency decisions under federal law, most of which decisions are now made in Washington at agency headquarters. This is a structure that places heavy burdens on everyone. In the Tellico case, for instance, the conservation group had to petition the Secretary of the Interior pursuant to federal regulations. A petition is a formal document, usually requiring a lawyer to draft, which must be supported by some evidence. After the petition is filed a hearing is often held, participation in which again requires skill, time, expert help, and money.

The Tellico Dam case also makes clear that courts will not arbitrate what is rea-

sonable for society. A decision that balances environmental, economic, and social values is a policy decision that belongs in the political arena where legislators and executive agencies operate. This in turn places burdens upon environmental and conservation organizations to develop and maintain a scientific, political, and lobbying presence with Congress as well as at EPA, NRC, Interior, OSHA, and the other specialized governmental agencies to which Congress has delegated its policy-making authority.

Congress, in delegating authority, has delegated responsibility as well. The NRC must determine safety of nuclear reactors; EPA must protect public health. In the Tellico Dam case, the Department of Interior was charged in the first instance to protect the endangered species and its habitat. There were obvious pressures against the decision favoring conservation where the threatening dam was nearly completed. But the lesson from the Tellico Dam case is that when the agency does act to protect environmental and conservation values, the court will sustain the action. The rule that prevents a court from substituting its policies for those of Congress or agencies operates to protect agency decisions that favor the environment as well as those that do not. This is an important lesson for environmental agencies, some of which are still in the formative stages and are yet uncertain just how far they can go and still be upheld in the courts. The Tellico Dam case tells them that they will be upheld and encourages them to fulfill Congressional policy.

---

1. Tennessee Valley Authority v. Hill, 46 L.W. 4673 (June 15, 1973).

Ross Sandler is a staff attorney for the Natural Resources Defense Council and edits *Overview—Law*.

LESSONS TO BE LEARNED FROM A BAD LAW

James J. Kilpatrick

In the familiar maxim, bad cases make bad law, but there is a second maxim drawn from the first: Bad laws breed bad law. That is one of several instructive lessons that might be gleaned from the Supreme Court's opinion of June 15 in TVA vs. Hill, et al. This was the Great Snail Darter case, and it had everything.

To refresh your recollection: Back in 1967, Congress authorized the Tennessee Valley Authority to begin work on the Tellico Dam and Reservoir Project along the Little Tennessee River. The idea was to improve the lives of the people in the area, to create a great lake for recreation, to generate a little electric power, and to develop the shoreline through new construction. It was pointed out at the time that the 33-mile reservoir, covering 16,500 acres of productive farmland, would obliterate other values, but no matter. Congress authorized the venture, and TVA went to work.

Six years later, building upon a couple of earlier laws, Congress adopted the Endangered Species Act of 1973. I intend no offense in remarking that it seemed the fashionable thing to do. This is how things work in Congress. Once it was fashionable to be anticommunist, and we got the Subversive Activities Control Board. Again, it was fashionable to support détente, and the board disappeared. We have had legislative fashions in consumerism, in space exploration, in civil rights. In the fall of 1973, environmentalism was in fashion, and people who had never met the word before in their lives were talking earnestly of "ecology." On a splendid wave of good intentions, Congress floated the Endangered Species Act to Mr. Nixon's desk. The vote in the Senate was 92–0, in the House, 390–12.

The purpose was altogether admirable. The idea was to halt the reckless and irresponsible march of what may provisionally be termed "progress" at the expense of the natural world around us. Americans, as a breed, have an ugly record in this regard. Long before the 1973 act was passed, we and our forebears had killed off the passenger pigeon and nearly eliminated the bison and such lovely creatures as the whooping crane and the ivory-billed woodpecker. In a heedless quest for material wealth, we polluted lakes, poisoned streams, paved over the countryside for parking lots, and sprayed defoliants to hell and gone. From an economic standpoint, much of this has been arguably good; from an environmental standpoint, much of this has invited disaster.

In any event, with a nearly unanimous cry of mea culpa, Congress passed the 1973 act. No one paid serious attention to a paragraph in Section 7. The paragraph authorized the Secretary of the Interior to identify, and publicly to proclaim, those species of animals, birds, fish, and plants he found to be endangered or threatened.

James J. Kilpatrick, "Lessons to Be Learned From a Bad Law," *Nation's Business*, August 1978, pp. 11–12. Reprinted by permission from Nation's Business, August, 1978. Copyright 1978 by Nation's Business, Chamber of Commerce of the United States.

The paragraph then imposed a flat and unqualified obligation upon "all other federal departments and agencies." Once they are put on notice of a Secretary's finding, they must take such action as may be necessary to ensure "that actions authorized, funded, or carried out by them do not jeopardize the continued existence of such endangered species. . . ."

While the Endangered Species Act was pending in Congress, late in the summer of 1973, a Tennessee ichthyologist, Dr. David A. Etnier, Jr., began exploring the Little Tennessee River in the area of the Tellico Dam. He found a previously unknown species of perch, a three-inch, tannish-colored overgrown minnow, the snail darter, *Percina Imostoma tanasi*. He estimated its population at 10,000 to 15,000.

Perhaps only an ichthyologist could love them. All told, some 130 species of darters are known to exist, 85 or 90 of them in Tennessee, and new species of darters recently have been identified at the rate of one a year. Nevertheless, opponents of the dam brought Dr. Etnier's discovery to the attention of the Secretary of the Interior, and on Nov. 10, 1975, with the dam 75 percent complete, the snail darter formally was pronounced to constitute an endangered species.

TVA officials, convinced that the 1973 law was not intended to apply to ongoing projects authorized before its enactment, kept working on the dam. Opponents sought an injunction to stop construction. A U.S. district court refused to enter such an injunction, but the Sixth Circuit in January, 1977, reversed. By that time, the dam was substantially complete. With the appellate decision, things at last ground to a dead halt. TVA appealed, and on June 15 the Supreme Court voted six to three to affirm the Sixth Circuit. "The snail darter won," said Justice Lewis F. Powell, Jr., from the bench. "He won 100 percent."

In my own view, for whatever it may be worth, Section 7 provides us with a good example of bad law—of extreme law. The section admits no room for compromise, no means for balancing values, no way to consider such realities as a $119 million nearly completed dam.

The section suffers from the vice of egalitarianism. All species are equally to be preserved. Falcons, eagles, grizzly bears, and whooping cranes carry no more weight than a couple of mud turtles, some subspecies of toad, and the Furbish lousewort.

Lesson number one to be learned from this affair is thus a lesson in statutory drafting. It is extremely doubtful that Congress ever intended Section 7 to be applied retroactively to projects far advanced toward completion. But if this was so, Congress failed to say it was so. Congress succumbed to the powerful gospel of environmentalism and wrote a bad law. And before the story is ended, unless we are careful, bad law will breed more bad law.

None of this is meant to criticize the court's majority opinion of June 15. On the contrary, Chief Justice Warren Burger and his colleagues merit applause for standing by the doctrine of judicial restraint even if their position produced absurd results. The majority found the language of the statute too clear to require much interpretation. The law set up an "irreconcilable conflict" between the dam and the darter, and under the law it was the dam and not the darter that was doomed. Congress had power to adopt the 1973 act; if the law was unwise, it was no business of the Supreme Court to pronounce it so.

"Once the meaning of an enactment is discerned and its constitutionality determined, the judicial process comes to an end. We do not sit as a committee of review, nor are we vested with the power of the veto," the opinion said.

That is sound doctrine. At the same time, there was something to be said for the dissent by Mr. Justice Powell, who objected that his fellow justices' view of "the plain intent of Congress" was not that plain to him. He thought the word "actions" in Section 7 could be reasonably construed so as to permit "some modicum of common sense and the public weal." Mr. Justice Powell observed that he could not believe Congress intended to halt construction on some vital defense project in order to preserve some newly discovered water spider. "I have little doubt," he concluded, "that Congress will amend the Endangered Species Act to prevent the grave consequences made possible by today's decision."

That was sound prophecy. The majority opinion no sooner was announced than Congressman Robin L. Beard of the Sixth District of Tennessee sprang into action. Mr. Beard, a consistent fellow, had been one of only four members of the House to vote against the original conference report of 1973. Now, he proposed to tie the House in knots by offering 682 amendments to the 1973 act—one for each species on the endangered list—in order to prevent its continued funding. On the Senate side, Tennessee's Howard H. Baker moved to set up review panels with authority to weigh the Secretary's proclamations against other public interests. Meanwhile, a staff writer for "The Washington Post" found a state of "pork panic" on Capitol Hill, as legislators saw nightmare visions of their own pet projects halted in mid-construction.

The 1973 act expires of its own terms on Sept. 30. A few general observations are in order. The intention of the Endangered Species Act was sound and good and farsighted. The sweep may have been too broad—there are an estimated 1.4 million full species of animals and 600,000 full species of plants in the world—but it is at least arguable that a protective act should sweep widely. We still know pathetically little about the cycles of life that sustain living things, and we are forever discovering in nature secrets that benefit mankind. It would be a pity—more than a pity, a disaster!—to see the act wiped out in reckless reaction to the Supreme Court's decision.

But there is this to be said on the other side: We err, we try to play God, in attempting to preserve every species and subspecies of every plant, bird, fish, and animal on earth. The history of this planet is in part the history of species appearing and disappearing, surviving and expiring according to the laws of natural selection. For aesthetic reasons, we surely have an obligation to preserve species of great beauty or great interest; for scientific reasons, we ought to fight for those endangered plants that may have medicinal value. And as a general rule, we ought not heedlessly to interfere with the life chain that sustains our fish and wildlife. But one subspecies of snail darter? Mr. Justice Powell rightly scoffed at putting a $119 million price tag on an unimportant, insignificant fish. The mammalian species known as Homo sapiens, Mr. Justice Powell seemed to be saying, deserves a little preservation, too.

The story may have a happy ending. At this writing, the TVA people are working on an alternative plan that Chairman S. David Freeman believes may provide even more benefit for the taxpayers than the original development plan. Efforts to transplant the snail darter into nearly identical Tennessee streams are continuing. Alarmed conservationists are rallying their scattered forces to plead for extension of the act without crippling amendments. Spokesmen for Interior are doing their best to mollify the suddenly aroused opposition. Reason may yet prevail.

Meanwhile, in the clear, cold waters of the Little Tennessee River, the snail darter, casting flickering shadows on the shallow gravel, provides a superlative textbook in politics and law.

ENDANGERED REVIEW BODY SEEMS TO BE IN THE CLEAR

John Walsh

A Cabinet-level review committee designed to have the last word on species-endangering federal projects appears to have survived the disenchantment of an influential sponsor, Senator Howard Baker (R-Tenn.).

Baker, the Senate Minority Leader, was cosponsor last year with Senator John Culver (D-Iowa) of an amendment creating a review body with the power to grant exemptions allowing the government to proceed with projects that had been found to threaten flora and fauna protected by the Endangered Species Act (ESA).

Baker had been given a case of home-state pique by the halting of construction on the Tennessee Valley Authority's Tellico Dam, on which some $100 million had already been spent. The action was taken under ESA provisions when the project was judged to threaten extinction to the snail darter, a tiny fish unique to the waters in the area where the dam was being built. The Culver-Baker amendment creating the review body was designed to provide flexibility for ESA when controversy arose over the law's extension last year. The review panel has six federal agency members and one vote is allowed to states involved. Five positive votes are required for an exemption.

In January, the review panel's first formal action was to deny an exemption to the Tellico project (*Science*, 23 February). Baker reacted by framing legislation to have the dam project exempted by direct congressional action and also to have the review council abolished by repeal of the appropriate section of the law.

At a 9 May final markup session of the Senate Environment and Public Works Committee on another extension of ESA, Baker offered an amendment to confer an exemption on the Tellico Dam project. The amendment failed by a final tally of 10 to 3. Baker did not put forward his amendment to abolish the review group. The committee reported out the bill extending ESA for 2½ years. Observers say that the decisiveness of the vote on the exemption in committee makes it unlikely that Baker will carry the fight to the Senate floor.

John Walsh, "Endangered Review Body Seems to Be in the Clear," *Science*, 204 (1979), 815.
Copyright 1979 by the American Association for the Advancement of Science.

ENDANGERED SPECIES MAY DETERMINE MAN'S FATE

"Humanity's fate is inextricably bound up with the fate of the great whales, the gorillas, the Furbish lousewort, and other endangered species," Stanford biologist Paul R. Ehrlich told the First International Congress on Research in Conservation Biology. He said that preserving other species was not simply a matter of compassion or of keeping them around for their aesthetic interest, but "a matter of maintaining the crucial life-support functions of ecological systems. These systems maintain the quality of the atmosphere, control our weather, create and maintain soils, provide fresh water, recycle nutrients essential to agriculture, provide food from the sea, dispose of our wastes, and provide a 'library' of genetic information from which future crops, domestic animals, antibiotics, spices, medicines, and tools for medical research can be drawn."

Ehrlich went on to point out that it is not just the destruction of species that is dangerous, but also the destruction of genetically distinct populations within species. "The rate of extinction in the last few decades has become vastly greater than the average extinction rate over the last several hundred million years. It is much too rapid for the normal evolutionary processes that create new forms of life to keep up with; species are disappearing many times more rapidly than new species are evolving. What we are seeing is a rapid depletion of Earth's stock of living things. Some scientists expect that as many as a million species will become extinct in the tropics alone by the turn of the century—somewhere between 10 and 20% of all the species on the planet. We do not know how many species can be exterminated before ecological systems are seriously disrupted, but the current tendency seems to be to keep experimenting until we find out. The folk 'wisdom' of economics tells us that we should continue to exploit the Earth wastefully for short-term gain and give no consideration to ecological constraints or to preserving long-term productivity of the planet. In short, the 'wisdom' of economics is actually insanity."

Ehrlich cited the mining law of 1872 as a prime example of a statute that was appropriate in its day, but is "lethally dangerous" in 1978. "The law says, in essence, that extracting minerals from public land can take precedence over all other values. The law is being used by giant conglomerates like Amax to chew up substantial portions of the western United States for short-term profit—destroying 'renewable' activities such as livestock grazing, forestry, recreation, and above all, the maintenance of those crucial ecosystem functions.

"It is important to remember that it is not just the decimation of large animals or known endangered species that threatens us—it is more importantly the ploughing under, paving over, strip-mining, submerging under tailings, mowing, herbiciding, pesticiding, and so forth of myriad unsung populations of unspectacular organisms that is the major threat. Killing off any given population or species will not necessarily produce a disaster, any more than removing a single rivet will cause an airplane to fall out of the sky.

"Endangered Species May Determine Man's Fate," *USA Today*, June 1979, p. 15. Reprinted with permission from *USA Today*; copyright 1979 by Society for the Advancement of Education.

But if we keep wiping out organisms, eventual catastrophe is as sure as if you keep removing rivets from the wing. And beware of those who say everything is fine until the wing actually comes off."

Ehrlich stressed the need for a new "strategy of conservation" to supplement the tactics already in use. He based the strategy on what he described as the "five iron laws" of conservation: "1) In conservation there is only successful defense or retreat, never an advance: a species or ecosystem once destroyed cannot be restored; 2) continued human population growth and conservation are fundamentally incompatible; 3) a growthmanic economic system and conservation are fundamentally incompatible; 4) the notion that only the short-term goals and immediate happiness of *Homo sapiens* should be considered in making moral decisions about the use of Earth is lethal, not only to nonhuman organisms but to humanity itself; and 5) arguments about the aesthetic value of nonhuman life forms, or their intrinsic interest, or appeals for compassion for what may be our only living companions in the universe mostly fall on deaf ears. Conservation must be promoted as an issue of *human well-being*, and, in the long run, *survival*."

Ehrlich urged conservationists to base their strategy on these laws and to put some of their effort not into protecting individual species or areas, but into combatting the forces that create the threats in the first place. "The public must come to understand that every time a population or species or other organism goes extinct, the tenure of *Homo sapiens* on this planet becomes a little less secure. When the bell tolls for the snail darter, it may also be tolling for us."

SNAIL DARTER VS. DAM
"PORK BARRELERS" WIN

Admitting that he was bowing to political pressures—which he presumably felt could weaken his bid for reelection—President Jimmy Carter signed into law a $10.8 billion public-works appropriation bill last week. In so doing, he removed the last obstacle standing in the way of completing the $145 million Tellico Dam project in Tennessee, famed for its role in the threatened extinction of the snail darter.

The continuing saga of the fish versus the dam has played before audiences large and small, from the Supreme Court (SN: 6/24/78, p. 403) and the Cabinet-level Endangered Species Committee (SN: 1/27/79, p. 55) to local affected homeowners. It has also figured prominently in both the threatened demise (SN: 10/7/78, p. 247) and later revision of endangered-species law. But this newest chapter introduces a specter that environmental lobbyists had hoped to elude—a complete and uncompromising exemption from all federal laws so that a "pork barrel" project might survive unabated.

The Tellico Dam has been the subject of intense and heated controversy since its inception around 1963. Supporters of the project have claimed that the recreational value of the dam reservoir, new construction jobs and the economic growth that would follow development of it's reservoir's scenic shoreline would aid economically depressed East Tennessee. And TVA, for whom the dam is being built, expects to save $2.7 million annually in electrical generating costs by diverting base-load capacity from coal and nuclear power plants to Tellico's somewhat less costly hydropower.

Opponents have countered, focusing on the natural, historical and cultural value of the river and its valley. For example, the dam reservoir will inundate some 5,600 acres of agricultural land and most of 280 archaeological sites—chronicling a history of human habitation dating back 10,000 years—that had been nominated to the national Register of Historic Places, in addition to seven sites already in the register. It will also partially flood a national landmark.

What's more, certain fish- and wildlife-habitat losses which will occur with the dam-reservoir development "are not fully accounted for in the TVA's comparisons of measured recreational benefits," according to a January 1979 cost-benefit analysis of the dam project by the staff of the new Endangered Species Committee.

In fact, when the Cabinet-level Endangered Species Committee held its first meeting, last January, its seven members voted unanimously against the dam on the grounds that finishing the already 90-percent-completed project was economically unjustifiable, irrespective of the snail-darter issue. At best there was a $.4 million annual net benefit for the dam over the originally free-flowing river, the new Endangered Species Committee's staff found. And Cecil Andrus, who chaired the committee, said his calculations showed a possible $.6 million annual net benefit for the river over the dam. Both calculations were arrived at before consideration

"Snail Darter vs. Dam: 'Pork Barrelers' Win," *Science News*, 6 Oct. 1979, p. 230. Reprinted with permission from *Science News*, the weekly news magazine of science, copyright 1979 by Science Service, Inc.

of the acknowledged but largely unmeasurable value (in dollars) of the archaeological sites and wildlife regions that would be lost due to the project.

But no sooner had the committee decision been tendered than Tennessee Senator Howard Baker vowed he would abolish the panel. Ironically, it was his bill that only months earlier had established this panel and empowered it to waive endangered-species law. In the end, Baker and other disgruntled members of Congress just wrote a blanket exemption for the Tellico Dam from all federal regulations—including Occupational Safety and Health Administration laws and workmen's compensation—and attached it as a rider to the public-works bill.

President Carter said he signed the bill "with regret" to avoid a "divisive veto battle" that might divert congressional attention—and undoubtedly support—from more pressing issues.

And what about the fish? Some 2,000 transplanted snail darters appear to be thriving in another Tennessee river.

TELLICO TRIUMPH
Defeat for the Snail Darter

It was the bane of Tennessee politicians and the butt of barroom jokes. For four years the lowly snail darter, a finger-size species of perch, blocked completion of the $116 million Tellico Dam project on the Little Tennessee River. Because the creature was found only in these waters, it was entitled to protection under the 1973 Endangered Species Act. But it also provided legal leverage for environmentalists who saw the dam as a pork barrel that would deluge 16,000 acres of fertile farm land and wipe out Indian historical sites.

Last week the snail darter met defeat. Congress had already voted to allow exceptions to the Endangered Species Act because of "irresolvable conflict," and Republican Howard H. Baker of Tennessee moved to apply this gambit to the snail darter. When that failed, Baker resolutely pushed again, and Tellico was tacked onto a $10.8 billion energy and water appropriations bill. President Carter, on record as opposing the dam, faced a bitter choice. The bill reportedly contained no other pork barrels that he had fought, and it kept alive his Water Resources Council, an independent body that judges future projects. Moreover, the Endangered Species Act was due for congressional review, and a Tellico veto might leave it endangered. Carter also felt a need to build good will for upcoming legislative battles. So he signed the bill, saying: "I accept, with regret, this action as expressing the will of the Congress."

Ironically, the snail darter may not be doomed after all. The U.S. Fish and Wildlife Service, which helped transplant much of the snail darter population to the nearby Hiwassee River, says that while their future is not yet assured, the fish are doing well so far. But the dam itself may not have a happy ending. Though Mayor Charles Hall of Tellico Plains (pop. 1,000) predicts the project will create 10,000 jobs over the next two decades, a new report by the Tennessee Valley Authority and the U.S. Department of the Interior concludes that the river and the farm land untouched would have brought even more jobs.

The study also finds that the dam's projected output of 23 megawatts of electricity will be offset by operational costs and rack up an annual $750,000 deficit. And the TVA, which lobbied vehemently for the dam throughout the 1960s and '70s, now admits that the project will not even provide the power for which it was built. But as bulldozers returned to the dam site for a last month of construction before the reservoir is filled, practicality seemed to have lost a last round to politics.

"Tellico Triumph: Defeat for the Snail Darter," *TIME*, 8 Oct. 1979, p. 105. Reprinted by permission from *Time*, The Weekly Newsmagazine; Copyright Time Inc. 1979.

154

PERSPECTIVE
The Triumph of Wrong

Robert Cahn

What went wrong? Why did winter's snail darter–Tellico Dam victory turn into fall's defeat? How did an issue that appeared permanently resolved in January get reversed?

Although some people, including President Carter, may rationalize that what happened is, in the long run, in the best interests of the nation and conservation, it may be that what was lost is far more important than what was gained.

In general, politicians and the press performed poorly in this matter. The performance of Congress was dismayingly shoddy, while the President sought political expediency instead of standing up for a matter of principle. The mass media failed to communicate the facts adequately and accurately to the American people.

When the issue was covered at all, it was played as the tiny, "worthless" fish against the big, important dam. National television news occasionally gave the issue thirty seconds or so, always from the fish-versus-dam angle. In six years, no large newspaper or national magazine sought to report fully the underlying issues—that the last unspoiled thirty-three miles of a large, clear-flowing river in Tennessee, the Little Tennessee, would be turned into an unneeded recreation lake; that the dam would add only a few megawatts of energy in an area that has no need for it; that the project was primarily a speculative real estate enterprise by the Tennessee Valley Authority; that it was an economic boondoggle from the start; that alternatives exist for providing economic development in the area without the dam; and that the snail darter will not necessarily survive because of transplant experiments.

Earlier in the year (see "Perspective" in *Audubon*, May 1979), it seemed to environmentalists that right had triumphed. A Cabinet-level committee had ruled the Tellico Dam project economically unjustified and had therefore refused to exempt it from provisions of the Endangered Species Act. The nearly finished dam was halted, the snail darter wrested from extinction, and a pristine valley saved from inundation.

Development interests, however, continued their efforts to use the snail darter to nullify the Endangered Species Act, and they were not sitting back and accepting defeat. As the May *Audubon* noted, "If our system does not allow for perception of the facts, and development forces use the snail darter as a caricature, then the law may be weakened even further. Unfortunately, rationality and the environmental ethic do not yet have the broad constituency they deserve."

Perhaps by looking at what happened we can learn some lessons for the future.

First off, Senator Howard Baker, acting more like a petulant child than a presidential candidate, sought to change the rules because he was losing the game. The Tennessee senator tried to scuttle his own creation, the Cabinet-level Endan-

Robert Cahn, "Perspective: The Triumph of Wrong," *Audubon*, November 1979, pp. 5, 8, 12. "Perspective: The Triumph of Wrong" by Robert Cahn is reprinted from *Audubon*. Copyright © 1979 The National Audubon Society. Used by permission.

gered Species Committee, which he had co-authored in legislation. Then, failing to get support, he introduced an amendment to exempt the Tellico Dam from provisions of the Endangered Species Act. He lost on the floor, 52–43.

On June 18th, in the House, John Duncan, the representative from the Tellico area, made his move. He chose a Monday afternoon when only a few congressmen were present, most of them Appropriations Committee members, there to take up routine committee appropriations in the multibillion-dollar energy and water development bill. Duncan had cooked up a scheme with some of his congressional colleagues. He knew that the minute he mentioned Tellico, someone would raise a point of order, because the House has a firm rule that forbids using an appropriations bill to change existing law.

Duncan nevertheless introduced an amendment which he had quietly placed in the hopper. During the clerk's reading of the amendment, Duncan stopped him as he was just about to state its substance. A minority member popped up by prearrangement to say that the minority had reviewed the amendment and accepted it.

Alabama Representative Tom Bevill, chairman of the Appropriations Subcommittee on Energy and Water Development, arose to say for the Democratic majority, "We have no objection." The chair called for a voice vote before the clerk could continue, and the amendment was agreed to. The whole process took forty-two seconds. The next morning, members of Congress read in the Congressional Record what had *not* been uttered on the floor—that the House had adopted an amendment directing TVA to complete construction of Tellico Dam and fill the reservoir, *notwithstanding* the Endangered Species Act and "all other laws"—clean air and water, dam safety,

labor, civil rights, or whatever laws would ordinarily apply in the building of a dam.

Later, some members, led by Louisiana's John Breaux and California's Paul (Pete) McCloskey, sought unsuccessfully to reverse the action. McCloskey, a Tellico Dam opponent who had been present when the amendment passed but had fallen victim to the trickery, told his fellow members in a floor speech that the process attacked the integrity of the House proceedings, and he warned them of "the danger of condemnation by the public if we adopt without reading an amendment of this degree of controversy."

After a bitter Senate debate pitting Baker against Iowa's Senator John Culver, the upper house voted 53–45 to have the objectionable House amendment removed. But the House, with many members needing Appropriations Committee approval for their own pet water projects, voted 258–156 to put the Tellico amendment back in. During floor debate, Duncan defended his earlier action, saying, "The House was full of people"; and Bevill stated baldly, "Three hundred members were sitting there." One impartial newsman sitting in the press gallery notes that there were between fifteen and twenty-five present at the time the Duncan amendment passed.

On September 10th, the Senate again took up the issue, after a good deal of Baker arm-twisting to change votes, countered by an intensive citizen environmental network on the other side. For some reason, Tellico was to Baker more than just a project to please the people back home. In debate, he claimed that the dam would be a great energy boon to the area, and that the snail darter was already successfully transplanted to other areas. He labeled the snail darter "an unfortunate symbol of environmental extremism."

Culver tried to present the facts: that this project would generate just 23 megawatts in a TVA power grid already producing 27,000 megawatts, and that, by TVA's own admission, the power is unneeded. Culver presented evidence that despite the claims of successful snail darter transplants the species is still endangered; that the transplants are experimental; that it will be years before it is known whether the transplants are successful; and that, as the Cabinet-level committee had determined, the project was economically unjustified. It would cost an additional $35 million to complete the dam and would cost annually $700,000 more than it would provide in benefits.

The debate before a sparsely occupied Senate chamber accomplished little for either side. The senators came from their offices to the floor for the vote without having listened to the debate, and, with one minute to go, Tellico opponents had a slight majority. But Baker went up and down the aisles, and in that last minute, six senators changed their votes. The dam advocates won, 48–44.

Unless the President vetoed the bill, all would be lost.

While the controversial Tellico amendment—a tiny part of a massive $10.6 billion energy and water appropriation—sat on the President's desk, environmental leaders laid their case before White House officials: The Tellico provision went against the President's policy and commitment to preserve the integrity of the Endangered Species Act and would open the door to similar actions. The blanket waiver of the Tellico Dam from all laws cuts deep into the heart of the legislative process and into the President's own water policy. The dam has been proved economically unsound and is not an energy issue. Flooding the Little Tennessee Valley, the original home of the Cherokee nation, would destroy historical and archeological resources, some of worldwide significance.

Sixteen thousand acres of prime farmland would be lost forever. Economically viable alternatives to the Tellico Dam are available in developing historical and recreational values of the Little Tennessee River Valley, and TVA has alternative plans for developing the area without the dam.

Environmentalists advocated that the President veto the bill and strongly assert his leadership with a message to Congress urging removal of the most objectionable parts. Meanwhile, the environmental groups promised to work diligently on Capitol Hill for votes to sustain the veto.

As the bill neared the signing deadline, a White House official passed the word to stop lobbying the President for a veto, and to start lobbying Congress to sustain a veto. So environmental lobbyists and a broad-based citizen coalition worked on House and Senate members.

Zygmunt Plater, the environmental law professor who has donated his time and legal efforts in leading the Tellico fight for six years, winning a Supreme Court case in the process, also worked night and day in Washington, meeting with House members and staffs. Toward the end of the ten-day presidential holding period, the head-by-head count showed a margin to sustain the veto in both chambers, although the President was being urged by a number of members to sign the bill.

Meantime, White House staffers were on the Hill looking for opportunities for the President to trade off the snail darter for votes on the Panama Canal, the Department of Education, and other issues coming up in Congress.

A few hours before the deadline, the President signed the bill without giving environmental leaders an opportunity to counter the advice he was getting from his staff.

It was a hard decision for the President to make, say his advisers. His heart said veto. But practical politics said sign. The same day, Representative Bevill had sneaked an identical Tellico rider past the House on a continued funding appropriation bill which the President would have had even greater difficulty vetoing. "Even if I vetoed this bill, Tellico exemptions would be proposed repeatedly in the future," Mr. Carter said in a statement released after he signed the bill. But as President, he said, he had to "balance many competing interests." And, he concluded, "I believe that avoiding a divisive veto battle will help focus congressional efforts on priority concerns."

The environmental community was shocked, disappointed, and angry. The President, they felt, had traded off the environment for the promise of congressional support on issues he considers of higher priority.

Brock Evans, director of the Sierra Club's Washington office, commented at a press conference: "The President has sent a clear message to anybody who worries about laws that stand in the way of the pork-barrel project: Don't worry about my views on it . . . I really won't veto it. All you have to do is talk to the chairman of the House Appropriations Subcommittee on Energy and Water Development. If you can fix it up with him, you can overturn any law on the book."

Evans' remark no doubt was colored by anger and frustration. Yet defeat on such a permanent matter as obliterating a species and its habitat is hard to take. We do not know at present whether the snail darter has some unique contribution to make in nature's interrelated scheme of things. And we may never find out. The snail darter is important for itself. But it also is important as an indicator of the habitats and values we should preserve. It is perhaps like the canaries the coal miners used to carry when working underground where lethal gases might be present—if the bird expires you'd better get out.

While it appears that the snail darter may be lost forever unless the experimental transplant succeeds in other rivers, and the Little Tennessee River Valley seems doomed to become a large lake, the fight to preserve the valley is being continued by the Cherokee Indians. Last month they went to court to block completion of the dam and flooding of the valley. The lake would destroy their sacred city of Echota, plus ten other major town sites and cemeteries the Cherokees claim, and thus violates their constitutional and other statutory rights.

More than a half-century ago, because of a congressional decision, conservationists lost a multi-year battle to stop the first dam's being built within a national park (Hetch Hetchy Dam in Yosemite). But a lesson was learned. No dam has been built since within any national park. Perhaps we can learn a similar lesson from the snail darter. Perhaps this will be the last time (as well as the first) that we consciously sacrifice a species or a habitat for political reasons.

THE PRICE OF TELLICO

Peter Matthiessen

In the late nineteenth century, a remnant band of Cherokees—descendants of those who had hidden in the Great Smokies in 1838 when the rest of the tribe was "removed" to Oklahoma—came down from the North Carolina mountains to a ceremonial place overlooking the valley of the Little Tennessee River. There, an old prophet, climbing onto a high stump and gazing out over the traditional home of the Cherokee people, received a vision of a dreadful day still several generations in the future when this valley would be flooded over, and the faces of countless buried ancestors would glimmer upward through the unnatural waters as through a floor of glass. Tearful and frightened, the old man told his people that when the river no longer ran free through the sacred valley, the Cherokee would be destroyed forever as a tribe.

The recent closing of TVA's Tellico Dam at the river's mouth has not only fulfilled this prophecy but affirms an older one that anticipates the white man's disruption of the earth's natural harmonies, with calamitous consequences for mankind. Although the project had been repudiated for a decade in the Congress and the courts as uneconomical, unlawful and unnecessary, it has now achieved through procedural tricks and political blackmail what it had never been able to win in a fair hearing.

The last stretch of free-flowing river in northeast Tennessee has now been stopped up like a clogged pork barrel, and under the mud of the 25th artificial lake within 60 miles will lie not only the last natural spawning beds of the small, pretty perch called the snail darter, but the hard-won homesteads of hundreds of evicted families, 16,000 acres of rich river-bottom farmland and a historical record perhaps as important as all these other losses put together.

Loss

I wish there had been time for all Americans to see this lovely valley, which I visited myself just a few weeks ago. In the soft, sad light of early November, the golden sassafras and yellow hickory, with the reds of black oak, tupelo and dogwood, and the clear whites and mossy greens of the rock walls at the river bends, were reflected like a memory in the clear, swift, quiet water that came down from the mountains; the day was filled with earth smells, muted beauties and a wistful resonance that echoed in the autumn calls of birds. "You don't have to be a Cherokee to feel the spiritual power here," murmured Roy Warren, an amateur archeologist and trout fisherman who fought hard against the loss of "the Little T."

From where we stood, just upriver from the Tellico stream (in Cherokee, *ade la eqwa* or "tellico" means "big money") near the site of the first British fort built west of the Appalachians, we could see the tattered cornfield that marked the buried village of Tuskegee, birthplace of Sequoyah, the great Cherokee teacher whose name has been commemorated by a national park as well as a mighty tree.

Farther upriver, Warren pointed out the

Peter Matthiessen, "The Price of Tellico," *Newsweek*, 17 Dec. 1979, p. 21. Copyright 1979, by Newsweek, Inc. All Rights Reserved. Reprinted by Permission.

sites of six other villages, including Tanasi (the original "Tennessee") and Chota, the last great sacred center of the Cherokee nation. In the eighteenth century, this tribe protected the beleaguered colonists of Virginia and Carolina from French-led Indians to westward, and sent warriors to help George Washington in the Big Sandy Expedition against the Shawnee. In 1814, the Cherokee set Andrew Jackson on the road to the White House by turning the tide in the battle of Horseshoe Bend against the Creeks, an act of friendship soon to be repaid by banishment on the "Trail of Tears" to Oklahoma.

Throughout the valley, the buried evidence of a great period—some of the hundreds of sites were thought to be more than 8,000 years old—was scarcely touched, despite the crude and hasty digs, grave desecration and plain looting that the threat of flooding had inspired. A report prepared for the TVA by Department of Interior archeologists (dated May 24, 1979, but mysteriously withheld until after the final Tellico appropriations were signed into law by President Carter on Sept. 25) ascribes "worldwide significance" to these sites, declaring that "the physical records of American prehistory present in Tellico cannot be matched in any other area this size in the continent."

"If the homeland of our fathers is covered with this water," said an 80-year-old medicine man named Lloyd Sequoyah, "it will cover the medicine and spiritual strength of our people because this is the place from which the Cherokee people came. When this place is destroyed, the Cherokee people cease to exist . . . then all the peoples of the earth cease to exist." His sister, Mrs. Emmaline Driver, had made a pilgrimage to the place where the old seer "made his last prophecy" upon the stump; his brother Ammoneeta, also a medicine man, lived in an abandoned cabin at Chota for five years and still made regular journeys there to perform the going-to-water purification, gather medicinal herbs and chant *idi-gawe-sti*, or sacred incantations.

Heritage

All three of these great-great-great-grandchildren of Sequoyah are full-blood Cherokees proficient in their language; so is Myrtle Driver, the young tribal interpreter of Big Cove, N.C., who introduced me to her elders. Not until these years of struggle to save the sacred valley, Myrtle said, had she realized how much her heritage still meant to her. In the words of Jimmie Durham, one of many Cherokees who had spoken publicly against the dam since 1965, "Is there a human being who does not revere his homeland, even though he may not return? . . . In our own history, we teach that we were created there, which is truer than anthropological truth because it was there that we were given our vision as the Cherokee people."

In 1967, the eastern Cherokee began protesting the backhoeing and bulldozing of sacred sites and ancestral graves. For Indians, the most dangerous sacrilege is to disturb the spirits of the dead. It will take some weeks before the flood waters reach the sacred land, and the Cherokee still carry on their fight for a hearing of their claim that the destruction of their sacred ground would deny religious rights guaranteed them under the First Amendment.

But the Tellico is a transgression against all of us. If the valley is filled, let them drain it again; let the dam stand as a monument, not to short-sightedness and greed, but to the wise avoidance of a national calamity. A beautiful river can be restored, rich farmland and historic sites can be recovered.

Eventually, the courts must grant a hearing, but in the absence of an injunction, the TVA has closed its dam and thereby transformed the "strong water" of the sacred river into *ama huli wotshi* or "dead water," the floor of glass of the old prophecy through which—perhaps in a matter of weeks—the faces of the ances-tors will appear, like pale dead leaves seen dimly through black ice.

Matthiessen's *The Snow Leopard* won a National Book Award this year.

Public Law 93-205—Dec. 28, 1973

AN ACT

December 28, 1973
[S. 1983]

To provide for the conservation of endangered and threatened
species of fish, wildlife, and plants, and for other purposes.

Be it enacted by the Senate and House of Representatives of the United
Endangered
Species Act of
1973. *States of America in Congress assembled.* That this Act may be cited as the
"Endangered Species Act of 1973".

TABLE OF CONTENTS

FINDINGS, PURPOSES, AND POLICY

SEC. 2. (a) FINDINGS.—The Congress finds and declares that—
(1) various species of fish, wildlife, and plants in the United States
have been rendered extinct as a consequence of economic growth and
development untempered by adequate concern and conservation;
(2) other species of fish, wildlife, and plants have been so depleted
in numbers that they are in danger of or threatened with extinction;
(3) these species of fish, wildlife, and plants are of esthetic, ecological, educational, historical, recreational, and scientific value to the
Nation and its people;
(4) the United States has pledged itself as a sovereign state in the
international community to conserve to the extent practicable the various species of fish or wildlife and plants facing extinction, pursuant
to—

Excerpts from Public Law 93-205, Dec. 28, 1973.

(A) migratory bird treaties with Canada and Mexico;

(B) the Migratory and Endangered Bird Treaty with Japan;

6 Stat. 1354.

(C) the Convention on Nature Protection and Wildlife Preservation in the Western Hemisphere;

1 UST 477.

(D) the International Convention for the Northwest Atlantic Fisheries;

4 UST 380.

(E) the International Convention for the High Seas Fisheries of the North Pacific Ocean;

(F) the Convention on International Trade in Endangered Species of Wild Fauna and Flora; and

(G) other international agreements.

(5) encouraging the States and other interested parties, through Federal financial assistance and a system of incentives, to develop and maintain conservation programs which meet national and international standards is a key to meeting the Nation's international commitments and to better safeguarding, for the benefit of all citizens, the Nation's heritage in fish and wildlife.

(b) PURPOSES.—The purposes of this Act are to provide a means whereby the ecosystems upon which endangered species and threatened species depend may be conserved, to provide a program for the conservation of such endangered species and threatened species, and to take such steps as may be appropriate to achieve the purposes of the treaties and conventions set forth in subsection (a) of this section.

(c) POLICY.—It is further declared to be the policy of Congress that all Federal departments and agencies shall seek to conserve endangered species and threatened species and shall utilize their authorities in furtherance of the purposes of this Act.

DEFINITIONS

SEC. 3. For the purposes of this Act—

(1) The term "commercial activity" means all activities of industry and trade, including, but not limited to, the buying or selling of commodities and activities conducted for the purpose of facilitating such buying and selling.

(2) The terms "conserve", "conserving", and "conservation" mean to use and the use of all methods and procedures which are necessary to bring any endangered species or threatened species to the point at which the measures provided pursuant to this Act are no longer necessary. Such methods and procedures include, but are not limited to, all activities associated with scientific resources management such as research, census, law enforcement, habitat acquisition and maintenance, propagation, live trapping, and transplantation, and, in the extraordinary case where population pressures within a given ecosystem cannot be otherwise relieved, may include regulated taking.

(3) The term "Convention" means the Convention on International

Trade in Endangered Species of Wild Fauna and Flora, signed on March 3, 1973, and the appendices thereto.

(4) The term "endangered species" means any species which is in danger of extinction throughout all or a significant portion of its range· other than a species of the Class Insecta determined by the Secretary to constitute a pest whose protection under the provisions of this Act would present an overwhelming and overriding risk to man.

(5) The term "fish or wildlife" means any member of the animal kingdom, including without limitation any mammal, fish, bird (including any migratory, nonmigratory, or endangered bird for which protection is also afforded by treaty or other international agreement), amphibian, reptile, mollusk, crustacean, arthropod or other invertebrate, and includes any part, product, egg, or offspring thereof, or the dead body or parts thereof. . . .

DETERMINATION OF ENDANGERED SPECIES
AND THREATENED SPECIES

SEC. 4. (a) GENERAL.—(1) The Secretary shall by regulation determine whether any species is an endangered species or a threatened species because of any of the following factors:

(1) the present or threatened destruction, modification, or curtailment of its habitat or range;

(2) overutilization for commercial, sporting, scientific, or educational purposes;

(3) disease or predation;

(4) the inadequacy of existing regulatory mechanisms; or

(5) other natural or manmade factors affecting its continued existence.

(2) With respect to any species over which program responsibilities have been vested in the Secretary of Commerce pursuant to Reorganization Plan Numbered 4 of 1970—

(A) in any case in which the Secretary of Commerce determines that such species should—

(i) be listed as an endangered species or a threatened species, or

(ii) be changed in status from a threatened species to an endangered species,

he shall so inform the Secretary of the Interior, who shall list such species in accordance with this section;

(B) in any case in which the Secretary of Commerce determines that such species should—

(i) be removed from any list published pursuant to subsection (c) of this section, or

(ii) be changed in status from an endangered species to a threatened species,

he shall recommend such action to the Secretary of the Interior, and the Secretary of the Interior, if he concurs in the recommendation, shall implement such action; and

(C) the Secretary of the Interior may not list or remove from any list any such species, and may not change the status of any such species which are listed, without a prior favorable determination made pursuant to this section by the Secretary of Commerce. . . .

INTERAGENCY COOPERATION

SEC. 7. The Secretary shall review other programs administered by him and utilize such programs in furtherance of the purposes of this Act. All other Federal departments and agencies shall, in consultation with and with the assistance of the Secretary, utilize their authorities in furtherance of the purposes of this Act by carrying out programs for the conservation of endangered species and threatened species listed pursuant to section 4 of this Act and by taking such action necessary to insure that actions authorized, funded, or carried out by them do not jeopardize the continued existence of such endangered species and threatened species or result in the destruction or modification of habitat of such species which is determined by the Secretary, after consultation as appropriate with the affected States, to be critical. . . .

Public Law 95-632
Approved 11/10/78; S. 2899.

Endangered Species Act Amendments—Amends the Endangered Species Act of 1973 to set forth procedures to be followed by the Secretary of the Interior and other Federal agencies in reviewing agency actions to assure that such actions do not jeopardize the continued existence of endangered or threatened species or result in the destruction or adverse modification of critical habitat. Establishes a procedure for the application for the review of an exemption from the prohibition against agency actions which jeopardize endangered or threatened species or critical habitat.

Provides that upon receipt of an application for such exemption the Secretary of the Interior shall notify the Governor of each State affected and request the Governors to recommend individuals to be appointed to a review board established pursuant to this Act, which will initially consider such applications and to the Endangered Species Committee, established by this Act, which shall review such applications if the review board determines that an irresolvable conflict exists. Defines "irresolvable conflict" as a situation in which the completion of agency action would jeopardize the continued existence of an endangered or threatened species or harm critical habitat.

States that a review board shall consist of three members: (1) one appointed by the Secretary; (2) one appointed by the President after consideration of any recommendations received from Governors of affected States; and (3) an administrative law judge. Stipulates that any determination by such board that an irresolvable conflict does not exist or that the applicant has not carried out specified responsibilities shall be considered final agency action. Stipulates that if the board determines that an irresolvable conflict does exist the board shall submit to the Committee a report containing specified information.

States that the Committee shall be composed of seven members: (1) the Secretary of Agriculture; (2) the Secretary of the Army; (3) the Chairman of the Council of Economic Advisors; (4) the Administrator of the Environmental Protection Agency; (5) the Secretary of the Interior; (6) the Administrator of the National Oceanic and Atmospheric Administration; and (7) an individual appointed by the President upon the recommendation of the Governors of the States to be affected by the exemption.

Authorizes the Committee to grant an exemption if: (1) there are no reasonable and prudent alternatives to the agency action; (2) the benefits of such action clearly outweigh the benefits of alternative courses of action consistent with conserving the species or its critical habitat, and such action is in the public interest; (3) the action is of regional or national significance; and (4) it establishes reasonable mitigation and enhancement

Public Law 95-632, Nov. 10, 1978. *Digest of Public General Bills and Resolutions,* Congressional Research Services, Library of Congress.

measures as necessary to mitigate the adverse effects of the agency action upon the endangered species, threatened species, or critical habitat concerned.

Prohibits the Committee from granting an exemption if the Secretary of State has determined the proposed agency action to be in violation of any international obligation.

States that an exemption shall not be considered a major Federal action for purposes of the National Environmental Policy Act of 1969.

Sets forth the procedure for judicial review of Committee decisions.

Declares that the President may grant exceptions to the requirements of the Act in major disaster areas.

Makes provisions for raptors held legally in captivity or in a controlled environment on the effective date of this Act.

Exempts certain imported antique articles from certain restrictions of the Act relating to possession and dealing in endangered species. Directs the Secretary of the Treasury, after consultation with the Secretary of the Interior, to designate one port within each customs region where such antique articles must enter the United States. Declares that any person who forfeited such imported antique articles to the United States before the enactment of this Act may, before the close of a one year period after enactment, make application to the Secretary of Interior for return of the article.

Directs the Committee, within 30 days after the enactment of this Act, to consider the exemption of the Tellico and Greyrocks Projects from the requirements of this Act.

Requires that for the imposition of a civil penalty for violation of the Act, the offense must have been committed knowingly and provides that a person acting in self-defense shall not have any penalty imposed.

Authorizes appropriations necessary to carry out the purposes of this Act.

Authorizes the Secretary of the Interior to enter into cooperative agreements with any State in the implementation of programs for the conservation of endangered and threatened species.

Revises the procedures to be followed by the Secretary of the Interior in issuing regulations under the Endangered Species Act of 1973 and directs the Secretary to review the endangered species list at least once every five years and to publish, in the Federal register, any final regulation which adds a species to the endangered list, not later than two years after the date of the regulations.

Requires the Secretary of the Interior to develop and implement plans for the conservation and survival of endangered and threatened species.

Directs the Secretary in determining the critical habitat of any endangered or threatened species to consider the economic impact of specifying an area as a critical habitat. Authorizes the Secretary to exclude such area from the critical habitat if it is determined that the benefits of exclusion outweigh the benefits of specifying the area as part of a critical habitat, unless it is determined that failure to designate such area as a critical habitat will result in the extinction of the species.

TENNESSEE VALLEY AUTHORITY, PETITIONER, v. HIRAM G. HILL, JR., ET AL.

On Writ of Certiorari to the United States Court of Appeals for the Sixth Circuit.

[June 15, 1978]

Syllabus

The Endangered Species Act of 1973 (Act) authorizes the Secretary of the Interior (Secretary) in § 4 to declare a species of life "endangered." Section 7 specifies that all "Federal departments and agencies shall, . . . with the assistance of the Secretary, utilize their authorities in furtherance of the purposes of [the] Act by carrying out programs for the conservation of endangered species . . . and by taking such action necessary to insure that actions authorized, funded, or carried out by them do not jeopardize the continued existence of such endangered species or result in the destruction or modification of habitat of such species which is determined by the Secretary . . . to be critical." Shortly after the Act's passage the Secretary was petitioned to list a small fish popularly known as the snail darter as an endangered species under the Act. Thereafter the Secretary made the designation. Having determined that the snail darter apparently lives only in that portion of the Little Tennessee River that would be completely inundated by the impoundment of the reservoir created as a consequence of the completion of the Tellico Dam, he declared that area as the snail darter's "critical habitat." Notwithstanding the near completion of the multimillion-dollar dam, the Secretary issued a regulation, in which it was declared that, pursuant to § 7, "all Federal agencies must take such action as is necessary to ensure that actions authorized, funded, or carried out by them do not result in the destruction or modification of this critical habitat area." Respondents brought this suit to enjoin completion of the dam and impoundment of the reservoir, claiming that those actions would violate the Act by causing the snail darter's extinction. The District Court after trial denied relief and dismissed the complaint. Though finding that the impoundment of the reservoir would probably jeopardize the snail darter's continued existence, the court noted that Congress, though fully aware of the snail darter problem, had continued Tellico's appropriations, and concluded that "[a]t some point in time a federal project becomes so near completion and so incapable of modification that a court of equity should not apply a statute enacted long after inception to produce an unreasonable result. . . ." The Court of Appeals reversed the District Court's judgment

Excerpts from "Tennessee Valley Authority v. Hiram G. Hill, Jr." *The United States Law Week*, Supreme Court Opinions, 46 (1978), 4673–89. Reprinted by special permission from *The United States Law Week*, copyright 1978 by The Bureau of National Affairs, Inc., Washington D.C.

and permanently enjoined completion of the project "until Congress, by appropriate legislation, exempts Tellico from compliance with the Act or the snail darter has been deleted from the list of endangered species or its critical habitat materially redefined." The court held that the record revealed a prima facie violation of § 7 in that TVA had failed to take necessary action to avoid jeopardizing the snail darter's critical habitat by its "actions." The court thus rejected the contention that the word "actions" as used in § 7 was not intended by Congress to encompass the terminal phases of ongoing projects. At various times before, during, and after the foregoing judicial proceedings, TVA represented to congressional appropriations committees that the Act did not prohibit completion of the Tellico Project and described its efforts to transplant the snail darter. The committees consistently recommended appropriations for the dam, sometimes stating their views that the Act did not prohibit completion of the dam at its advanced stage, and Congress each time approved TVA's general budget, which contained funds for the dam's continued construction. *Held:*

1. The Endangered Species Act prohibits impoundment of the Little Tennessee River by the Tellico Dam.

(a) The language of § 7 is plain and makes no exception such as that urged by petitioner whereby the Act would not apply to a project like Tellico that was well under way when Congress passed the Act.

(b) It is clear from the Act's legislative history that Congress intended to halt and reverse the trend toward species extinction—whatever the cost. The pointed omission of the type of qualified language previously included in endangered species legislation reveals a conscious congressional design to give endangered species priority over the "primary missions" of federal agencies. Congress, moreover, foresaw that § 7 would on occasion require agencies to alter ongoing projects in order to fulfill the Act's goals.

(c) None of the limited "hardship exemptions" provided in the Act would even remotely apply to the Tellico Project.

(d) Though statements in appropriations committee reports reflected the view of the committees either that the Act did not apply to Tellico or that the dam should be completed regardless of the Act's provisions, nothing in the TVA appropriations measures passed by Congress stated that the Tellico Project was to be completed regardless of the Act's requirements. To find a repeal under these circumstances, as petitioner has urged, would violate the "cardinal rule ... that repeals by implication are not favored." *Morton* v. *Mancusi*, 417 U. S. 535, 549.

2. The Court of Appeals did not err in enjoining completion of the Tellico Dam, which would have violated the Act. Congress has spoken in the plainest words, making it clear that endangered species are to be accorded the highest priorities. Since that legislative power has been exercised, it is up to the Executive Branch to administer the law and for the judiciary to enforce it when, as here, enforcement has been sought.

549 F. 2d 1064, affirmed.

Burger, C. J., delivered the opinion of the Court, in which Brennan, Steward, White, Marshall, and Stevens, JJ., joined. Powell, J., filed a dissenting opinion, in which Blackmun, J., joined. Rehnquist, J., filed a dissenting opinion.

Mr. Chief Justice Burger delivered the opinion of the Court.

The questions presented in this case are (a) whether the Endangered Species Act of 1973 requires a court to enjoin the operation of a virtually completed federal dam—which had been authorized prior to 1973—when, pursuant to authority vested in him by Congress, the Secretary of the Interior has determined that operation of the dam would eradicate an endangered species; and (b) whether continued congressional appropriations for the dam after 1973 constituted an implied repeal of the Endangered Species Act, at least as to the particular dam.

I

The Little Tennessee River originates in the mountains of northern Georgia and flows through the national forest lands of North Carolina into Tennessee, where it converges with the Big Tennessee River near Knoxville. The lower 33 miles of the Little Tennessee takes the river's clear, free-flowing waters through an area of great natural beauty. Among other environmental amenities, this stretch of river is said to contain abundant trout. Considerable historical importance attaches to the areas immediately adjacent to this portion of the Little Tennessee's banks. To the south of the river's edge lies Fort Loudon, established in 1756 as England's southwestern outpost in the French and Indian War. Nearby are also the ancient sites of several native American villages, the archeological stores of which are to a large extent unexplored.[1] These include the Cherokee towns of Echota and Tennase, the former being the sacred capital of the Cherokee Nation as early as the 16th century and the latter providing the linguistic basis from which the State of Tennessee derives its name.[2]

In this area of the Little Tennessee River the Tennessee Valley Authority, a wholly owned public corporation of the United States, began constructing the Tellico Dam and Reservoir Project in 1967, shortly after Congress appropriated initial funds for its development.[3] Tellico is a multipurpose regional development project designed principally to stimulate shoreline development, generate sufficient electric current to heat 20,000 homes,[4] provide flatwater recreation and flood control, as well as improve economic conditions in "an area characterized by underutilization of human resources and outmigration of young people." Hearings before a Subcommittee of the House Committee on Appropriations, 94th Cong., 2d Sess., at 261. Of particular relevance to this case is one aspect of the project, a dam which TVA determined to place on the Little Tennessee, a short distance from where the river's waters meet with the Big Tennessee. When fully operational, the dam would impound water covering some 16,500 acres—much of which represents valuable and productive farmland—

thereby converting the river's shallow, fast-flowing waters into a deep reservoir over 30 miles in length.

The Tellico Dam has never opened, however, despite the fact that construction has been virtually completed and the dam is essentially ready for operation. Although Congress has appropriated monies for Tellico every year since 1967, progress was delayed, and ultimately stopped, by a tangle of lawsuits and administrative proceedings. After unsuccessfully urging TVA to consider alternatives to damming the Little Tennessee, local citizens and national conservation groups brought suit in the District Court, claiming that the project did not conform to the requirements of the National Environmental Policy Act of 1969 (NEPA), 42 U. S. C. § 4331 *et seq.* After finding TVA to be in violation of NEPA, the District Court enjoined the dam's completion pending the filing of an appropriate Environmental Impact Statement. *Environmental Defense Fund* v. *Tennessee Valley Authority*, 339 F. Supp. 806 (ED Tenn. 1972), aff'd, 468 F. 2d 1164 (CA6 1972). The injunction remained in effect until late 1973, when the District Court concluded that TVA's final Environmental Impact Statement for Tellico was in compliance with the law. *Environmental Defense Fund* v. *Tennessee Valley Authority*, 371 F. Supp. 1004 (ED Tenn. 1973), aff'd, 492 F. 2d 466 (CA6 1974).[5]

A few months prior to the District Court's decision dissolving the NEPA injunction, a discovery was made in the waters of the Little Tennessee which would profoundly affect the Tellico Project. Exploring the area around Coytee Springs, which is about seven miles from the mouth of the river, a University of Tennessee ichthyologist, Dr. David A. Etnier, found a previously unknown species of perch, the snail darter, or *Percina Imostoma tanasi*.[6] This three-inch, tannish-colored fish, whose numbers are estimated to be in the range of 10,000 to 15,000, would soon engage the attention of environmentalists, the TVA, the Department of the Interior, the Congress of the United States, and ultimately the federal courts, as a new and additional basis to halt construction of the dam.

Until recently the finding of a new species of animal life would hardly generate a cause celebre. This is particularly so in the case of darters, of which there are approximately 130 known species, eight to 10 of these having been identified only in the last five years.[7] The moving force behind the snail darter's sudden fame came some four months after its discovery, when the Congress passed the Endangered Species Act of 1973, 87 Stat. 884, 16 U. S. C. 1531 *et seq.* 1976 ("Act"). This legislation, among other things, authorizes the Secretary of the Interior to declare species of animal life "endangered"[8] and to identify the "critical habitat"[9] of these creatures. When a species or its habitat is so listed, the following portion of the Act—relevant here—becomes effective:

"The Secretary [of the Interior] shall review other programs administered by him and utilize such programs in furtherance of the purposes of this Act. All other Federal departments and agencies shall, in consultation with and with the assistance of the Secretary, utilize their authorities in furtherance of the purposes of this Act by carrying out programs for the conservation of endangered species and threatened species listed pursuant to section 4 of this Act and *by taking such action necessary to insure that actions authorized, funded, or carried out by them do not jeopardize the continued existence of such endangered species and threatened species or result in the destruction or modification of habitat of such species* which is determined by the Secretary, after consultation as appropriate with the affected States, to be critical." 16 U. S. C. § 1536 (emphasis added).

In January 1975, the respondents in this case[10] and others petitioned the Secretary of the Interior[11] to list the snail darter as an endangered species. After receiving comments from various interested parties, including TVA and the State of Tennessee, the Secretary formally listed the snail darter as an endangered species on November 10, 1975. 40 Fed. Reg. 47505–47506; see 50 CFR § 17.11 (i). In so acting, it was noted that "the snail darter is a living entity which is genetically distinct and reproductively isolated from other species." 40 Fed. Reg., at 47505. More important for the purposes of this case, the Secretary determined that the snail darter apparently lives only in that portion of the Little Tennessee River which would be completely inundated by the reservoir created as a consequence of the Tellico Dam's completion. *Id.*, at 47506.[12] The Secretary went on to explain the significance of the dam to the habitat of the snail darter:

> "[T]he snail darter occurs only in the swifter portions of shoals over clean gravel substrate in cool, low-turbidity water. Food of the snail darter is almost exclusively snails which require a clean gravel substrate for their survival. *The proposed impoundment of water behind the proposed Tellico Dam would result in total destruction of the snail darter's habitat.*" *Ibid.* (emphasis added).

Subsequent to this determination, the Secretary declared the area of the Little Tennessee which would be affected by the Tellico Dam to be the "critical habitat" of the snail darter. 41 Fed. Reg. 13926–13928; see 50 CFR § 17.81. Using these determinations as a predicate, and notwithstanding the near completion of the dam, the Secretary declared that pursuant to § 7 of the Act, "all Federal agencies must take such action as is necessary to insure that actions authorized, funded, or carried out by them do not result in the destruction or modification of this critical habitat area." 41 Fed. Reg., at 13928; 50 CFR, at § 17.81 (b). This notice, of course, was pointedly directed at TVA and clearly aimed at halting completion or operation of the dam. . . .

II

We begin with the premise that operation of the Tellico Dam will either eradicate the known population of snail darters or destroy their critical habitat. Petitioner does not now seriously dispute this fact.[17] In any event, under § 4 (a) (1) of the Act, 16 U. S. C. § 1533 (d), the Secretary of the Interior is vested with exclusive authority to determine whether a species such as the snail darter is "endangered" or "threatened" and to ascertain the factors which have led to such a precarious existence. By § 4 (d) Congress has authorized—indeed commanded—the Secretary to "issue such regulations as he deems necessary and advisable to provide for the conservation of such species." 16 U. S. C. § 1533 (d). As we have seen, the Secretary promulgated regulations which declared the snail darter an endangered species whose critical habitat would be destroyed by creation of the Tellico Reservoir. Doubtless petitioner would prefer not to have these regulations on the books, but there is no suggestion that the Secretary exceeded his authority or abused his discretion in issuing the regulations. Indeed, no judicial review of the Secretary's determinations has ever been sought and hence the validity of his actions are not open to review in this Court.

Starting from the above premise, two questions are presented: (a) would TVA be in violation of the Act if it completed and operated the Tellico Dam as planned?; (b) if TVA's actions would offend the Act, is an injunction the appropriate remedy for the violation? For the reasons stated hereinafter, we hold that both questions must be answered in the affirmative.

(A)

It may seem curious to some that the survival of a relatively small number of three-inch fish among all the countless millions of species extant would require the permanent halting of a virtually completed dam for which Congress has expended more than $100 million. The paradox is not minimized by the fact that Congress continued to appropriate large sums of public money for the project, even after congressional appropriations committees were apprised of its apparent impact upon the survival of the snail darter. We conclude, however, that the explicit provisions of the Endangered Species Act require precisely that result.

One would be hard pressed to find a statutory provision whose terms were any plainer than those in § 7 of the Endangered Species Act. Its very words affirmatively command all federal agencies "to *insure* that actions *authorized, funded,* or *carried out* by them do not *jeopardize* the continued existence" of an endangered species or "*result* in the destruction or modification of habitat of such species. . . ." 16 U. S. C. § 1536. (Emphasis added.) This language admits of no exception. Nonetheless, petitioner urges, as do the dissenters, that the Act cannot reasonably be interpreted as applying to a federal project which was well under way when Congress passed the Endangered Species Act of 1973. To sustain that position, however, we would be forced to ignore the ordinary meaning of plain language. It has not been shown, for example, how TVA can close the gates of the Tellico Dam without "carrying out" an action that has been "authorized" and "funded" by a federal agency. Nor can we understand how such action will "*insure*" that the snail darter's habitat is not disrupted.[18] Accepting the Secretary's determinations, as we must, it is clear that TVA's proposed operation of the dam will have precisely the opposite effect, namely the *eradication* of an endangered species.

Concededly, this view of the Act will produce results requiring the sacrifice of the anticipated benefits of the project and of many millions of dollars in public funds.[19] But examination of the language, history and structure of the legislation under review here indicates beyond doubt that Congress intended endangered species to be afforded the highest of priorities.

When Congress passed the Act in 1973, it was not legislating on a clean slate. The first major congressional concern for the preservation of the endangered species had come with passage of the Endangered Species Act of 1966, 80 Stat. 926, repealed 87 Stat. 903 (1973).[20] In that legislation Congress gave the Secretary power to identify "the names of the species of native fish and wildlife found to be threatened with extinction," § 1 (c), 80 Stat. 926, as well as authorization to purchase land for the conservation, protection, restoration, and propagation of "selected species" of "native fish and wildlife" threatened with extinction. § 2 (a)–(c), 80 Stat. 926–927 (1966). Declaring the preservation of endangered species a national policy, the 1966 Act directed all federal agencies both to protect these species and *"insofar as is practicable and consistent with the[ir] primary purposes,"* § 1 (b), 80 Stat. 926 (1966), "preserve the habitats of such threatened species on lands under their jurisdiction." *Ibid.* (Emphasis added.) The 1966 statute was not a sweeping prohibition on the taking of endangered species, however, except on federal lands, § 4 (c), 80 Stat. 938 (1966), and even in those federal areas the Secretary was authorized to allow the hunting and fishing of endangered species. § 4 (d) (1), 80 Stat. 928 (1966).

In 1969 Congress enacted the Endangered Species Conservation Act, 83 Stat. 275 (1966), repealed 87 Stat. 903 (1973), which continued the provisions of the 1966 Act while at the same time broadening federal involvement in the preservation of endangered species. Under the 1969 legislation, the Secretary was empowered to list species "threatened with world-wide extinction," § 3 (a), 83 Stat. 275 (1969); in addition, the importation of any species so recognized into the United States was prohibited. § 2, 83 Stat. 275 (1969). An indirect approach to the taking of endangered species was also adopted in the Conservation Act by way of a ban on the transportation and sale of wildlife taken in violation of any federal, state, or foreign law. Section 7 (a)–(b), 83 Stat. 279 (1966).[21]

Despite the fact that the 1966 and 1969 legislation represented "the most comprehensive of its type to be enacted by any nation"[22] up to that time, Congress was soon persuaded that a more expansive approach was needed if the newly declared national policy of preserving endangered species was to be realized. By 1973, when Congress held hearings on what would later become of the Endangered Species Act of 1973, it was informed that species were still being lost at the rate of about one per year, 1973 House Hearings, at 306 (statement of Stephen R. Seater, for Defenders of Wildlife), and "the pace of disappearance of species" appeared to be "accelerating." H. R. Rep. No. 93–412, 93d Cong., 1st Sess., 4 (1973). Moreover, Congress was also told that the primary cause of this trend was something other than the normal process of natural selection:

"[M]an and his technology has [sic] continued at any ever-increasing rate to disrupt the natural ecosystem. This has resulted in a dramatic rise in the number and severity of the threats faced by the world's wildlife. The truth in this is apparent when one realizes that half of the recorded extinctions of mammals over the past 2,000 years have occurred in the most recent 50-year period." 1973 House Hearings, 202 (statement of Asst. Secy. of Interior).

That Congress did not view these developments lightly was stressed by one commentator:

"The dominant theme pervading all Congressional discussion of the proposed [Endangered Species Act of 1973] was the overriding need *to devote whatever effort and resources were necessary* to avoid further diminution of national and worldwide wildlife resources. Much of the testimony at the hearings and much debate was devoted to the biological problem of extinction. Senators and Congressmen uniformly deplored the irreplaceable loss to aesthetics, science, ecology, and the national heritage should more species disappear." Coggins, Conserving Wildlife Resources: An Overview of the Endangered Species Act of 1973, 51 N. D. L. Rev. 315, 321 (1974). (Emphasis added.)

The legislative proceedings in 1973 are, in fact, replete with expressions of concern over the risk that might lie in the loss of *any* endangered species.[23] Typifying these sentiments is the report of the House Committee on Merchant Marine and Fisheries on H. R. 37, a bill which contained the essential features of the subsequently enacted Act of 1973; in explaining the need for the legislation, the report stated:

"As we homogenize the habitats in which these plants and animals evolved, and as we increase the pressure for products that they are in a position to supply (usually unwillingly) we threaten their—and our own—genetic heritage.
"*The value of this genetic heritage is, quite literally, incalculable.*

. . . . .

"From the most narrow possible point of view, *it is in the best interests of mankind to minimize the losses of genetic variations.* The reason is simple: they are potential resources. They are keys to puzzles which we cannot solve, and may provide answers to questions which we have not yet learned to ask.
"To take a homely, but apt, example: one of the critical chemicals in the regulation of ovulations in humans was found in a common plant. Once discovered, and analyzed, humans could duplicate it synthetically, but had it never existed—or had it been driven out of existence before we knew its potentialities—we would never have tried to synthesize it in the first place.
"Who knows, or can say, what potential cures for cancer or other scourges, present or future, may lie locked up in the structures of plants which may yet be undiscovered, much less analyzed? . . . Sheer self-interest impels us to be cautious.
"*The institutionalization of that caution* lies at the heart of H. R. 37. . . ." H. R. Rep. No. 93–412, 93d Cong., 1st Sess., 4–5 (1973). (Emphasis added.)

As the examples cited here demonstrate, Congress was concerned about the *unknown* uses that endangered species might have and about the *un-*

foreseeable place such creatures may have in the chain of life on this planet. . . .

It is against this legislative background[29] that we must measure TVA's claim that the Act was not intended to stop operation of a project which, like Tellico Dam, was near completion when an endangered species was discovered in its path. While there is no discussion in the legislative history of precisely this problem, the totality of congressional action makes it abundantly clear that the result we reach today is wholly in accord with both the words of the statute and the intent of Congress. The plain intent of Congress in enacting this statute was to halt and reverse the trend toward species extinction, whatever the cost. This is reflected not only in the stated policies of the Act, but in literally every section of the statute. All persons, including federal agencies, are specifically instructed not to "take" endangered species, meaning that no one is "to harass, harm,[30] pursue, hunt, shoot, wound, kill, trap, capture, or collect" such life forms. 16 U. S. C. §§ 1532 (14), 1538 (a)(1)(B). Agencies in particular are directed by §§ 2 (c) and 3 (2) of the Act to "use *all methods* and procedures which are necessary" to preserve endangered species. Id., §§ 1531 (c), 1532 (2) (emphasis added). In addition, the legislative history undergirding § 7 reveals an explicit congressional decision to require agencies to afford first priority to the declared national policy of saving endangered species. The pointed omission of the type of qualifying language previously included in endangered species legislation reveals a conscious decision by Congress to give endangered species priority over the "primary missions" of federal agencies. . . .

(B)

Having determined that there is an irreconcilable conflict between operation of the Tellico Dam and the explicit provisions of § 7 of the Endangered Species Act, we must now consider what remedy, if any, is appropriate. It is correct, of course, that a federal judge sitting as a chancellor is not mechanically obligated to grant an injunction for every violation of law. This Court made plain in *Hecht Co.* v. *Bowles*, 321 U. S. 321, 329 (1944), that "[a] grant of *jurisdiction* to issue compliance orders hardly suggests an absolute duty to do so under any and all circumstances." As a general matter it may be said that "[s]ince all or almost all equitable remedies are discretionary, the balancing of equities and hardships is appropriate in almost any case as a guide to the chancellor's discretion." Dobbs, Remedies 52 (1973). Thus, in *Hecht* the Court refused to grant an injunction when it appeared from the District Court findings that "the issuance of an injunction would have 'no effect by way of insuring better compliance in the future' and would [have been] 'unjust' to [the] petitioner and not 'in the public interest.' " 321 U. S., at 326.

But these principles take a court only so far. Our system of government is, after all, a tripartite one, with each Branch having certain defined functions delegated to it by the Constitution. While "[it] is emphatically the province and duty of the judicial department to say what the law is," *Mar-*

bury v. *Madison*, 5 U. S. 137, 177 (1803), it is equally—and emphatically—the exclusive province of the Congress not only to formulate legislative policies, mandate programs and projects, but also to establish their relative priority for the Nation. Once Congress, exercising its delegated powers, has decided the order of priorities in a given area, it is for the Executive to administer the laws and for the courts to enforce them when enforcement is sought.

Here we are urged to view the Endangered Species Act "reasonably," and hence shape a remedy "that accords with some modicum of common-sense and the public weal." *Post*, at 2. But is that our function? We have no expert knowledge on the subject of endangered species, much less do we have a mandate from the people to strike a balance of equities on the side of the Tellico Dam. Congress has spoken in the plainest of words, making it abundantly clear that the balance has been struck in favor of affording endangered species the highest of priorities, thereby adopting a policy which it described as "institutionalized caution."

Our individual appraisal of the wisdom or unwisdom of a particular course consciously selected by the Congress is to be put aside in the process of interpreting a statute. Once the meaning of an enactment is discerned and its constitutionality determined, the judicial process comes to an end. We do not sit as a committee of review, nor are we vested with the power of veto. The lines ascribed to Sir Thomas More by Robert Bolt are not without relevance here:

"The law, Roper, the law. I know what's legal, not what's right. And I'll stick to what's legal. . . . I'm *not* God. The currents and eddies of right and wrong, which you find such plain-sailing, I can't navigate, I'm no voyager. But in the thickets of the law, oh there I'm a forester. . . . What would you do? Cut a great road through the law to get after the Devil? . . . And when the last law was down, and the Devil turned round on you—where would you hide, Roper, the laws all being flat? This country's planted thick with laws from coast to coast—Man's laws, not God's—and if you cut them down . . . d'you really think you could stand upright in the winds that would blow then? Yes, I'd give the Devil benefit of law, for my own safety's sake." Bolt, A Man for All Seasons, Act I, at 147 (Heinemann ed. 1967).

We agree with the Court of Appeals that in our constitutional system the commitment to the separation of powers is too fundamental for us to preempt congressional action by judicially decreeing what accords with "commonsense and the public weal.' " Our Constitution vests such responsibilities in the political Branches.

Affirmed.

Mr. Justice Powell, with whom Mr. Justice Blackmun joins, dissenting.

The Court today holds that § 7 of the Endangered Species Act requires a federal court, for the purpose of protecting an endangered species or its habitat, to enjoin permanently the operation of any federal project, whether completed or substantially completed. This decision casts a long shadow over the operation of even the most important projects, serving vital needs of society and national defense, whenever it is determined that continued operation would threaten extinction of an endangered species or its habitat. This result is said to be required by the "plain intent of Congress" as well as by the language of the statute.

In my view § 7 cannot reasonably by interpreted as applying to a project that is completed or substantially completed[1] when its threat to an endangered species is discovered. Nor can I believe that Congress could have intended this Act to produce the "absurd result"—in the words of the District Court—of this case. If it were clear from the language of the Act and its legislative history that Congress intended to authorize this result, this Court would be compelled to enforce it. It is not our province to rectify policy or political judgments by the Legislative Branch, however egregiously they may disserve the public interest. But where the statutory language and legislative history, as in this case, need not be construed to reach such a result, I view it as the duty of this Court to adopt a permissible construction that accords with some modicum of commonsense and the public weal. . . .

II

Today the Court, like the Court of Appeals below, adopts a reading of § 7 of the Act that gives it a retroactive effect and disregards 12 years of consistently expressed congressional intent to complete the Tellico Project. With all due respect, I view this result as an extreme example of a literalist[10] construction, not required by the language of the Act and adopted without regard to its manifest purpose. Moveover, it ignores established canons of statutory construction.

A

The starting point in statutory construction is, of course, the language of § 7 itself. *Blue Chip Stamps* v. *Manor Drug Stores*, 421 U. S. 723, 756 (1975) (POWELL, J., concurring). I agree that it can be viewed as a textbook example of fuzzy language which can be read according to the "eye of the beholder."[11] The critical words direct all federal agencies to take "such action [as may be] necessary to insure that actions authorized, funded or, carried out by them do not jeopardize the continued existence of . . . endangered species . . . or result in the destruction or modification of [a critical] habitat of such species. . . ." Respondents—as did the Sixth Circuit—read these words as sweepingly as possible to include all "actions" that any federal agency ever may take with respect to any federal project, whether completed or not.

The Court today embraces this sweeping construction. *Ante*, at 29–32. Under the Court's reasoning, the Act covers every existing federal installation, including great hydroelectric projects and reservoirs, every river and harbor project, and every national defense installation—however essential to the Nation's economic health and safety. The "actions" that an agency would be prohibited from "carrying out" would include the continued operation of such projects or any change necessary to preserve their continued usefulness.[12] The only precondition, according to respondents, to thus destroying the usefulness of even the most important federal project in our country would be a finding by the Secretary of the Interior that a continuation of the project would threaten the survival or critical habitat of a newly discovered species of water spider or amoeba.[13]

"[F]requently words of general meaning are used in a statute, words broad enough to include an act in question, and yet a consideration of the whole legislation, or of the circumstances surrounding its enactment, or of the absurd results which follow from giving such broad meaning to the words, makes it unreasonable to believe that the legislator intended to include the particular act." *Church of the Holy Trinity* v. *United States*, 143 U. S. 457, 459 (1892).[14] The result that will follow in this case by virtue of the Court's reading of § 7 makes it unreasonable to believe that Congress intended that reading. Moreover, § 7 may be construed in a way that avoids an "absurd result" without doing violence to its language.

The critical word in § 7 is "actions" and its meaning is far from "plain." It is part of the phrase: "actions authorized, funded or carried out." In terms of planning and executing various activities, it seems evident that the "actions" referred to are not all actions that an agency can ever take, but rather actions that the agency is *deciding whether* to authorize, to fund, or to carry out. In short, these words reasonably may be read as applying only to *prospective actions, i.e.,* actions with respect to which the agency has reasonable decision-making alternatives still available, actions *not yet* carried out. At the time respondents brought this lawsuit, the Tellico Project was 80% complete at a cost of more than $78 million. The Court concedes that as of this time and for the purpose of deciding this case, the Tellico dam project is "completed" or "virtually completed and the dam is essentially ready for operation", *ante*, 1, 2. See n. 1, *supra*. Thus, under a prospective reading of § 7, the action already had been "carried out" in terms of any remaining reasonable decision-making power. Cf. *National Wildlife Federation* v. *Coleman*, 529 F. 2d 359, 363 and n. 5 (CA5), cert. denied *sub nom. Boteler* v. *National Wildlife Federation*, 429 U. S. 979 (1976). . . .

III

I have little doubt that Congress will amend the Endangered Species Act to prevent the grave consequences made possible by today's decision. Few, if any, Members of that body will wish to defend an interpretation of the Act that requires the waste of at least $53 million, see n. 6, *supra*, and denies the people of the Tennessee valley area the benefits of the reservoir that Congress intended to confer.[19] There will be little sentiment to leave this dam standing before an empty reservoir, serving no purpose other than a conversation piece for incredulous tourists.

But more farreaching than the adverse effect on the people of this economically depressed area is the continuing threat to the operation of every federal project, no matter how important to the Nation. If Congress acts expeditiously, as may be anticipated, the Court's decision probably will have no lasting adverse consequences. But I had not thought it to be the province of this Court to force Congress into otherwise unnecessary action by interpreting a statute to produce a result no one intended.

[1]This description is taken from the opinion of the District Judge in the first litigation involving the Tellico Dam and Reservoir Project. *Environmental Defense Fund* v. *Tennessee Valley Authority*, 339 F. Supp. 806, 808 (ED Tenn. 1972). In his opinion, "all of these benefits of the present Little Tennessee River Valley will be destroyed by impoundment of the river. . . ." *Ibid.* The District Judge noted that "the free-flowing river is the likely habitat of one or more of seven rare or endangered species." *Ibid.*

[2]See *Amicus Curiae* Brief of the Eastern Band of Cherokee Indians, at 2. See also Mooney, Myths of the Cherokee and Sacred Formulas of the Cherokee, 19th Annual Report of the Bureau of American Ethnology (1900); H. Timberlake, Memoirs, 1756–1765 (Watauga Press 1927); A. Brewer and C. Brewer, Valley So Wild: A Folk History (East Tenn. Historical Soc'y 1975).

[3]Public Works Appropriations Act, 1967, 80 Stat. 1002, 1014.

[4]Tellico Dam itself will contain no electric generators; however, an interreservoir canal connecting Tellico Reservoir with a nearby hydroelectric plant will augment the latter's capacity.

[5]The NEPA injunction was in effect some 21 months; when it was entered TVA had spent some $29 million on the project. Most of these funds have gone to purchase land, construct the concrete portions of the dam, and build a four-lane steel span bridge to carry a state highway over the proposed reservoir. 339 F. Supp., at 808.

[6]The snail darter was scientifically described by Dr. Etnier in the Proceedings of the Biological Society of Washington, Vol. 88, No. 44, at 469–488 (Jan. 22, 1976). The scientific merit and content of Dr. Etnier's paper on the snail darter were checked by a panel from the Smithsonian Institution prior to publication. See App., at 111.

[7]In Tennessee alone there are 85 to 90 species of darters, App., at 131, of which upward to 45 live in the Tennessee River system. *Id.*, at 130. New species of darters are being constantly discovered and classified—at the rate of about one per year. *Id.*, at 131. This is a difficult task for even trained ichthyologists since species of darters are often hard to differentiate from one another. *Ibid.*

[8]An "endangered species" is defined by the Act to mean "any species which is in danger of extinction throughout all or a significant portion of its range other than a species of the Class Insecta determined by the Secretary to constitute a pest whose protection under the provisions of this chapter would present an overwhelming and overriding risk to man." 16 U. S. C. § 1532 (4).

"The act covers every animal and plant species, subspecies, and population in the world needing protection. There are approximately 1.4 million full species of animals and 600,000 full species of plants in the world. Various authorities calculate as many as 10% of them—some 200,000—may need to be listed as Endangered or Threatened. When one counts subspecies, not to mention individual populations, the total could increase to three to five times that number." Keith Shreiner, Associate Director and Endangered Species Program Manager of the U. S. Fish and Wildlife Service, quoted in a letter from A. J. Wagner, Chairman TVA, to Chairman, House Committee on Merchant Marine and Fisheries, dated April 25, 1977, quoted in

Wood, On Protecting an Endangered Statute: The Endangered Species Act of 1973, 37 Federal Bar Journal 25, 27 (1978).

[9]The Act does not define "critical habitat," but the Secretary of the Interior has administratively construed the term:

" 'Critical habitat' means any air, land, or water area (exclusive of those existing man-made structures or settlements which are not necessary to the survival and recovery of a listed species) and constituent elements thereof, the loss of which would appreciably decrease the likelihood of the survival and recovery of a listed species or a distinct segment of its population. The constituent elements of critical habitat include, but are not limited to: physical structures and topography, biota, climate, human activity, and the quality and chemical content of land, water, and air. Critical habitat may represent any portion of the present habitat of a listed species and may include additional areas for reasonable population expansion." 50 CFR § 402.02, 43 Fed. Reg. 874.

[10]Respondents are a regional association of biological scientists, a Tennessee conservation group and individuals who are citizens or users of the Little Tennessee Valley area which would be affected by the Tellico Project.

[11]The Act authorizes "interested persons" to petition the Secretary of the Interior to list a species as endangered. 16 U. S. C. § 1533 (c)(2); see 5 U. S. C. § 553 (e).

[12]Searches by TVA in more than 60 watercourses have failed to find other populations of snail darters. App. 36; 410–412. The Secretary has noted that "more than 1,000 collections in recent years and additional earlier collections from central and east Tennessee have not revealed the presence of the snail darter outside the Little Tennessee River." 40 Fed. Reg. 47505. It is estimated, however, that the snail darter's range once extended throughout the upper main Tennessee River and the lower portions of its major tributaries above Chattanooga—all of which are now the sites of dam impoundments. See Hearings on Public Works for Water and Power Development and Energy Research Appropriation Bill, 1978, before a Subcommittee of the House Committee on Appropriations, 95th Cong., 1st Sess., Pt. 4, 240–241 (1977) (Statement of witness for TVA); Hearings on the Endangered Species Act, before a Subcommittee of the Senate Committee on Environmental and Public Works, 95th Cong., 1st Sess., 291 (1977); App. 139.

[17]The District Court findings are to the same effect and are unchallenged here.

[18]In dissent, MR. JUSTICE POWELL argues that the meaning of "actions" in § 7 is "far from 'plain,' " and that "it seems evident that the 'actions' referred to are not all actions that an agency can ever take, but rather actions that the agency is *deciding whether* to authorize, to fund, or to carry out." *Post,* at 10. Aside from this bare assertion, however, no explanation is given to support the proffered interpretation. This recalls Lewis Carroll's classic advice on the construction of language: "When *I* use a word," Humpty Dumpty said in a rather scornful tone, "it means just what *I* choose it to mean—neither more nor less." Through the Looking Glass, in the Complete Works of Lewis Carroll, 196 (1939).

Aside from being unexplicated, the dissent's reading of § 7 is flawed on several counts. First, under its view, the words "or carry out" in § 7 would be superfluous since all prospective actions of an agency remain to be "authorized" or "funded." Second, the dissent's position logically means that an agency would be obligated to comply with § 7 only when a project is in the planning stage. But if Congress had meant to so limit the Act, it surely would have used words to that effect, as it did in the National Environmental Policy Act, 42 U. S. C. §§ 4332 (2) (A), (C) (1970).

[19]The District Court determined that failure to complete the Tellico Dam would result in the loss of some $53 million in nonrecoverable obligations; see *supra,* at 10. Respondents dispute this figure, and point to a recent study by the General

Accounting Office, which suggests that the figure could be considerably less. See GAO Study, *supra*, at 8 n. 13, at 5–14; see also Cook, Cook & Gove, The Snail Darter and the Dam, 51 National Parks & Conservation Magazine 10 (1977); Conservation Foundation Letter, at 1–2 (April 1978). The GAO study also concludes that TVA and Congress should explore alternatives to impoundment of the reservoir, such as the creation of a regional development program based on a free-flowing river. None of these considerations are relevant to our decision, however; they are properly addressed to the Executive and Congress.

[20]Prior federal involvement with endangered species had been quite limited. For example, the Lacey Act of 1900, 31 Stat. 187, partially codified in 16 U. S. C. §§ 667e and 701 (1976), and the Black Bass Act of 1926, 16 U. S. C. § 851 *et seq.* (1976), prohibited the transportation in interstate commerce of fish or wildlife taken in violation of national, state or foreign law. The effect of both of these statutes was constrained, however, by the fact that prior to passage of the Endangered Species Act of 1973, there were few laws regulating these creatures. See Coggins, Conserving Wildlife Resources: An Overview of the Endangered Species Act of 1973, 52 N. D. L. Rev. 315, 317–318 (1973). The Migratory Bird Treaty Act, passed in 1918, 16 U. S. C. § 703 *et seq.* (1976), was more extensive, giving the Secretary of the Interior power to adopt regulations for the protection of migratory birds. Other measures concentrated on establishing refuges for wildlife. See, *e.g.*, Land and Water Conservation Fund Act of 1965, 16 U. S. C. § 4601–4 *et seq.* See generally M. Bean, The Evolution of National Wildlife Law (1977).

[21]This approach to the problem of taking, of course, contained the same inherent limitations as the Lacey and Black Bass Acts, discussed, *supra*, at 19–20, n. 20.

[22]Hearings on Endangered Species before a Subcommittee of the House Committee on Merchant Marine and Fisheries, 93d Cong., 1st Sess., 202 (1973) (statement of Asst. Secy. of the Interior) (hereinafter cited as 1973 House Hearings).

[23]See. *e.g.*, 1973 House Hearings, at 280 (statement of Rep. Roe); *id.*, at 281 (statement of Rep. Whitehurst); *id.*, at 301 (statement of Friends of the Earth); *id.*, at 306–307 (statement of Defenders of Wildlife). One statement, made by the Assistant Secretary of the Department of the Interior, particularly deserves notice: "[I] have watched in my lifetime a vast array of mollusks in southern streams totally disappear as a result of damming, channelization, and pollution. It is often asked of me, 'what is the importance of the mollusks for example in Alabama.' I do not know, and I do not know whether any of us will ever have the insight to know exactly why these mollusks evolved over millions of years or what their importance is in the total ecosystem. However, I have great trouble being party to their destruction without ever have gained such knowledge." *Id.*, at 207.
One member of the mollusk family existing in these southern rivers is the snail, see 12 Encyclopedia Britannica 326 (15th ed.), which ironically enough provides the principle food for snail darters. See *supra*, at 7, 10–11, n. 16.

[29]When confronted with a statute which is plain and unambiguous on its face, we ordinarily do not look to legislative history as a guide to its meaning. *Ex parte Collett*, 337 U. S. 55, 61 (1949), and cases cited therein. Here it is not *necessary* to look beyond the words of the statute. We have undertaken such an analysis only to meet MR. JUSTICE POWELL'S suggestion that the "absurd" result reached in this case, *post*, at 1, is not in accord with congressional intent.

[30]We do not understand how TVA intends to operate Tellico Dam without "harming" the snail darter. The Secretary of the Interior has defined the term "harm" to mean "an act or omission which actually injures or kills wildlife, including acts which annoy it to such an extent as to significantly disrupt essential behavioral

patterns, which include, but are not limited to, breeding, feeding or sheltering; *significant environmental modification or degradation which has such effects is included within the meaning of 'harm.'*" 50 CFR § 17.3 (1975). (Emphasis added); see S. Rep. No. 307, 93d Cong. 1st Sess., 7 (1973).

[9]Attorney General Bell advised us at oral argument that the dam had been completed, that all that remains is to "close the gate," and to complete the construction of "some roads and bridges." The "dam itself is finished. All the landscaping has been done. . . . It is completed." Tr. of Oral Arg. 18.

[10]See Frank, Words and Music, 47 Colum. L. Rev. 1259, 1263 (1947); Hand, The Speech of Justice, 29 Harv. L. Rev. 617, 620 (1916).

[11]The purpose of this Act is admirable. Protection of endangered species long has been neglected. This unfortunate litigation—wasteful for taxpayers and likely in the end to be counterproductive in terms of respondents' purpose—may have been invited by careless draftsmanship of otherwise meritorious legislation.

[12]Opinion of the Court, *ante*, at 29–31. At oral argument, respondents clearly stated this as their view of § 7:

"QUESTION: . . . Do you think—it is still your position, as I understand it, that this Act, Section 7, applies to completed projects? I know you don't think it occurs very often that there'll be a need to apply it. But does it apply if the need exists?

"MR. PLATER: To the continuation—

"QUESTION: To complete projects. Take the Grand Coulee dam—

"MR. PLATER: Right. Your Honor, if there were a species there—

.   .   .   .   .   .

"—it wouldn't be endangered by the dam.

"QUESTION: I know that's your view. I'm asking you not to project your imagination—

"MR. PLATER: I see, Your Honor.

"QUESTION:—beyond accepting my assumption.

"MR. PLATER: Right.

"QUESTION: And that was that an endangered species might turn up at Grand Coulee. Does Section 7 apply to it.

"MR. PLATER: I believe it would, Your Honor. The Secretary of the Interior—

"QUESTION: That answers my question.

"MR. PLATER: Yes, it would." Tr. of Oral Arg. 57–58.

[13]Under the Court's interpretation, the prospects for such disaster are breathtaking indeed, since there are hundreds of thousands of candidates for the endangered lists:

"The act covers every animal and plant species, subspecies, and population in the world needing protection. There are approximately 1.4 million full species of animals and 600,000 full species of plants in the world. Various authorities calculate as many as 10% of them—some 200,000—may need to be listed as Endangered or Threatened. When one counts subspecies, not to mention individual populations, the total could increase to three to five times that number." Keith Shreiner, Associate Director and Endangered Species Program Manager of the U. S. Fish and Wildlife Service, quoted in a letter from A. J. Wagner, Chairman TVA, to Chairman, House Committee on Merchant Marine and Fisheries, dated April 25, 1977, quoted in Wood, On Protecting an Endangered Statute: The Endangered Species Act of 1973, 37 Federal Bar Journal 25, 27 (1978).

[14]Accord, *e.g., United States* v. *American Trucking Assns.*, 310 U. S. 534, 543 (1940); *Armstrong Co.* v. *Nu-Enamel Corp.*, 305 U. S. 315, 333 (1938); *Sorrells* v. *United States*, 287 U. S. 435, 446–448 (1938) (collecting cases); *United States* v.

Ryan, 284 U. S. 167, 175 (1931). The Court suggests, *ante*, at 32 n. 33, the precept stated in *Church of the Holy Trinity* was somehow undermined in *Crooks* v. *Harrelson*, 282 U. S. 55, 60 (1931). Only a year after the decision in *Crooks*, however, the Court declared that a "literal application of a statute which would lead to absurd consequences is to be avoided whenever a reasonable application can be given which is consistent with the legislative purpose." *Ryan, supra,* at 175. In the following year, the Court expressly relied upon *Church of the Holy Trinity* on this very point. *Sorrells, supra,* at 448. The real difference between the Court and myself on this issue arises from our perceptions of the character of today's result. The Court professes to find nothing particularly remarkable about the result produced by its decision in this case. Because I view it as remarkable indeed, and because I can find no hint that Congress actually intended it, see pp. 12–15, *infra*, I am led to conclude that the congressional words cannot be given the meaning ascribed to them by the Court.

[19]The Court acknowledges, as it must, that the permanent injunction it grants today will require "the sacrifice of the anticipated benefits of the project and of many millions of dollars in public funds." *Ante*, at 19.

Answers to Selected Problems

Many of the problems presented in the book are such that there is not one correct answer. Thus the answer we provide is often only one of several possible solutions. You won't find answers for every problem. Our aim has been to leave some items for you to resolve in discussions with your teacher or tutor. We have, however, provided enough answers to enable you to check your understanding as you read through the chapters.

1-1. 1. Categorization
      2. Compare/contrast
      3. Categorization
      4. Sequence
      5. Causes or effects
1-2. 2. overly simplistic, an overworked topic
      4. an overworked topic
      6. This topic is of reasonable complexity, but possibly rather broad. Information should be readily available. The topic is not worn out.
      8. The topic is reasonably complex, but could be handled if the causes are relatively few in number. Information should be available in a college library. The topic is not worn out.

2-1. 1. Sports: *a)* by number of players (individual, team)
                 b) by degree of contact (no contact = tennis; moderate contact = basketball; much contact = football)
      2. College students:
                 a) by year in school (freshman, sophomore, junior)
                 b) by major in school (agriculture, engineering, history)
      3. Pets: *a)* by size (large pets: dogs, horses; medium-size pets: cats, rabbits; small pets: mice, birds)
                 b) by domesticity (very social: dog; less social: cats; non-social: turtle)
2-2. 1. speed
         grace
         sound
2-3. None of the evidence seems sufficient to convict Jones. However, you could arrange the evidence in categories based on quality—on

how convincing the evidence for Jones's guilt seems. We suggest four categories:

1. *Irrelevant evidence*

   Witness: Lucky Louie denies meeting Jones

   Witness: Betty Wilson bought encyclopedias

   Exhibit: sales receipt for encyclopedias

   (The above facts have nothing to do with the case.)

2. *Evidence that Jones is not guilty*

   Exhibit: footprint, size 9D

   Exhibit: tennis shoe, size 9D

   Exhibit: Jones's footsize: 6A

   (Since Jones's footsize doesn't match the print at the scene of the crime, this suggests someone else stole the chickens and is perhaps trying to frame Jones.)

3. *Relevant (but weak) evidence for guilt*

   Exhibit: bucket with chicken feathers

   Witness: Sheriff arrests Jones at dinner table

   Exhibit: chicken bones on plate

   Exhibit: lab reports showing grease on Jones's hands and face

   (The above evidence is circumstantial. Jones might have bought chickens from a farmer.)

   Witness: Farmer Smith swears two chickens are missing.

   (This establishes that a crime was committed, but says nothing about Jones.)

4. *Relevant (and more convincing) evidence for guilt*

   Witness: Suzie Bell White sees Jones with two chickens.

   (This is strong evidence against Jones.)

   Witness: Sheriff testifies there was mud on Jones's floor with chicken droppings.

   (Places Jones in the area of live chickens, but is still circumstantial.)

   Exhibit: Jones's police record

   Witness: Dr. Mindbender testifies about Jones's obsession.

   (This gives Jones a motive and may suggest that he was inclined to steal chickens.)

2-4. 1. *a)* weekly
   b) bi-weekly
   c) monthly
   d) quarterly
   2. *a)* annual
   b) perennial
   c) biennial
   3. *a)* mesomorph
   b) ectomorph
   c) endomorph

2-5. 1. *a)* Bike Nuts: bikers who ride $1,000 bikes and pedal seventy miles in five hours or less; Bike Nuts aren't interested in scenery

   b) Amiable Amateurs: bikers who ride for fun all year around and enter to test their stamina

   c) Togetherness Families: families of bikers who treat the affair as an extended family picnic

   d) Senior Cyclers: older bikers, some of whom take turns riding tricycles

   e) Handlebar Hedonists: bikers interested in drinking beer and looking for mates

2. *a)* Meddling: The teacher intervenes in instruction.

   b) Modeling: The teacher instructs by example.

   c) Muddling: The teacher lets students make discoveries on their own.

3. *a)* Preparation: investigating the problem

   b) Incubation: letting ideas gel

   c) Illumination: discovering a solution

   d) Verification: testing the validity of the solution

2-6. 1. "Backward" is the most offensive term. The other terms might be offensive to some people.

2. All of these labels are potentially offensive.

2-7. 1. *a)* impromptu

   b) memorized

   c) read

   d) extemporaneous

2. *a)* nuclear explosion

   b) population expansion

   c) environmental destruction

3. *a)* fumbling stage

   b) functioning stage

   c) fluency stage

4. *a)* creole hypothesis

   b) dialect hypothesis

2-8. This is one answer:

air pollution (point 1)
fertilizer runoff (point 4)
feedlot runoff (point 7)
potato plant discharge (point 5) } pollution control
erosion from building construction (point 2) } erosion control
erosion from joy riders (point 8)
landfill overflow (point 6) } sanitation control
septic tank overflow (point 3)

} areas of inadequate reforms by weak city council (point 9)

2-9. 1. first   5. fifth

2. seventh   6. fourth

3. sixth   7. third

4. second

2-10. 1, 2, 4, 6. In writing on subject 3 you might break down each method of persuasion into steps, but the main method of development would be comparison/contrast.

2-11. 1. Estendian Revolution
   July 1, 1845
   July 6, 1845
   July 7, 1845
   August 15, 1845
   September 19, 1845

2. Crump's Presidency
   September 30, 1845
   February 6, 1890

3. Rutabaga Reaction
   March 3, 1890
   March 10, 1890
   September 1890

4. The Rise of Rutabaga Diplomacy
   March 16, 1930
   May 19, 1931
   June 10, 1931

2-12. One possibility is as follows:

I. Nuclear Fission
   A. Process and substances involved
      1
      7
   B. History
      9
      2
   C. Feasibility
      8
      15
      12
   D. Safety risk
      16

II. Nuclear Fusion
   A. Process and substances involved
      4
      6
   B. History
      10
   C. Feasibility
      11
      14
      5
      13
   D. Safety risk
      3

Another possibility is:
I. Process and substances involved
    A. Nuclear fission
       1
       7
    B. Nuclear fusion
       4
       6
II. History
    A. Nuclear fission
       9
       2
    B. Nuclear fusion
       10
III. Feasibility
    A. Nuclear fission
       8
       15
       12
    B. Nuclear fusion
       11
       14
       5
       13
IV. Safety risks
    A. Nuclear fission
       16
    B. Nuclear fusion
       3

2-13. Here are some sample answers.
1. Cause 1: Declining economic situation
   Cause 2: Increased competition to get into professional schools
   Cause 3: Grade inflation (Students fear that now they have to get an A to stand above the crowd when before a B would do.)
2. Cause 1: A historical tradition of man's desire to go "back to nature" (information might come from reading in the Romantic Movement)
   Cause 2: Growing concern for the environment (fear of chemical pollution)
   Cause 3: Growing concern for nutrition (tied in to improved research techniques)
   Cause 4: Commercial exploitation by makers of "natural" products
3. Cause 1: Poor city planning
   Cause 2: Flight to the suburbs

Cause 3: Prejudice (fear of certain racial communities in the central city)

Cause 4: Fear of violence in the city

4. Cause 1: Chemical pollution (toxic chemicals affect breeding)

Cause 2: Poaching

Cause 3: Human engineering (eagles die from landing on power lines)

Cause 4: Encroachment of civilization on eagle habitat

3-1. 2. There are several possible orders for this set of points.

Order: *b, a, e, d, f, c*

Reason: In this order you would first discuss the organismic model, then the mechanistic model.

or

Order: *b, d, a, f, e, c*

Reason: In this order you would compare the two models by discussing first the extent of man's activity, second the locus of behavioral control, and finally the view of development.

3. Order: *b, a, c*

Reason: from least desirable to most desirable approach

4. Order: *b, d, c, a*

Reason: Although it is not chronological, this order would best trace the development of place value in numeration systems.

3-2. 2. Order: *b, a, c*

Reason: from lowest degree (1) to highest degree (3)

3. Order: *a, d, b, c*

Reason: The categories are arranged from ambition for intangible rewards (personal happiness) to ambition for tangible rewards (money).

4. Order: *a, e, b, d, c*

Reason: from smallest to largest unit of administration

5. Order: *c, b, d, a, f, e*

Reason: degree of sophistication (this is a matter of opinion)

3-3. 1. Suggested final order: *b, c, d, e, a*

Reason: You want to concentrate on city problems, so you might want to save the most important aspects of the topic for last. Moreover, city problems are related to health problems at the other levels, so it makes sense to discuss the other problems first as background.

2. Suggested final order: *a, c, b*

Reason: You discuss extremes first, middle ground last; this highlights the reasonableness of the position you support.

3. Suggested final order: *c, b, a*

Reason: Because the emphasis is on large companies you should discuss them last. The discussion of smaller companies provides contrasting background information.

4. Suggested final order: *a, d, b, c*

   Reason: By dealing with the extremes first you can hope to convince a reader that a medium- or small-size pet would be best. Then you can point out special disadvantages of medium-size pets, and end by discussing the virtues of small pets.

5. Suggested final order: *a, b, c, d, e*

   Reason: The logical order—from smallest form of ocean life to largest—seems most sensible for this topic.

3-4. Complete laissez-faire approach

Informed consumer approach

Optimum consumer approach

National planning approach

The approaches seem to differ most significantly in terms of the degree of freedom they could allow potential Ph.D. students. Organizing them from completely nonrestrictive of freedom to very restrictive helps you to understand how one approach differs from another.

It seems likely that President Fleming would have decided on an alternative order. If he presented the points in the order they are listed above, he would have to discuss the approach he was pushing (optimum consumer) immediately before he discussed national planning. The impression given would be that his proposal was only a notch on the line away from socialism. This might upset many Americans.

For President Fleming's purpose the "extremes first, middle ground last" order would be effective, because it would suggest that his "optimum consumer" approach is a good compromise that takes into account both the demands of individuals and the needs of society.

The actual order used in the speech was:

Complete laissez-faire approach

National planning approach

Informed consumer approach

Optimum consumer approach

4-1. 1. *b*

2. *b*

3. *a*

4. *a*

5. *b*

6. *b*

7. *b*

8. *b*

4-2. Note: the answers below are suggestions only.

1. There should be both national and international laws to save whales from extinction.

   (The writer is going to mention the need for national and international controls as necessary to save whales from extinction.)

2. Today's children are less creative and less inquisitive than children in the past. This suggests that parents are too strict with their children.
(The writer will use information on declining creativity and inquisitiveness to argue that parents should be less strict.)

3. Art is an aspect of our cultural heritage and a part of our everyday lives; therefore, knowing something about art is important.
(The writer is going to support the opinion that art is important by showing that it is part of our heritage and everyday experience.)

4. It is important to eat well if one is to maintain a sound body, healthy intellect, and cheerful attitude.
(The writer will show how eating habits are linked to physical, mental, and emotional well-being.)

4-3. 2. The money allotted for women's athletic programs has doubled in the past two years. This recent encouraging show of support, however, does not change the fact that women's athletic teams at the University of_____have been shabbily financed and shabbily coached for years.

3. Although I have friends who are satisfied with the education they received in high school, I feel my high school teachers could have tried a little harder to provide their students with an interesting and practical education.

4. I am aware of the arguments against court-ordered busing, but I am still in favor of it. I feel it is the only way to achieve peace and justice in this country.

5. Although I am aware that Governor Johnston and the Council on Crime Deterrence have arrived at a contrary conclusion, the research I have conducted suggests that the threat of the electric chair does not stop people from committing the violent crimes of rape and murder.

4-4. 1. The techniques used in these two advertisements to promote Smirnoff Vodka are similar in mood, appeal, and language; moreover, both build on the good reputation of the product.

2. To operate a fireworks stand and make a profit, one must observe government regulations, be conscious of safety problems, and find good, reliable help.

3. Although compost heaps have drawbacks, they provide a useful way for gardeners to recycle waste, improve their soil, and do something with their spare time.

4. To develop a physical fitness program, one should follow a plan that begins with moderation and gradually progresses to strenuous conditioning. (Note: the points that "Many people like sports..." and "Exercising is an important part of keeping healthy" can be handled in the paper's introduction.)

5-1. 1, 4

5-2.   1. The average American knows that people carry their driver's license in their wallets; a visitor from Burma might not know this.
2. The average American knows what jury duty is and that it is not thought of as work. A Burmese who didn't know anything about jury duty might be confused as to why going to do one's duty was not going to work.
3. The average American knows that many drugstores have a soda fountain where milk shakes are sold. A Burmese, thinking drugstores sold only drugs, might find these sentences incoherent.
4. Most Americans know that the golden arches are the symbol for McDonald's. A visitor from Burma might be unable to see the connection between McDonald's and arches.

5-3.   1. This gap is bridgeable by someone who knows that Ernest Hemingway liked bullfights.
2. This gap is bridgeable by someone who knows that bedridden patients who are not moved can develop lung problems.
3. This gap is bridgeable by someone who knows the three-second rule in basketball.

5-4.   2. *a)* 1
       b) 2
       c) thesis
   3. *a)* 2
       b) thesis
       c) 3
       d) 1

5-5.   1. *a)* Some regulatory agencies are bad because they are inefficient.
       b) Other agencies are bad because the bureaucrats running them lack an understanding of the industries they are regulating.
   2. *a)* The lack of fairness of Jones's approach.
       b) The high cost of Jones's approach.
   3. *a)* differences of territory
       b) differences of religion
   4. *a)* The spirit that swept over Poland and East Germany after the accords.
       b) The spirit that swept over Czechoslavakia.
   5. *a)* The violation of adult rights.
       b) The even worse situation concerning the rights of young people.

5-6.   1. The first major cause of alienation is personal habit.
2. In addition to personal habit, people are often singled out because of physical disability.
3. Mental disabilities...
4. Often, people may be singled out because of race.
5. Finally, people may be singled out because of their beliefs or ideologies.

5-7.   *however, on the other hand, consequently, as a result*

5-11. Line 11

Signal word—"however"—indicates contrast with preceding idea.

Lines 17–20

Thesis statement—allows reader to predict the main points of the paper.

Lines 21–23

Topic statement. Use of key label "sensorimotor period" provides link with thesis. This sentence and the next present the major idea of the paragraph.

Lines 31–33

The phrase "next stage" signals a shift to a subtopic that follows in logical order from the preceding point. This sentence and the next present the major idea of the paragraph (topic statement).

Line 33

"But" signals a contrast.

Line 35

"For example" signals an illustration.

Line 52–55

This topic statement reflects both the main idea of the preceding paragraph (preoperational child focuses on one aspect) and the main idea of the following paragraph (concrete operational child focuses on several aspects).

Line 64

"On the other hand" signals a shift to a contrasting point.

Lines 69–72

These two sentences are the topic statement indicating a shift to a new topic, the formal operational period.

Lines 78–79

This sentence summarizes the main idea of the paper—that Piaget maintains that children advance through four stages.

Lines 81–83

"Thus" signals a conclusion (that children aren't "little adults"). The use of the phrase "little adults" ties the conclusion to the same phrase in the introduction.

Line 83–86

The final sentence points beyond the paper to educational implications.

5-12. Your answers need not be the same as the ones below to be correct. In the original paper, the following words were used:

1. implements
2. solar devices
3. first
4. applied
5. Another major
6. drying grain
7. dry grain
8. dry its grain
9. One problem
10. second problem
11. applicability
12. efficiency
13. third
14. economy
15. One reason
16. second reason
17. conventional energy
18. conventional energy

LB2369 .H33
Hashimoto, Irvin Y. (Irvi
Strategies for academic writin

010101 000

0 2002 0019264 5

YORK COLLEGE OF PENNSYLVANIA 17403